FEAR NO EVIL!!!

BY
VERNON STEVE WEAKLEY

c Copyright 2002, Vernon Steve Weakley
This book may not be reproduced in any form without the written consent of the author.

AN IMPRINT OF
ZWORLD-NET PUBLISHING INC.
ISBN 0-9712310-2-8 /// A SPECIAL PAPERBACK EDITION

FEAR NO EVIL!!!

Published by ZWORLD-NET PUBLISHING Inc. in conjunction with VSW Publishing inc. //// ISBN 0-9712310-2-8 //// A SPECIAL PAPERBACK EDITION. V.S. WEAKLEY, Copyright 2002 by Vernon Steve Weakley. All rights reserved. Printed in the United States of America. No part of this book may be used or reproduced or transmitted in any manner (electronic, or mechanical, including but not limited to photocopying, recording, or by any information storage and retrieval system, etc.) whatsoever without written permission except in the case of brief quotations embodied in critical articles and reviews. For information, address ZWORLD-NET PUBLISHING Inc. VSW Publishing Inc. 2103 Linea Del Pino Blvd. Houston TX. 77077 //// or EMAIL ZWORLDNET @ AOL.COM.

ZWORLD-NET books may be purchased for educational, business, personal, or sales promotional use. To order please visit WWW.VERNON.WEAKLEY.COM or E:MAIL the Publisher at ZWORLDNET@AOL.COM or write or call the Special Markets Department, VSW Publishing Inc. 2103 Linea Del Pino Blvd. Houston Tx. 77077 //// 281 589-7421.

FIRST EDITION:

Book Concept By Langston (Pooh) D'angelo & Shinika Washington, Dijon Stevens and Kristine Stevens.

EDITORS:

PEYCHAUD LITERARY PRODUCTIONS INC. NEW ORLEANS LOUISIANA, CAROL DAVIS WILSON AND FINAL EDIT, Z-WORLD-NET PUBLISHING STAFF.

OTHER WORKS BY THE AUTHOR:

"STANDING AT THE EDGE OF MADNESS," - IS AN INCREDIBLE STORY ABOUT A YOUNG BLACK KID GROWING UP IN THE DEEP SOUTH WHO HAS SEVERAL LIFE THREATENING ENCOUNTERS WITH RACISM DURING THE CIVIL RIGHTS ERA. ITS PRIMARY STORY LINE IS BASED ON A TRUE HISTORICAL EVENT CENTERING AROUND THE MURDERS AND SHOOTINGS OF INNOCENT COLLEGE STUDENTS AT JACKSON STATE COLLEGE BY ROGUE MEMBERS OF THE MISSISSIPPI HIGHWAY PATROL. ON MAY 14, 1970.

" THE PARADOX " - A BOOK THAT DETAILS THE MANY DEFINING EVENTS THAT WILL LEAD TO MANKIND'S DEMISE AT THE BEGINNING OF THE NEW MILLENNIUM.

WORK IN PROCESS BY THE AUTHOR:

" AND WHEN WE SAY OUR LAST GOOD-BYE " - IS ABOUT THE LEGEND, HISTORY AND THE WILD, WILD ADVENTURES OF THE MIGHTY MEN OF OMEGA PSI PHI FRATERNITY.

" THE QUOTA " - THE STORY OF A YOUNG, DASHING BLACK CIA AGENT RECRUITED WHILE IN COLLEGE TO ELIMINATE THREATS TO AMERICA BY HOSTILE COUNTRIES.

" AND THEN, UP POPS THE DEVIL " IS A VIBRANT LOVE STORY ABOUT A YOUNG COUPLE WHOSE BLISS IS CONSTANTLY BEING DERAILED BY THE DEVIL IN ORDER TO ROB THE WORLD OF TRUE LOVE.

............*Acknowledgments*...............

FROM THE AUTHOR:

This book is dedicated in loving memory of my grandparents, Jeff and Clara Stevens. The love, compassion, happiness, guidance, and raw fortitude they passed on to me and generations to come charged our spirit, and will be with us forevermore. Without the precious life lessons they lovingly passed on to us, we truly would not have the wings to soar.

I also dedicate this book to my beloved mother, Lola Weakley, who has been my rock, teacher, anchor, eternal love, and strength throughout my life. She taught me how to hold my head up and be strong, proud, wise, tenacious and yet kind and gentle in successfully navigating this world and its many difficulties and challenges.

This book is also dedicated to my beautiful aunt Dollie who has shown me the true meaning of devotion and loyalty. For without her encouragement, counseling and understanding, my caged spirit may have never found the courage to run free.

To my brothers Donald and Stanley, my sister Cheryl, my deceased uncles Jeff and Joe, my loving daughter Shinika and my little grandson Pooh Langston, my aunt Maxine and old friends Rosalind, Lee Arthur, Joe and Ruby who have anchored and supported me throughout my life, I say thanks for enabling me to experience true love, blossom, see the forest far beyond the trees and ultimately realize my purpose.

Each of the people above played a major role in helping me become the man I am today. They all gave me a sense of worth and inner strength that has helped me to pick myself up off the floor time and time again, and succeed. I want to thank them all for their unwavering love, faith, patience, tolerance and guidance throughout the years.

I also want to give a special word of thanks to Thelma Dennis, John Williamson, Alita Carter, Georgia Madison, Carol Davis Wilson, Patricia Wycoff, Martha Valdez, Alma Burks, Patricia Booker, Sharon Finney, Olivia Carter, Beverly Dickerson, Sue Step, Wanda Hill, Charles Boyd, Bubba Greene, Shirley Prince, Constance Slaughter Harvey and my brothers, the mighty, mighty men of Omega Psi Phi Fraternity Inc.

I want all of my friends and supporters to know that I greatly appreciate the kindness they have shown me. You are indeed special and heaven sent. You mean the world to me and I will always love you and never forget your unchanging support and encouragement. Thank You! Thank You! Thank You!

And finally, but certainly not least, I want to thank the Heavenly Father, the Holy Spirit and Jesus my Lord and personal savior for saving, loving and blessing a poor wretch like me. **For without God's magnificent grace, I would truly be lost!**

FEAR NO EVIL!!!

####### *Introduction* #######

"***FEAR NO EVIL***," IS A STORY OF AMERICA AT ITS BEST AND WORST. IT IS ABOUT THE TRIALS AND TRIBULATION OF A POOR BLACK SOUTHERN MAN AND HIS FAMILY IN MISSISSIPPI DURING THE TURBULENT CIVIL RIGHTS ERA, STRUGGLING TO RISE AND ULTIMATELY SUCCEED IN SPITE OF THE MANY CHALLENGES SET BEFORE THEM BY A BRUTALLY RACIST SYSTEM, EAGER TO REVEL IN THEIR FAILURE.

ITS MESSAGE IS SIMPLE AND CLEAR. IT IS ONE OF HOPE AND THE PROMISE OF TOMORROW FOR THOSE WHO HAVE FAITH, AND YES, THE COURAGE TO REALIZE TRUTH AND LOOK BEYOND THE NAYSAYERS AND SEEMINGLY INSURMOUNTABLE OBTACLE THE WORLD HAS PLACED BEFORE THEM WHO DARE TO ASPIRE TO RISE UP, REGARDLESS OF THEIR CIRCUMSTANCE AND THE BITTER CONSEQUENCES, AND BE THE BEST THAT THEY CAN BE!!!

THIS STORY CHRONICLES EACH QUIVERING TEAR, HEARTBREAK AND SHATTERED DREAM IN THIS FAMILY'S INCREDIBLE ODYSSEY AND OFFERS AN ESCAPE TO ALL WHO HAVE EXPERIENCED THE UGLY FACE OF RACISM AND/OR INJUSTICE, FOUGHT THE GOOD FIGHT AND, HAVING FAILED OR SUCCEEDED, EVEN AFTER HAVING THE FULL WEIGHT OF THE SYSTEM COME CRASHING DOWN ON THEM, CHOSE TO CONTINUE THE PERILOUS JOURNEY BECAUSE IT HAD TO BE DONE.

"FEAR NO EVIL," TAKES A HARD LOOK AT RACISM IN AMERICA PAST AND PRESENT DAY AND OFFERS A RAY OF HOPE TO THOSE WHO ARE OBJECTIVE ENOUGH TO SEE AND EXPERIENCE IT THROUGHOUT ITS TEAR STAINED PAGES. WHILE ITS STORY LINE BEGINS AND FOCUSES TO A DEGREE ON A SOUTHERN STATE IN THE DEEP SOUTH, NO ONE SHOULD MAKE THE MISTAKE OF BELIEVING THAT ITS PREMISE IS NOT COMMON TO EVERY STATE, CITY, ONE HORSE TOWN AND SLEEPY LITTLE HAMLET IN AMERICA. FOR, YOU SEE, "FEAR NO EVIL" IS A STORY OF US ALL. IT IS ABOUT CHEERING FOR THE UNDERDOG, WHICH AT SOME POINT IN TIME, WE WILL ALL BECOME. THEREFORE, ITS PREMISE IS UNIQUE TO NO ONE, NO ONE RACE, GEOGRAPHICAL REGION OR RELIGIOUS BELIEF. IT IS THE ETERNAL DREAM OF AMERICA.

ALTHOUGH THE STORY LINE AND EVENTS IN THIS BOOK ARE EXTREMELY ENTERTAINING, SOMETIMES FUNNY, EYE OPENING, AND OFTEN INSPIRING, BE ADVISED THAT THIS BOOK ALSO HARBORS MANY HIDDEN UNIVERSAL TRUTHS AND NOT SO EASY TO LOOK AT SIDES OF HUMAN NATURE THAT MAY CHALLENGE AN UNKNOWING READER.

ADDITIONALLY, FOR THE RECORD, THE AUTHOR WANTS THE WORLD TO KNOW THAT MISSISSIPPI AND THE DEEP SOUTH IN PARTICULAR, HAS NOW OVERCOME ITS MONSTROUS PAST RACIAL PROBLEMS AND IS AN IDEAL

PLACE IN WHICH TO RAISE ONE'S FAMILY. WITH A LOT OF SOUL SEARCHING, HARD WORK AND TEARS, MISSISSIPPI HAS CLEARLY EMERGED AS ONE OF THE TRUE LEADERS IN AMERICA WHERE POSITIVE RACE RELATIONS ARE CONCERNED.

BE ALSO ADVISED THAT MANY OF THE BASED IN TRUTH STORIES CONTAINED IN THIS BOOK ARE FROM THE AUTHOR'S PERCEPTION AS TAKEN FROM HIS MEMORY OF WHAT OCCURRED, AND/OR FROM THE PERCEPTION OF OTHERS WHO ALSO EXPERIENCED THE FULL WEIGHT OF THE THEN BRUTALLY RACIST MISSISSIPPI SYSTEM. HAVING MADE THE STATEMENTS ABOVE, THE AUTHOR WANTS THE WORLD TO KNOW THAT THIS BOOK IS NOT MEANT TO BE A VEHICLE TO MALIGN ANY PERSON, RACE, STATE, AGENCY, POLITICAL SYSTEM, BELIEF SYSTEM, AND/OR WAY OF LIFE. THE AUTHOR MERELY SEEKS TO SHARE THE EVENTS THAT SHAPED AND MOLDED HIM DURING THIS PERIOD IN HIS LIFE.

SOME NAMES IN THIS BOOK HAVE BEEN CHANGED AND/OR WITHHELD TO PROTECT THE INNOCENT, AND/OR THE DIGNITY OR PRIVACY OF SOME INDIVIDUALS. IN ADDITION, ALTHOUGH THIS BOOK IS BASED IN TRUTH, BE CLEARLY ADVISED THAT SOME INCIDENTS MAY HAVE BEEN ENHANCED TO CLARIFY AND PERPETUATE THE BOOK'S POSITIVE STORY LINE MORAL.

IN CONCLUSION, "FEAR NO EVIL," WILL MAKE YOU SEE FAR BEYOND THE PAIN OF STRUGGLE, SWEAT AND SACRIFICE TO A DISTANT CALM THAT RESIDES WITHIN THE SPIRIT OF EACH PERSON. IT IS INDEED A MAGIC CARPET RIDE TO FREEDOM!! PREPARE YOURSELF MY FRIEND, FOR A JOURNEY FROM WHICH YOU WILL NEVER RETURN!!!

FEAR NO EVIL!!!

CHAPTER	CONTENTS	PAGE

1. THE COLD, HARD REALITY OF IT ALL 01
2. CURSED BY A FEW BAD APPLES 06
3. THE PEACEFUL LITTLE ISLAND 09
4. THE SEED...13
5. ONE COURAGEOUS WOMAN.................................19
6. SWORN TO PROTECT AND SERVE.........................24
7. THE BLACK MARIAH..28
8. BIG WOMAN WHERE FORTH ARTH THOU...................33
9. THE BEAST THAT FEEDS ON ITS YOUNG...................41
10. THE DEATH OF INNOCENCE...................................46
11. THE TEARS OF A CHILD...50
12. THE AWAKENING...53
13. THE WIZARD OF OZ..60
14. AND THEN THERE WAS LITTLE OLE ME...................67
15. MR. SLICK..71
16. THE LEGEND OF BAD BOBBY...................................75
17. YA'LL PLEASE SAVE MR. HARVEY.........................81
18. THE SHOWDOWN ON OAKLEY STREET...................86
19. AH, FOR THE LOVE OF A PRETTY GIRL...................90
20. MAN, WHAT WAS I THINKING ABOUT...................94
21. MS. NIGG'S WHISKEY HOUSE................................99
22. THE REAL POWER 106
23. THE BLACK POLICE...111
24. YEP, PAY BACK IS A MOTHER...............................117
25. BOY, YOU TALKING ABOUT SOME FUN...................121
26. THE CHICAGO CONNECTION...................................128
27. IF YOU THINK YOU HAVE IT TOUGH......................134
28. CRUISING FOR A BRUISIN.......................................137
29. THE MOMENT OF TRUTH...141
30. OUT OF THE MOUTHS OF BABES............................146

FEAR NO EVIL!!!

CHAPTER	CONTENTS	PAGE
31.	A LITTLE TOO CLOSE TO HOME	150
32.	OBAAY	153
33.	THE BOYS IN THE BAND	159
34.	THE MAD DASH	164
35.	A SHORT DETOUR DOWN MEMORY LANE	168
36.	GROOVIN, ON A SUNDAY AFTERNOON	173
37.	OH, DON'T WORRY	178
38.	WE TOLD YA WE WERE GOING TO GIT YA!	181
39.	YOU CAN RUN BUT YOU CAN'T HIDE	187
40.	OBAAY POPS UP AGAIN	190
41.	THE SNEAKY FBI	194
42.	THE HURT	203
43.	THE EVIL POWERS THAT BE	213
44.	NO GREATER LOVE	219
45.	MAN, JUST HOW DID WE SURVIVE THE 60s & 70s	225
46.	THE POWER OF A MOTHER'S PRAYERS	233
47.	SPEAK TO ME LORD, SPEAK TO ME	239
48.	THE LITTLE MIRACLE	244
49.	THE SHIRT OFF YOUR BACK	249
50.	THE MUSIC BUSINESS	257
51.	THE PROFESSIONAL	266
52.	THE RISING STAR	273
53.	THE KKK	283
54.	AND THEN THE LIGHTS WENT ON	293
55.	THE TRUTH CAN REALLY HURT SOMETIMES	298
56.	SHOOT FIRST AND ASK QUESTIONS LATER	301
57.	TOE TO TOE WITH THE KKK	305
58.	THE VERY LAST STRAW	308
59.	EPILOG...SO WHERE DO WE GO FROM HERE?	317

FEAR NO EVIL!!!

x

FEAR
NO
EVIL!

****
****
******
**
*

BY
VERNON STEVE WEAKLEY

CHAPTER ONE

THE COLD, HARD REALITY OF IT ALL!

I've been told that I was born during a Chicago blizzard in the wee hours of the morning on December 7th, 1950, nine years removed from Pearl Harbor day. Hum, one has to wonder if my tumultuous birth on this infamous day was a prelude of things to come in my life? Rather than wallow in the negative, I choose to be forever positive and look frantically for the silver lining. As crazy as this may sound, I consider myself indeed blessed to have been raised as a small child in the deep South during the calm before the civil rights storm and eventually during the famous civil rights era. This experience gave me a better prospective on life that would make me appreciate my highs as well as my lows, no matter the circumstance.

Being raised in the deep South during the civil rights era afforded me an opportunity to see the absolute worst in people, especially where racism is concerned. I learned that the human species is capable of grotesque cruelty to its own.

Segregation and the diabolical evil of racism in the deep South in 1950 were rampant. Blacks were openly beaten, as I was told by my grandparents, for little more than innocently wandering into the wrong Whites only area at that point in time in America's history. Many Blacks were openly lynched in my home state of Mississippi for no more than the wrong glance. It's no secret, and there was no secret to be made of it. For at that time there was no shame in this thing called racism in the sick land, in which I was raised as a child. It was common knowledge in the deep South that there was a big difference in Black and White. White was the color of purity, righteousness and all that was sacred. And black was seen as an ugly thing, worthy of nothing but disdain, burden, ridicule and pain.

Blacks at this point in America's history were lynched and beaten for no reason other than the color of their skin. Second class citizen would have been a positive title for Black people in that day and age. Not only were we not second class citizens, we were so far down the ladder in terms of the pecking order that it would serve no good purpose to classify our station at this stage in America's history.

The concept of integration was like a fleeting idea that no one in the deep South could even dream about in the year 1950, much less, aspire to achieve. In a few short years though, things would indeed change. Integration would move to the fore and be more than a fleeting thought indulged by FOOLS AND SOON TO BE DEAD MEN. This thing, this haunting song called integration, was like an infant struggling to take its first steps without the aid of an adult trying to help it up and give it balance.

Black Americans knew of freedom as a result of the success of Blacks in Europe, in far away places like France. Hearing of it was like someone describing the sweet taste of chocolate ice cream to a child who had never experienced it. The anticipation to finally taste it and feel it oozing away in your mouth was pure exhilaration. As a result of being told how great it was to have actually tasted it by those who had been in the war, it made us here in the states want it oh so badly. We could almost taste it in our mouths as they had! The problem was however, that White America was not quite ready for this elusive and risky thing called freedom for Black Americans.

It is true, hearing about something that you have been told you cannot have is sheer torment. Perhaps it would have been better if we had never had our curiosity peaked. Black Americans wanted freedom so dearly in the late forties as a people, but the problem was, were we truly ready to risk it all to achieve it. And then the fifties finally arrived. With this new age, (the baby boom period) came a daring that fed and filled a few like Medger Evers and Martin Luther King with courage and thoroughly frightened at first, the rest of us. The intoxicating call of freedom was suddenly here in America and all around us. Believe me, things were getting ready to change.

You could feel the hunger for freedom in the air and see it in every Black person's anxiously waiting, nervous face. All that was needed now were the martyrs (Black and White) to bravely rip the pin hole, give their blood and knowingly offer their lives up for the cause. And come, bleed and die they did.

The Freedom Riders that fearlessly came into the South made clear the soon to be bloody path to which we would all be drawn. There was no turning back once it began. Although we could all smell death in the air, we still went towards it anyway, and yes, naively like little innocent lambs to their slaughter.

Mississippi's own courageous native son, Medgar Evers, felt the fatal sting of an assassin's bullet. John Kennedy's and his younger brother Bobby's lives were taken with a bloody exclamation mark that shook the entire world. Tears flowed from all of our eyes as a result of these events and stained our faces forever. Even till this very day, many of us know exactly where we were when the news of these tragedies ripped through our minds. Of course, it will be the same way for the terrible tragedy that America was forced to endure on September 11, 2001. None of us will ever forget the horror our weeping eyes and minds were forced to bear witness to! Oh what pain we endure for the freedom we now, seemingly take so much for granted.

I recall having a young person in the year 2000 ask me what was wrong with Black people back in those days, the fifties, sixties and prior? Did they not have dignity and courage? Why would proud, strong, able bodied Black men allow themselves to be dragged out of their homes and killed at the whim of White people. And how could Medger Evers, a well-known seemingly irreplaceable pillar of the Black community be shot down by a White man who boldly strolled without fear no doubt, into the middle of his neighborhood in the bosom of the safety of his friends and neighbors and calmly fire the fatal shots to extinguish such a valuable son?

Before answering the young man who had asked me this numbing question, I paused long and hard, carefully thought through my answer and with all the courage I could muster, told him, that "when there was a choice between seeing your wife, and small kids savagely killed and giving up your own life so they could live on, most good and decent men would gladly step out of their homes, when there is no other option, when called out in the dead of night into this terrible fate. That was the dilemma that Black men faced in those days. There was no other choice that made sense." Justice in those days in the deep South was an illusion thoroughly hidden by white sheets, and those who had the might and yes, ugliness and seething evil within them to even think of such a crime, much less on carry it out with such glee.

Courage comes in a lot of different forms. The courage to willingly give up your life and die so that others, who you love so dearly may live, is probably the greatest courage and love of all. Jesus Christ gave this sparkling example to us by dying for mankind's sins on the cross. He could have easily averted his fate with a simple nod of his head. Or, merely uttered the words and ten thousand angels would have instantly come to his rescue. But he didn't because of the boundless depths of his love for us all.

If you really want to hear something funny, in my naive heart, I truly believe that the overwhelming number of White people in the deep South at that time in America's history (the sixties and before then) really liked Black people. That's not to say that the hard core haters didn't exist, because they did. And they indeed made their presence known. They went about their evil racist tasks as if it was their God given calling.

CHAPTER TWO

CURSED BY A FEW BAD APPLES

The Klan and many other racist organizations like them, set the South ablaze with their hatred and violence, and in my view, gave the majority of good people (both White and Black) in the South a bad name. The deep South in America as far as the rest of the world was concerned, was a hideous place, filled with ignorant, barefooted, tobacco chewing rednecks and uneducated Blacks who did not have the sense to get out of a hard driving rain, much less have sense enough to flee this terrible existence like many had before them. This was what the world at that time openly thought about the deep South, and Mississippi in particular, given the sick images that were in the forefront of the news media in that day and time.

All of this negativity and lingering bad publicity occurred because of a stupid few. Sad, but true. My premise that most White people deep down inside really like Black people in general is a curious phenomena that was present in the deep South at that day in time. The good White folks in the South liked to keep Black folks close, as if KEEPING THEM OH SO NEAR and wearing them around their neck like a big red bow tie, or rubbing their heads would bring them good luck. The odd thing though, was that it was obvious that there indeed was a bond between them. Whites however, insisted that Blacks know their place, stay in their place and be happy and obedient like little children while they were in their presence.

The evidence was undeniable and overtly obvious for all the world to see. Blacks were welcomed into their homes to be their servants, nannies caring for their precious children, cook their food for them and even care for them on their dying bed. Or better still, be the best companion and coon hunting buddy for even the biggest Nigger haters and Klan's men across the South.

So yes, whether we will admit it or not, there was an incredibly mysterious bond behind closed doors and in the small communities throughout the deep South between Blacks and Whites. Although this powerful bond was a potential bridge that could have been used to grow into a positive path. It was denied its natural growth and could span no further.

I've also been mystified at how the biggest racists and outwardly bigoted public figures dating back to slavery time could have numerous Black mistresses and long-time lovers without fear or shame. They boldly ventured into our Black neighborhoods and/or slaves' row in those days to take their pleasure with our women.

What a contrast on the other hand, if a Black man in the deep South wanted to get killed or let's just say wanted for whatever crazy reason to commit suicide, all he had to do was cast a curious eye at any White woman. And believe me, any White woman would truly do. He would quickly get his wish and meet his maker in tall order. It was no secret that Black people were fair game for any little excuse in the deep South during this period.

It was no wonder that many Blacks ran from the South in great numbers during this time. There was no way that dignity could remain, in such a twisted environment. Black people ran completely out of their shoes from the South to cities like Chicago in droves. Although slavery has been abolished for years, I consider myself and many, many more like me to be no more than modern day runaway slaves. I eventually, like many others before me, took flight from an intolerable system in the deep South, that many who remain there, would even deem a curse. I am not alone in my circumstance. No, No, NO, I am not alone. Black flight from the South has occurred for hundreds of years. Young Blacks have fled to many northern states like shivering migratory birds. The only difference is, that with the exception of occasional visits to be with and/or bury love ones, they left with no intention of ever returning back to the South to make it their home. And why shouldn't they run and never plan to return? The only future that they could see in the deep, deep South at that point in America's history promised only diminished dignity, poverty and/or an agonizing death at the end of a stiff rope.

CHAPTER THREE

THE PEACEFUL LITTLE ISLAND

And now, imagine if you will a quiet family of seven, gleefully oblivious to all around them. Adrift like a peaceful island in the midst of an angry sea. That is what it was like growing up in the Stevens/Weakley household for a small child. This setting was no accident or dream. It was a skillfully crafted, unchanging still life portrait created by God working through my grandparents and mother to protect those that were most precious to them from the cruel world. Inside our walls, my brothers, sister and I as small children, saw no evil, spoke no evil and willingly warmed ourselves in this God spun cocoon that nourished us, oh so safely, to adulthood.

No matter how loud the commotion outside our home, or how awful the murder, mayhem and drunkenness got in the streets just outside of our doorway, inside our warm protecting walls was a deafening quiet that seemed to scream to the world about it, that these people will not, and shall not be disturbed. Aside from my grandmother and aunt Dollie, (who were the self-appointed screaming sirens for our family) everyone else barely spoke above a whisper.

Although all around us just outside our doorway was violence and unbelievable poverty, as children, we knew not of it.

We also knew no hardship, no sorrow, and no pain and were told to dream of only those things that represented the best of what life had to offer.

Now that I am adult and can look back on those days, I, in some ways feel ashamed that my family was so blessed while many others around us withered away in poverty and hopeless despair. Please do not misunderstand what I am saying. I was glad for what we had. I only wish that others around us had been as blessed as we were. My family was definitely not rich financially; quite the contrary, we were a long, long way from it. But in spite of our lack of material wealth, we somehow seemed to always have the best of all things. We were indeed blessed and whether the old adage that ignorance is bliss applied to us or not, we merrily went about our lives with a smile.

We were told by our mom and grandparents to dream only the dreams of kings, and of good things. As a result of this positive implanted seed, we faithfully strived to become these things.

My personal thanks, in aiding us along this journey, go out to a very special lady who worked at a public library at the end of the street from our home named Vivian Romans.

Many a day, as small children, my grandfather would walk my brother Stanley and me down to the library and turn us over to this wonderful lady. She challenged us to read a book weekly and like an anxious mother hen, carefully watched over us to make certain that we stayed the course. It was there that we eventually got lost in the many wonders that the world, through these books, had to offer. Along with my brother and a few of our playmates, I floated effortlessly around the world in our journeys. From these journeys, we better understood the many life principles that our parents were teaching and instilling in us.

Reading books created a solid foundation of understanding and reasoning that has remained with us all for a life time. The wealth that we were so graciously blessed with in taking these incredible journeys have constantly replenished us.

This lifelong blessing and limitless replenishing intellectual oasis sprung from our parents and the beautiful smiling face of a great lady named Ms. Roman.

It is very true, one good person can indeed make all the difference in the life of a child. Ms. Roman was a critical piece of the God spun puzzle that made up our lives. She, along with our parents, set our feet on the path of knowledge that would sustain and fuel us when we eventually ventured away from our nest.

I recall as a child, my mom sharing that she was advised by a well respected man in our community, and many other prominent people, to move the family away from our so called "terrible neighborhood." They said, "Lola, you will never be able to raise your kids in such a terrible environment. Nothing good will ever become of them as a result of the terrible weight that your decision to remain here has cursed them with!"

They lamented that "the blight of the neighborhood would win in the long run and drag you and your kids down with it." But guess what! They were all proven wrong!!

With God's grace of course, my mother and grandparents came through like gang busters and proved all of the naysayers incorrect. The amazing thing is that we, my brothers, sister and I, all grew to be reasonably successful, when many of the so called silver spoon kids fell quickly to ruins by the wayside.

Even though they were well outside of the trash and human devastation that their parents called our neighborhood, they were indeed sucked in from their rich gated communities and many, even to this day, are hopeless drug addicts and alcoholics right there in the very ghettos that their now long deceased, well-to-do parents bemoaned. I do not think being rich was their curse. I truly believe however, looking down on those with less than they was what brought God's ironic wrath on them.

It's funny how so many people who have very little hands on knowledge of the ghetto in the world today, instantly associate failure and the absolute worse about people who live there. The truth is that there are many, many, decent, hard working, good people who reside there. And, an even bigger truth is that many great people, although some may not openly admit it today, sprung from these humble beginnings.

As I grew older and moved ever farther outside the nurturing, blessed walls of our home, I came to know of the horrors out in the so-called high society world that we had been so mercifully sheltered from.

My older brother Stanley once told me long after I reached adulthood, how my mother practically cried her eyes out when I moved out of our home my junior year in college to take an apartment on the edge of Jackson State College. Of course, being the great consoling person he is, he was able to allay my sweet mother's fears and convince her that all would be okay. Although time would prove him right, I wish now that I am an adult, that I had stayed for a while longer. And, in doing so, slipped many of the direct hits and bruises I received oh so young in life while out there foolishly rushing to experience the world. And now, as an older man myself with a child of my own, I find myself worrying about my daughter. For I now know the endless depths of my mother's fears and worries, and have experienced for myself the many painful tears that I caused my mother to cry.

My dear mother cried when I flew away from the nest because she felt that even though I was leaving the so-called terrible ghetto, that I would not be safe. How ironic!! She was right though. I learned of the worst of life after leaving the loving and safe arms of my little family nest there at 131 W. Oakley Street.

CHAPTER FOUR

THE SEED

My grandfather, Jeff Stevens, ran a successful pool room in downtown Jackson and was well respected in our community! I remember him as a very well-dressed, extremely proud, handsome man with a strong jaw. While most of my neighbors would say he was a quiet, no nonsense type of guy, I knew him as a loving, playful man who never missed an opportunity to make me smile. He was a decent, hard working, God fearing man who was constantly helping our neighbors with their troubles. He kept many of our wayward friends from going to jail, with just an assuring word to the White arresting officer. Anyone possessing the power to avert this terrible tragedy for a neighbor was held in high regards by his community. I think it would be safe to say that my grandfather was an invaluable asset to us all.

At that point in time in Jackson Mississippi's history there was no such thing as Black policemen. Justice was dispensed to Blacks purely at the discretion and occasional mercy of White people.

My grandfather was also the perfect role model for all of the kids in our neighborhood. And, as far as the other kids were concerned, he was like their second dad. If they were blessed enough to have a dad around at all. Oddly enough, this was my situation as well because my father died when I was a very small child. I never really knew him. So, my grandfather not only took up the slack for my brothers, sister and me, but the entire neighborhood as well.

As my grandfather walked home from work each day, kids would dance and play around him as if he was the Pied Piper. He gave us kids most of his spare time and went many steps further by helping a lot of my friends' families out financially. My grandfather also gave out plenty of good, sound advice when it was needed. People (both Black and White) loved and respected him.

I recall as a small child, our front porch being filled to the brim with people from our neighborhood coming over to visit with my grandfather. It was like a daily ritual for most of them. And Friday night, oh man, what a time they would have watching the Gillette Friday night fights and many other regularly scheduled television programs, like cowboy shows. You talking about some funny stuff!

Don't even let there be a big gun battle or showdown. The whole block, especially the men, would predict and anticipate it happening weeks before it would actually occur. And when it finally went down! Whee!!! All you would hear was, "I told you so! Didn't I tell ya!! I knew he would have to kill that sucker!" They all would be in an uproar about how their favorite cowboy hero shot it out with the bad guy! My grandfather and his friends, Mr. Buck, Mr. Blue and many more would talk about it and act it out on our front porch for weeks. What a hilarious sight! They really had fun!

Being the first in our neighborhood to have a television, made it an absolute necessity for us to share our God given blessings with all. That being the case, imagine if you will, the commotion that this new fangled invention caused in our little dirt poor neighborhood.

People would come from miles around to sit on our front porch and watch the television inside our living room through one of our big front windows. My grandfather laid down the law and made certain that no one got too rowdy at these gatherings. He made it absolutely crystal clear that if you were going to be at his house, you were going to respect his family, home, and most especially the women and children. Now his definition of too rowdy, was a different story entirely. Let's just say there was no loud cursing or hands being put on each other!

Our neighborhood had a lot of tough people in it. Some had killed many people. They also could get sloppy, falling down drunk at the drop of a hat if you let them. The operative world in that last sentence is LET THEM! My grandfather did not play that stuff at all. He kept everyone in line without raising his voice above a whisper and/or repeating himself. They all gathered on our front porch on these Friday nights to enjoy the TV at our humble house. But, you know what? No one ever got to far out of line or challenged my grandfather during these high energy, emotionally charged events. The one thing we all did though, was have a lot of fun at these gatherings.

My mom, aunt and grandmother were the true jewels of our family. They were beautiful ladies with a lot of Indian blood in them. My grandmother was a thin framed, light-skinned lady with long flowing gray hair down her back. Feisty wouldn't begin to describe her. She could hold her own with the best of them, when she had to, in a fight or cursing spree. As tough and as feisty as she was though, I never once heard her and my grandfather argue.

My grandfather treated my grandmother like a queen. She in turn returned his open display of respect and love by showering him with tenderness, devotion and the utmost in affection. Even as kids we noticed as well as all of our neighbors how much in love they were. The love that they constantly showed each other was unbelievably contagious. Couples who were having trouble in their marriage, in my opinion, came to our house just to see how two people in love should treat each other. And, as a result of their time around my grandparents, their own relationships were made much better.

My grandparents would go out of their way and give their last to feed anyone in our neighborhood who needed a helping hand. And in our neighborhood, it seemed as if every one needed a helping hand. Down and out people seemed to always be getting a plate of food, clothes and/or money from our side kitchen door. Over the years they always seemed to come back when they finally got up on their feet to thank my grandmother and grandfather for helping them when nobody else would.

I often hear people talk about the sins of the father being passed down from generation to generation. While others may wrestle with this dilemma in a negative sense, my family, I am absolutely certain, has been tremendously blessed the opposite way over the years by God as a result of the unselfish charity my grandfather, grandmother, Mom, aunts and uncles have extended eagerly to others. The effect of 'Sins of the Father' can be devastating. Many people out there who are having a hard time and can't understand why, may need to closely examine and research this circumstance where their lives and past family histories are concerned.

I am truly blessed and thank God that I have always had positive blessings that generously flowed to me. I believe that these blessings have occurred to a large degree because of the family members and generations that came before me that have happily done God's work to help anyone who needed a hand. For those who always seem to be having the worst of life heaped on them and they truly don't understand why, I recommend that when they pray they also ask God to mercifully remove any sins or things that their past generations may have done to offend him and/or anger him.

God is indeed merciful. Sometimes it's just a matter of knowing what to pray for. Not knowing that you had a sin sent down the line to you, could cause a person to easily over look this factor in their prayers. If you are sincere, God will answer your prayers and lift the burdens/curse that have been sent down the line to you from a previous person or generation. The key is knowing that you should, just to be on the safe side, also pray for forgiveness for sins of your fore fathers etc.. I learned this from my mom.

My dear sweet mother, who was just as beautiful as my grandmother in my opinion, didn't inherit her mother's tough side. She is very kind-hearted and rather laid back. My most vivid childhood memory of my mother is of her working hard in her sewing room from sun up to sun down. I also remember her taking off in a mad dash to the many homes of the sick people in our neighborhood to help them. She was the one that everyone in our little neighborhood seemed to call on when they or one of their family members were sick or on their death bed. My mom never complained when the call came. She just gathered her coat and purse and quickly hurried where she was needed. She is blessed with a gift of soothing people and making them feel better, regardless of their predicament or the final outcome!

My father died when I was a very small child. I don't remember anything about him. My mom was left to raise four small kids without the help of a husband. She was a natural at the job. She could lay out your faults and screw-ups going back to birth in a manner that tugged at your heart strings.

There was no talking your way into innocence or creating a shadow of doubt that would allow you to get away with a caper. My mom had the power to see right through your shenanigans. The old television lawyer, Perry Mason, who was famous for breaking people down on the witness stand and making them confess to their every sin and fault, had nothing on her. When my Mom got through talking to you, there was doubt as to why you should not have done whatever it was you had screwed up. She could bring tears to our eyes with the hurt and the disappointment in you that filled her eyes, when she counseled us when we had done wrong as children.

While my mother did not spare the rod when we were kids, when it came down to it in most instances it just wasn't necessary because she could wound you, oh so deeply, emotionally when you had done wrong, by just talking to you. At the end of one of her long talking sessions, we kids, would be eager to just jump on the bed, assume her little 45 degree angle wiping position to get it all over with.

My aunt Dollie chose not to follow my grandmother and Mom into the seamstress profession. She chose, as her final life work to be a beautician. Pictures of aunt Dollie as a teenager and young adult show an incredibly beautiful thin person. But I think I will always love and remember her as still beautiful and classy mind you, but slightly on the overweight side. Just to show you how attractive my aunt is, I can easily recall one of the many times she has been singled out for her beauty. Once the mother of Phylicia

Rashad, the famous television star who is best known for her role as Clare Hustible on the old Cosby show, while on a speaking engagement in Houston Texas, a few years ago, picked aunt Dollie out of the crowd and spoke in length in giving her glowing compliments. She professed to be awestruck at aunt Dollies incredible beauty only but a few years ago, just prior to the writing on this book.

Aunt Dollie at that time was in her late sixties. You would not be able to tell it though from looking at her. She has a youthful Indian heritage look, beautiful skin, great hair, incredible facial features and a drop dead gorgeous, radiant smile that would knock your eyes out. Ms. Rashad's mother went on and on about how uniquely beautiful aunt Dollie was and how incredibly rich her Indian features and heritage were. So when I say that aunt Dollie is fat, don't take that to mean that she isn't top notch. She is and has always been the class and belle of the ball. She was and still is my favorite relative. She and I just seemed to always have this magical connection. This connection has continually fueled my self-esteem all of my life.

CHAPTER FIVE

ONE COURAGEOUS WOMAN TAKES A STAND

One of the scariest times for me as a very young child growing up in Mississippi involved my aunt Dollie. My aunt at that point in her life was a housekeeper for a well-to-do White family that lived across town far removed from the Black community. She at that point in time in her life was somewhat on the overweight side.

On this particular hot summer's day, she was riding the city bus home from working in the home of her White employer. In the fifties and prior, Blacks were forced to ride in the back of the bus. It was here at the back of the bus that many housekeepers shared their stories and marveled at the strange things their White employers did. Oddly enough, in spite of the indignities they faced being the so-called hired help, it was glaringly apparent from their stories that their lives were very similar in that that they all wielded enormous power in their White households. As if to validate their authority, some of the housekeepers would excitedly show off large sums of money that their White employers would entrust them with to pay bills and so forth before returning back to their households.

It was also here, at the back of the bus, that many fortified their resolve, as my aunt did, to somehow get themselves away from this demoralizing occupation. While they felt that they were blessed to even have a job during these tough hand-to-mouth times in the fifties, it was even tougher to daily undergo the bitter sting of racism and indignity that they encountered just because of the times they lived in. The South during this day and age was seething with hatred of Black people by a very vocal number of Whites who unfortunately ruled the day. Blacks who were blessed enough to even get a seat at the back of the bus on their ride home would often have to stand and give up their seat to White people if the they wanted them.

On this particular ill fated day, my aunt Dollie was one of the unlucky ones. She was not able to get a seat, so she had to stand and desperately cling to the jumbling and tumbling bus' ceiling straps to keep from falling when it made a rough turn.

Somewhere during that bus' long, hot, bumpy journey, the Devil reared his awful head. A White man decided, for whatever crazy reason, that he would go back to the back of the bus and harass the Black people.

Most of the buses running from the many affluent White neighborhoods in Jackson ran right smack dab through the heart of the poor Black neighborhoods. They carried mostly Black women who were nannies or housekeepers. This evil White man decided, I guess for fun that day, that he would boot Black people off the back of the bus with his foot or knee as they got off.

My aunt had finally been able to get a seat as others had gotten off the bus. Although she was getting a much needed rest from her bumpy standing ordeal, her relief grew quickly into a different kind of anxiety as she watched this hurtful and demoralizing scene unfold before her very eyes. She said she found herself frozen in time, unable to do anything at that very moment, forced to watch this mean uncaring man boot off several of the poor ladies that were her friends.

These ladies were good, decent, hard working people who in some instances were old, tired and sick. She felt so sorry for them. They certainly did not deserve this type of evil treatment. Many violently stumbled down the awkward bus stairs onto their faces on the street pavement after not being able to catch their balance from the force of the blow they had received. After each incident, the White man would laugh out loud and look around at everyone as if to encourage the other White people on the bus and some frightened and/or confused Blacks, to join in laughing with him. Sadly enough, many people did join in laughing with him.

Aunt Dollie said, as she watched this awful scene repeat itself over and over as her get off point rapidly approached, she decided that this was her MOMENT OF TRUTH! Although she knew what the terrible consequences would be, she decided that she would FEAR NO EVIL and would just have to pay them that day. She made up her mind that there was no way in hell this guy was going to get away with treating her in this fashion!

Aunt Dollie said she sat with clenched fists, folded arms and puffed mouth waiting for her turn to come. In our family we have come to learn that when aunt Dollie's anger got to this point, she was about to blow! The mighty volcano, Mount St. Helen, had nothing on her. She got madder and madder and madder as her bus stop drew near.

When her bus stop finally came, my aunt Dollie was like a ticking time bomb ready to explode. The muscles in her arms, fists, legs and face were tense and as hard as steel. There was no way that she would let herself be abused as the other housekeepers had been. She slowly got up and walked to the door.

True to form, as aunt Dollie got in the bus rear exit doorway, the White man wasted no time putting his entire leg, foot first, into her behind. He kicked and then pushed her with all he had. But, this time, rather than see a person shooting out of the bus from the sheer force he had exerted, aunt Dollie didn't move an inch. She had wisely grabbed the inside door rail and braced herself. She then quickly turned to face the man! As she turned, she pulled a ten-inch butcher's knife from her purse and started slashing with all her might at this evil man. As she would swing to stab at him, he frantically backed up toward the front door to avoid being cut to shreds.

People both Black and White were screaming to the top of their lungs in sheer terror, falling down to the floor of the bus and to the sides of each aisle to get out of the way of her mighty swings. With each powerful blow from aunt Dollie's arm, he would just barely avoid being slashed into pieces. That White man will probably never know how blessed he was that day.

I don't know if I can do this part of the story justice. It really takes Aunt Dollie to tell it to you. Although this situation definitely was not funny, my aunt Dollie would have us all falling all over ourselves with laughter, at the way she acted it out and told this story.

The man, as she described it, was stumbling, half running, falling backward with his hands and arms flailing away like a rag doll at break neck speeds towards the front of the bus. He was screaming and using the bathroom in his pants at the same time with aunt Dollie swinging at him each step of the way. As soon as the hand with the butcher's knife would come down toward him, her other balled fist would come over the top of her head and hit him full blast.

The guy was moving so fast that he backed completely off of the bus with aunt Dollie all over him screaming and cursing at the top of her lungs. The man, once he slammed and bounced on the hard street pavement, began crawling backwards on the ground, doing the back stroke and anything else he could do to get away from aunt Dollie and keep her off of him. He finally, thanks to the Lord, was able to pick himself up and take off running. All of this occurred in a matter of seconds! Aunt Dollie got off the bus after him, but decided to quickly get back on it and not chase after him. The man kept running as fast as he could down the street. He was screaming to the top of his lungs as he ran, "Help, Please don't let her kill me yawl! Please don't let her kill me!!"

Lucky for aunt Dollie, she just barely made it back on to the bus before the White bus driver hastily closed the door. The Black people as well as some of the White people on the bus were cheering aunt Dollie to the top of their lungs. The remaining White people on the bus who were not cheering for her were cowering in utter fear. Aunt Dollie was cursing and literally foaming at the mouth with anger. She kept screaming out loud, "Oh how I wish I could have cut that Son Of A Bitch in two."

The bus driver, who was scared stiff as well, stopped the bus at the next stop, excitedly jumped out and ran to the first phone booth he could find and called the police. He quickly returned after making his call and continued down his route. As they drove down the street, they passed the White man who had caused the trouble bent over from exhaustion, crying, bleeding and throwing up whatever he had eaten in the last couple of days as a result of his traumatic ordeal.

He was bleeding from injuries from falling and stumbling to get the hell off that death machine. Lucky for him aunt Dollie had not connected with the blade of her butcher's knife. Every thing else though, that she threw at him, namely those left hooks of hers and kicks had hit this guy as he moved backwards blindly to get away from her. This included the stairs and steel rails inside the bus. The man, as they bean to pass him, began to scream for the bus driver to pull the bus over. He said he had called the police and they were on their way. Everyone on the bus, including aunt Dollie stayed in their seats. The Jackson police were there in mere seconds. They immediately began to talk to the man who had started the trouble.

CHAPTER SIX

SWORN TO PROTECT AND SERVE?

In case you are not familiar with Mississippi police in the fifties, I'll fill you in and tell you that any Black person going to jail in that dark day and time, even for a regular arrest could be beaten senseless by the all White Jackson police force. Some of the dirty little tricks they used in those days was to either take you off and beat the living crap out of you before they took you to jail, beat you in the paddy wagon as they drove you to jail, beat you in a darkened elevator at the police station, or, if they didn't intend for you to ever leave again, beat you to death or lynch you in the wee hours of the morning while you were helpless in your jail cell.

Aunt Dollie was in extreme danger. She had committed the ultimate sin by attacking a White man in the deep South. As I said earlier, aunt Dollie was a rather big woman. To add to her terrible dilemma, big Black people seemed to be a particular juicy target of abuse by the Jackson police force in that day and time. It was as if a big person's demise signaled a great victory of sort for the policeman who could bring them to their knees without the assistance of another officer.

The paddy wagon came a few seconds after the police arrived. The paddy wagon and the extremely brutal and evil

White policemen who drove it in Jackson had its own sort of history and ugly meaning for the Black community. It was nicknamed the Black Mariah. I'll tell you this, it was the utmost in terror on wheels. It was jet black, had rough jagged edges, big ugly wheels and was as heavy and as solid as a tank.

On many occasions, THE SICKENING MOANS AND CRIES OF ITS OCCUPANTS COULD BE HEARD AS IT SLOWLY CREPT THROUGH THE STREETS of the Black community. Everyone in Jackson knew that when the Black Mariah showed up on the scene, some poor Black person was going to be beaten unmercifully. Just seeing it drive through your neighborhood was enough to cause the weak of heart to throw up or send chills down your spine. It didn't matter what people were doing, when the Black Mariah drove through their street, people froze in their tracks, and just silently stared at it.

As the Black Mariah came to a stop, one of the White arresting officers grabbed and threw aunt Dollie to the ground. He began to curse her and loudly announce "NIGGER YOUR ASS IS GRASS." Everyone on the bus looked down in their seat or away from what was happening. Neither the Black nor White people on the now parked bus said a word. Then the two burly White policemen who had driven the Black Mariah snatched aunt Dollie up by her hair, throat and arms and slung her up against the side of the paddy wagon as if to use its immovable bulk as a weapon.

Aunt Dollie said she stuck to the side of the paddy wagon as if it had super glue on it to keep from bouncing back towards the officers. She then turned her head away from them and braced herself for the blows that were about to come. All of a sudden, the White man who had started the trouble limped up to the Black Mariah drivers and said, "That's right, whip that Niggers ass." The White people on the bus all of a sudden started to shout through the open windows to the police that the man had gotten what he deserved. The people on the bus also began to laugh at him!

One of the regular city police directed the bus driver, with several giant sweeping motions of his hand to get off the bus. They quickly got his side of the story. Although still obviously unnerved, the bus driver, to his credit, honestly told the policemen what had happened. The bus driver and many of the other people on the bus knew my aunt Dollie as a regular rider. Some of the White people on the bus also began to tell the officers by talking from their seat out of the window that she didn't start the trouble. The Black people on the bus kept their heads faced downward and didn't say a word.

The White man who was still wiping blood from his hand, knees and forehead began to tell the Black Mariah drivers that aunt Dollie had pulled a knife on him and tried to kill him. He went on to say that he hadn't done anything to provoke her.

He boldly announced in an excited voice to the police, "I only ran because I didn't want any of the good White people on the bus to get hurt." He went on to foolishly say he was trying to trick Aunt Dollie outside so that he could teach her a lesson.

One of the police at that moment burst out laughing and told the White guy "Sir, you're a disgrace to the White race." You let a big fat greasy Nigger like this kick your ass." He was pointing at Aunt Dollie as he told the man this. The police were obviously having a laugh at his expense. Although humiliating to Aunt Dollie and the other Black people of the bus, it kind of took the edge off of the policeman's anger for a moment. Even the usually stone faced drivers of the paddy wagon began to laugh. This was a relief in itself. Black Mariah drivers usually never cracked a smile.

Aunt Dollie said that during this time, she didn't say a word. She had her hands folded over her chest and was breathing very hard and staring at the man who had started the trouble, with a look that would kill. Aunt Dollie was still propped up against the outside door of the paddy wagon hoping that she would at least get a chance to tell her side of the story.

After the policeman finished taking the bus driver's statement, they again spoke to the man who had caused the trouble in private. It was as if they did not want anyone to hear what he was saying. They then proceeded to tell aunt Dollie she was under arrest. Keep in mind, that at this point aunt Dollie had been pretty peaceful during the time the police were there. She knew that any anger, resistance or comments from her to the man who started the trouble would only make a very bad situation worse. It took all she could muster to keep her temper and adrenaline from kicking in and causing her to loudly scream out what had really happened. But she controlled this burning urge.

One of the Black Mariah drivers announced that aunt Dollie was going to jail regardless of whose fault it was. He then pointed toward the paddy wagon's door and loudly shouted "GET YOUR ASS UP IN THERE NIGGER," as aunt Dollie reached for one of the door rails to get in, the other driver pushed her violently from behind into the paddy wagon. At this point aunt Dollie realized that she was in big trouble. The bus with all of the witnesses and people who were on her side was pulling off. It would now be just her, the man, the two White arresting police officers and the two Black Mariah drivers.

It was at this point that she also realized that the White police were not laughing anymore. This incident had suddenly taken a wrong turn down a steep, dark and scary alleyway!

CHAPTER SEVEN

THE BLACK MARIAH

Aunt Dollie figured this was it. She was now all alone and completely vulnerable. But to her surprise, the driver who had threw her in the paddy wagon gave her a weird "your time is going to come look" and quickly slammed the paddy wagon door in her face. The sound that heavy metal door made was ear piercing. It seemed to shut aunt Dollie off from the world. It also seemed to suck all of the courage and calmness she had had up until this point, out of her. She began to tremble. She quickly went to sit down. She said sitting in the Black Mariah waiting to see what would happen next was like being engulfed by death. The air was still and musty. The seats were cold and wet with what she thought was urine. Aunt Dollie had never been inside the Black Mariah before and she would never want to be in it again.

The two regular policemen and the Black Mariah drivers stood outside in earshot of the door talking with the man who had started the trouble. He apparently said something they didn't like because one of the paddy wagon drivers surprisingly out loud announced "So you're not scared of this big fat Nigger huh?" He then, before the stuttering man could get a word out, flung open the paddy wagon door and began to throw him in with aunt Dollie. Aunt Dollie said she stood up and quickly moved up to the door entrance. She had a look on her face to let the man know that she was going to finish the job she had started as soon as he got inside.

She told me that at that very moment she felt like she could have slaughtered the whole world without any remorse!

Aunt Dollie said what happened next, although it was not funny not even one bit at that moment, was the funniest thing she had ever witnessed up until that point in her life. The White man, who they had now gotten ready to toss up in the paddy wagon with her, began to wildly hold on to the side of the door of the paddy wagon for dear life. He started to cry uncontrollably and scream at the top of his lungs, "Please don't! Please don't put me in there with that crazy Nigger! Please don't put me in there!" Aunt Dollie said, that he was struggling so hard not to let them put him in with her that he put both feet on the edge of the door seal to prevent the officers from throwing him in with her. That's just how afraid he was. It was a pitiful sight!!

After a few minutes of pushing and shoving and the man pleading with them, they finally let him go. They were only pretending they were going to put him in with aunt Dollie. He just didn't know how blessed he was that day!! After all the trouble he had caused, if they would have put him in there, I guarantee you that only one person would have survived the trip!

The police decided to let the man go!! They abruptly told him, "Get your sorry ass on away from here!" They then, very roughly, pushed him away from the paddy wagon toward the street. They looked in at Aunt Dollie one more time as they laughed out loud at the man, and then slammed the paddy wagon door.

It would have been nice if the evening would have ended at this point, but it didn't! As I said earlier, the Jackson police in those days would beat Black people unmercifully. It was not uncommon to not be able to recognize a loved one after they came home from jail, because they had been beaten so badly.

Somewhere in her long journey to the police station in the back of the dark paddy wagon, aunt Dollie decided that day that she had had enough of being mistreated and abused by the Mississippi justice system. She stood at the door of the Black Mariah, holding the small window bars peering out as it drove along for the world to see. People stared at her and pointed at her as she passed. Anyone else may have been totally embarrassed by being in the back of the patty wagon but aunt Dolly said she felt proud. She had finally stood up for what she believed was right.

Aunt Dollie told me that the paddy wagon seemed to float over the streets of Jackson in slow motion as it made its way to the police station. She likened it to a funeral procession. Black people that they passed, stopped dead in their tracks and gazed at the paddy wagon with an eerie look, as if they knew what was about to happen to her. In any case, she made up her mind during her ride that she was not going to just stand there and take a whipping as many Blacks before her had. She tearfully came to terms with the fact that this decision could cost her, her life.

All of Jackson was a buzz with the news of what had happened to her on the bus. Our family was very well know throughout Jackson and respected for being law-abiding citizens. The word that aunt Dollie had been the person on the bus quickly made its way to our household. My grandparents contacted our family lawyer and the police station to see if we could quickly get aunt Dollie released. But this wasn't to be. Although we were absolutely certain that aunt Dollie was in their custody, no one at the police station would admit they had her at that point. You can imagine the fear my family felt at this time.

Aunt Dollie said they rode her around Jackson for a while and then as night came, they headed to the police station. The police station she said looked to her like an ancient castle, dark and shrouded in shadows as they pulled up to it. The entryway they pulled into was at the rear of the station. The paddy wagon came to a dead stop. It sat motionless for a few quiet minutes. She assumed the drivers were filling out some type of paper work. She nervously moved close to the door's little small window and peeked out. All she could see was a rather fat, White policeman standing with his hands folded across his chest looking towards her. He stood as stiff as a board. At first, he didn't appear to be real. He looked more like a lifeless wax statue in an old eerie museum. Occasionally he exhibited some life signs by moving his head to spit chewing tobacco onto the dirty concrete floor every few seconds or so. She assumed this odd looking character was the jailer because he had a large round metal rack of keys attached to his belt.

Then all of a sudden, he began to give her his full attention. Up until this point he had not even acknowledged the fact that she was there. It was if he was content to allow her to examine him from head to toe and soak him in completely with her eyes. But then, all of a sudden, his eyes glared at her and rolled back in his head like a shark getting ready to bite down on a piece of raw meat. He looked at her with glassy red eyes, as if she was his evening supper. As the Black Mariah's door swung open, two additional, burly White policeman with nightsticks appeared as if from nowhere and stood off to the side of the Black Mariah's door with their nightsticks held over their heads. It was as if they wanted a vantage point from which to attack her.

One of the Black Mariah drivers quickly slung open the door and roughly grabbed aunt Dollie by her dress collar and snatched her outside. As he pulled her out of the paddy wagon, the paddy wagon drivers jokingly called the other positioned officers over and told them what happened. Aunt Dollie fell to the hard concrete floor and stayed there. She was now completely surrounded by several White officers with nightsticks in their hands whose evil piercing eyes were quickly bouncing back and forth between her and the two animated Black Mariah drivers.

Several other officers arrived on the scene. They eagerly

walked over to listen to the Black Mariah driver's conversation. As the driver told the story, one of the policeman looked at her and said, "Oh she's a bad Nigger huh!" One little short policeman boldly walked over next to aunt Dollie and looked her in the eyes and said, "Let me teach this Nigger a lesson!" Another tall, slightly fat officer walked in behind him. He sarcastically said, "I think you'd better let me handle this one Shorty, as he booted him slightly out of the way with his knee! He then loudly commented while looking back towards the other officers, "She is too much woman for you!! Oh, but she is just the way I like em, fat and greasy!' The rest of the onlooking officers, burst out laughing at the short policeman as well as the officer who made the comment!" The short officer's face turned blood red with anger and embarrassment. He tensed up, looked up at the big officer, paused for a second and then quickly turned and walked away. The other officer's laughter grew even louder as he moved away.

CHAPTER EIGHT

BIG WOMAN, BIG WOMAN, WHERE FORTH ARTH THOU?

The tall officer who had cracked the joke on the short officer told her, in a very rough, deep tone, " Get up Nigger!" She quickly got up as he directed. He pointed his hand as if to motion for her to move toward the open elevator. Aunt Dollie said that she guessed that since she was a woman they didn't feel the need to go through the motion of handcuffing her at this point. Another rather burly policeman quickly moved out of the crowd of officers and got on the elevator before them. He had an unbelievable scowl on his face. His eyes were piercing. He looked her up and down as if he was sizing her up for a beating. As they got in the elevator, it immediately started upward.

The other police officer was facing her. He was the one who had taken her away from the short policeman. His eyes were frozen on her. He was looking aunt Dollie dead in her eyes, as if he wanted to kill her. The other guy moved to the back of the elevator as if he was getting a better position in which to strike at her. He began to kick the back of the elevator with the back of his foot real loud. It made a loud annoying thump! Aunt Dollie turned her head slightly towards him to try and get a better view of him. As her eyes moved towards him, he seemed to slowly begin to circle away from her to avoid her nervous stare. He appeared to be trying to conceal his fist behind his back. He also had a look on his face, as if to say, "I can't wait to get this ass whipping started." All of a sudden the officer at the front stopped the elevator and cut-off the light. Cutting the light off on the elevator was obviously the signal that both men had been waiting for. IT INITIATED A WILD FREE FOR ALL for all three combatants! Aunt Dollie said she hoped the two officers did not think they would be the only ones doing the ass whipping. There was no way in hell she was going to let them beat her without putting up a fight.

The police were swinging their fists wildly and kicking Aunt Dollie with their knees as well. Even though they were getting some good licks in on her, she said that in a weird sort of way, she didn't mind because she was getting her licks in too. She was screaming at the top of her lungs and hitting, kicking and clawing the officers with everything she had. SHE HAD HELD HER ANGER AND RAW ADRENALINE IN FOR SO LONG, THAT IT FELT GOOD TO NOW EXPLODE AND RELEASE IT ALL ON THESE TWO GUYS.

The heat being generated from the fight caused the temperature in that elevator to quickly rise! It was incredibly stuffy and hot. Aunt Dollie said, it didn't bother her though. As a matter of fact, it was just the way she liked it! It helped her to really get loosened up, so she could throw some nasty, down South haymakers that were going to hurt for weeks. It was elbows and fists flying all over the place.

Aunt Dollie said her fingernails and balled fists were digging into these guys big time. Of course their licks were landing too. But, they only caused her to concentrate just that much harder and as a result, get deeper into her own primal rage. They may have been bad, but for this moment in time, all she could think of was showing them in no uncertain terms that they had indeed met their match that day! As far as aunt Dollie was concerned, this was her moment in time! There was not going to be a tomorrow for her, nor was she looking for one! She said when a lick they threw connected she dug deeper inside herself and inwardly screamed, "Is that all you got? AND, HOW DARE YOU HIT ME MOTHERFUCKER!"

Aunt Dollie said that she could tell the two officers were getting tired and running out of steam. They definitely were not in good shape, and it showed. Their punches were now moving slow and beginning to feel like powder puffs. She thought to herself, "It's time to show these two White boys what real pain feels like! To this point the fight had only lasted a few minutes or more!! Aunt Dollie began to crank it into high gear and started to lay it on hot and heavy. She knew what a good knock down, hit em below the belt, spit in their face, life and death, hand to hand fists fight looked liked because her first husband, Ivy, had been a tough as leather airborne paratrooper. She learned to give as good as she got in her marital battles with him. She had learned a good ass kicking trick or two from my uncle Ivy.

All of a sudden, a thundering head butt she landed, surprised one of the now slow moving officers and dropped him to his knees at her feet with a loud noise that sounded like a ton of bricks slamming into a wooden floor. She quickly grabbed the fallen officer around the neck, snatched him to his feet and again drove him head first into the back of the elevator. Aunt Dollie said the fight was so fierce that she was coming out of her clothes. But she didn't care, because she was undressing these suckers as well with her right hooks. She now had them bouncing off the sides of the elevator with her pile driving punches like popcorn in a old hot stove!

One of the policeman screamed, "Wait a gotdamn minute here now! Wait a got damn minute!! This Nigger hit me in my eye??" The action all of a sudden ceased. They were all breathing incredibly hard and heavy and sweating unbelievable. One of the officers, who both were huffing and puffing away uncontrollably, after a few seconds, was finally able to cut the light on. When the light came on, aunt Dollie had one guy's head under her armpit. She had been rabbit punching him in his face. The other one, she had pinned against the front of the elevator door with her feet in his crouch and stomach. He was looking like he was having a heart attack and couldn't breathe. The guy had literally turned blue. The other one was bleeding like a stuck pig from several deep cuts over his eyes and nose. Aunt Dollie also had bruises and cuts but nothing like these two guys. They were in real bad shape.

Apparently during the scuffle and screaming someone hit the elevator stop button and caused it to move upward. As it got to the floor it opened. The guy pinned to the door shot out like a cannon. There was a crowd of police and some detectives gathered outside of the door. They were silent for a second with a look of amazement, then they all began to laugh.

Aunt Dollie said the guy she had the choke hold on began to cry like a baby. He was making this rapid squealing sound like an ambulance. All three of them were wringing with sweat. Some of the other officers ran in and pulled them all apart. That took a few seconds itself because aunt Dollie had a death grip on these guys. An officer who looked liked he may have been in charge, walked up at the moment and screamed, "What the hell is going on here? I told you guys about this shit!" He continued by screaming even louder, "Get this prisoner to her jail cell now!"

The two totally exhausted and battered officers limped away from the elevator and disappeared down the hallway as if they were about to die. It was also very obvious that they were very embarrassed by the ass whipping they had received. Everyone on the floor was laughing at the officers about what happened, even the inmates.

Another more compassionate officer began to help aunt Dollie to put her clothes on straight. He asked, ma'm are you okay? Do you need medical attention? Aunt Dollie quickly responded. No I'm okay! But they may need some though! (She was talking about the two officers she had been fighting with) I'll be better once I get my breath! Aunt Dollie said she then began to break into a big sarcastic Sunday-go-to meeting smile. And then she thanked the gentlemen officer kindly who had walked in and was assisting her. She then followed up with "Now which way is my jail cell sir, in a very proper, ringing sounding voice?"

Although she was bruised and beat up bad, She acted as if nothing had happened. She again thanked the officer kindly who had helped her and proceeded to walk by herself in the direction he had pointed. Everyone else watching seemed to be frozen in utter amazement. Aunt Dollie said, "I know this sounds crazy, but I was not going to let them take my dignity away from me any further. After a few feet of walking by herself, the jailer appeared and escorted her to her jail cell.

Aunt Dollie said that rather than sit in her cell, she just stood there standing with her fists balled up for hours. No one other than people making jokes about what had happened approached her cell. She stood anyway though, with her fists still balled, just to let them know that she was ready for round two, if anyone wanted to try something. It was in the wee hours of the morning, when she realized that the fighting part of her ordeal was more than likely over. It was at this point she burst into tears.

While all of this was funny years later when aunt Dollie told it, as a child of five, I was so scared for her. My grandfather and our lawyer went to get her out. We all (my family) were at my mom's house waiting for hours for them to get aunt Dollie out of jail. Boy, you talk about frightened. Aunt Dollie was my favorite aunt. I had spent a lot of time with her. I knew she would stand her ground if they messed with her. I also knew that standing her ground would get her in big trouble.

Sitting there waiting with the rest of my family and listening to my grandmother and some of our neighbors talk about Mississippi racism that night was something I'll never forget. They talked about the Ku Klux Klan and the lynching of Emit Teal and other poor Blacks in the South. Those scary, awful stories brought tears to my eyes and had chills running through me that made me tremble uncontrollably. Everyone was so worried about aunt Dollie that they never noticed me, a five year old child, sitting in the corner about to go into shock.

I recall saying to myself where is this great God that my Mom and Grandparents always told me was so good and was everywhere watching over his people. How could he let these mean people be so cruel and mistreat Black people like this?

They continued to share stories that night. They talked about the Mississippi Highway Patrol and how they would stop innocent Blacks on the highway and beat them senseless, and, in many cases mercilessly kill Blacks. They also talked about the Jackson police and the many atrocities they had ruthlessly perpetrated on Black people. Even with the terrible things I was hearing them say, no one, the adults rather, seemed afraid. It was if this was something they had gotten used to. They talked as if all Blacks were born to be mistreated by White people. I could not understand this at all.

I remember thinking to myself, "When I am grown, no one is going to treat me this way. I would die fighting this type of evil."I kept wondering to myself why were my parents, grandparents and neighbors putting up with this nonsense. My grandfather and grandmother did not take any stuff off anybody. But why were they comfortable with this situation? I struggled to listen closer and try to understand what I was missing. There had to be something in their words or eyes that would give me a clue as to what principle or religious practice they were abiding by that I just wasn't getting. They seemed resolute in the fact that they had to bide their time and fight the system in their own way.

They went on to talk about the many Blacks that fled Mississippi to the North to get away from this awful thing called racism. My grandmother said that our family could have easily chosen to leave, but we didn't. She went on to say that our family didn't run away from problems. My grandparents, according to my grandmother, insisted on staying and working to make Mississippi a better place for all its citizens. She went on to say that the Lord would eventually make the White man in America come to his senses and realize that what he is doing to the Black man is down right evil and wrong. She said that Black people are a part of God's master plan and purpose.

My grandmother kept repeating this over and over. She felt that everything that was happening in America was happening for a good reason. Not a bad reason! Hum, I thought to myself, will I ever be able to understand what my grandmother was talking about. At that point in time it just did not make sense to me!

That night was a long one. It was one of the few times as a small child I was able to stay up all night. I kept asking if aunt Dollie was okay. Each time I asked, everyone quickly said "yes, your aunt will be back with you, laughing and playing with you as she always does." Now I know they were telling me this to calm me. But I took it to heart. I would not be able to face any reality other than the fact that aunt Dollie was safe and not dead as I kept thinking.

Earlier that night, one of the ladies on the bus came by to tell us what happened. She seemed so proud of what aunt Dollie had done. I was so confused by this. I walked up to her while everyone was talking to her, interrupted and innocently asked in a non-accusatory tone as only a child can, why didn't you help aunt Dollie?" It got deathly silent in the room. The lady hesitated for a second, hung her head and then slowly walked away without saying a word. What had just happened, as I came to understand later on in life, could be called the curse of the Black race at that time in the South! We could feel proud when one of us took a stand, but we could not muster up the courage to take a stand with them.

Aunt Dollie was eventually released. On one hand, I really admired her for what she had done, but on the other hand, I was angry with her for putting her life in danger. Lucky for her and all of us, she came home with no serious injuries. They did not let me see her for a few days because of how bad she looked.
But I did get a chance to talk to her over the phone the next day. That phone call was all I needed to renew my faith. It's true. The Lord does look after his people and will intervene when necessary. Oddly enough, he looked out for my aunt Dollie and

didn't allow her to be killed as had many, many others before her who had dared to stand up to injustice and racism in the South.

CHAPTER NINE

THE BEAST THAT FEEDS ON ITS YOUNG

A Beast that feeds on its young is truly a strange, bewildering contradiction. How could a mother who lovingly gives life to her young, nurture it through the many pains of its birth and childhood, and then, without conscience or shame, devour it so that it can be made stronger? This strange paradox has tormented me for much of my life. Why would God allow such a monstrous creature to exist?

As bothersome as this paradox is, I do know this! This Beast does exist! It is clever and has learned how to hide itself deep within the evil of racism. It does this so that it may be allowed to continue to feed, without shame and remorse, on those who do not have the courage to stand up to it and/or do the right thing. Sadly enough, our precious children are usually its first unsuspecting victims. America in many cases has raised and nurtured its precious young, just to offer them up for its own selfish gain. How can a nation so strong and so deeply rooted in religion and human rights principles be rendered so helpless and blinded by the disease called racism.

Many faint of heart have chose to look away and ignore

the pain that this terrible beast has caused. Some would even go so far as to deny its very existence. But, if you believe nothing else, I say this! It lives! It lives and breathes. I saw it myself, with my own very eyes.

My personal trial by fire with this Beast was as a young child growing up in Mississippi. This experience left me with painful scars that are still with me to this very day. Even though I suffered tremendously and felt its horrible sting, I count myself as one of the lucky ones, because I did survive! Those who are devoured are lost forever. They are marked with an apathy, hopelessness, and perpetual failure that cripples them for the rest of their lives.

My first experience with racism growing up in the deep South was in the first grade in Mississippi. My elementary school was the one of the oldest Black schools in the state. It is now known as Smith Robinson Elementary. It still stands to this very day as a hard, cold reminder for the many Blacks that survived it. It was cold, dark and dank. The chairs we were forced to sit in were hard and full of splinters. Our books were old hand-me-downs from the White schools that should have been sent straight to the garbage dump. They were in such bad shape that we had to cover them with newspaper and glue then with homemade paste, just to keep the pages from flying away.

Our teachers were severely underpaid, overworked and lacked the resources to do their jobs properly. Even though they tried desperately to save us, they often fell short, because they too were past victims of this terrible system. Please don't get me wrong! The one thing I don't want anyone to do is to take what I say to mean that our teachers were not hard working and dedicated, because they were. They had to be, to be able to achieve the degree of success they did, especially with the few resources they had to work with.

From my school you could see the Mississippi Capitol building. Its shadow cast itself over our playground as if it was a enormous medieval castle. It was and still is a beautiful building with a gigantic golden eagle soaring above it.

As kids playing innocently only a few hundred yards from this great building, we often wondered what important things went on there. We knew whatever it was it had to be good, because adults never did anything to harm their kids. We all felt oh so safe, playing in the shadows of such a magnificent symbol as that mighty eagle. As kids, we would say that if anyone tried to bother us, that the Mississippi capitol building's mighty golden eagle would swoop down and save us. Oh how innocent and naïve we were! If I only knew then, what I have come to know about the things that went on inside the capitol building!

The year was 1956, long before anyone who I personally knew, had heard of equal rights and Freedom Riders. Mississippi, along with several other Southern states stood proud in their beliefs and held them up boldly before the nation. Racial superiority in Mississippi was not only perceived, it was the law of the land.

All of Mississippi's schools were segregated during this time in America's history. SEPARATE BUT EQUAL was the battle cry of Mississippi's smooth talking White politicians as they puffed on their big cigars in Washington and bragged to their fellow Congressmen about how they had their colored citizens in line and cowering in fear of them.

The funny thing was, as poor as Mississippi was as a state; these guys and their cronies were filthy rich. They lived in enormous mansions, owned thousands of acres of prime real estate and boldly flaunted their wealth for the entire world to see.

You would think that the poor Whites, who were an overwhelming majority in Mississippi, would catch on to this scam and right the system for no other reason than to improve their own lot! But this was not the case! For they too were victims, just as its Black citizens. They were too blinded by the racist scam perpetrated by the rich White powers brokers to realize that they too were on the menu. The evil of racism has many different twists and snares in it. If you are not standing for what's right, you can easily be blind-sided by it, as were many of the South's poor White citizenry in the fifties and early sixties.

Mississippi's public water fountains and restrooms were clearly marked, "White Only" during this time. Blacks dared not venture into these sacred areas, because they knew that it could easily cost them their lives. This was not a bluff, but a cold hard fact that on any given day could be supported by local news stories that intentionally went into graphic details of the beatings, lynchings, and murders of its Black citizens.

As sad as this era was, little Black children still innocently played and dreamed of becoming much more than the present situation offered them. Even with the violence and evil of racism that surrounded us everyday, many of us survived and went on to fulfill our dreams and promises. I was one of those children.

When I was a small child, my mother made the decision to move with my brothers and me from Chicago back to a condition that she prayed would get better. My mother enrolled us in the Mississippi School System confidant that God would protect us from the evil of racism. My mom would always say, "God is in control, in spite of what Satan say or do!" My Mother must have been right, because it could be the only explanation why so many of us made it through that hellhole known as the Mississippi School System during this period in its blood soaked history.

My grandparents were Jeff and Clara Stevens. They, along with my mom, taught us that everyone deserved to be treated with dignity and respect, regardless of race, color or status. This was not a recommended mode of behavior in our household, it was the code our family lived by. My parents believed in doing what was right and they taught me and my brothers and sister to do the same thing. Although the storms of racism, alcoholism, murder, and prostitution, raged just outside of our front door, my grandparents and mother made certain that it didn't hurt our family. They protected me and my brothers and sister from the evils of racism when we were at home. Their words of wisdom and our faith in God protected us when we were away at school.

My mother, her mother and generations of mothers before them were seamstresses. They fixed and made clothes for Black and White people all across the city of Jackson. Apparently, they were very good at it, because my brothers and sister and I never wanted for anything. In fact, I am a little ashamed to admit that compared to everyone else in our neighborhood we were widely considered by our neighbors to be well off.

As a result of the sewing my mother did, it was not unusual for White people with their families to be at our house for hours at a time, no matter what time of day or night. Their kids and I would play together as if we were family. We had a great time. We had an extremely happy childhood. Their kids would be outside playing with us while the White adults would be inside with my grandparents and mother laughing and having a good time.

My grandparents were well respected by Blacks and Whites in our community. It was nothing for my grandparents to take in a person (Black or White) who needed help. My grandparents were constantly scraping up food and clothing and were always finding ways to protect downtrodden people in our neighborhood until they could get on their feet. My parents strongly believed that when you did the Lord's work that those blessings would come back to your present family and future generations for many years to come. This is a belief that still stands in my family to this very day. The latter must be true because my family has been blessed beyond reason many times over, through the years.

The lessons learned from my parents and the environment in which I was raised, in an odd way, hindered me. While it was a very happy atmosphere, devoid of racism, it did not prepare me for the up close and personal racial injustice I would experience going off to school in the first grade. But, as an adult, I must admit that I am glad that my mother did enroll us into the Mississippi School System. It gave me the life experiences and mental toughness to rise above the many challenges that I have faced throughout my adult life. I would venture to say that the same is true of many others out in the world today!

CHAPTER TEN

THE DEATH OF INNOCENCE

My first grade teacher's name was Ms. Shelby. She was dedicated, loving and bent on teaching us everything there was to know about the world. One day she decided to take us on a field trip to the Mississippi Rodeo Parade. Smith Robinson Elementary was within walking distance of Capitol Street and the Governor's mansion. The parade route always went down Capitol Street and put on a big show in the front of the Mansion. I recall how excited we all were to go on this adventure. This trip was all we could talk about for days. Here we were thirty little Black kids and one Black female teacher, excitedly making posters and pictures about what we would see on our trip.

We kids were blessed because Ms. Shelby was a big hearted teacher who loved her job. She was just as excited as we, because it was also her first time going to the s Rodeo Parade. I think she was more excited about going on the field trip than we were. We all fantasized out loud to each other and made up stories about the animals, marching bands, and the dignitaries we were going to see when we finally got there. My personal favorite was the marching bands. I had heard that the bass drum as it passed you, would make your whole body shake from the vibrations of the potbellied instrument. It had to be incredible. Man, I could not wait to experience this! We planned on getting there early and getting the best possible spot. We left the school almost two hours before the parade was supposed to start.

On the walk to Capitol Street, a few of my friends and I noticed that there were only White people around us. I also noticed that Ms. Shelby grew more nervous as we got closer to Capitol Street. Here we were, little Black kids holding hands to keep from getting lost, but yet, nevertheless, there we were lost in a sea of White faces. Other than ourselves, there was not another Black face to be seen.

Getting to the parade very early enabled us to get a good spot right across the street from the Governor's Mansion. It was a moderate winter's day. Cold, but not too cold. We were all bundled up as if it was twenty below. Hey, we weren't about to let the cold spoil our fun!

I noticed immediately after we arrived that the White people in our area seemed to not want to get close to us. Although, it was extremely crowded on the parade route, it was as if we were on our own private little island. An invisible barrier of a couple of feet seemed to separate us from the multitudes. Everyone stared at us kids as if they were angry with us. We were very perceptive as kids. And, as kids will do, we asked Ms. Shelby why were the people so mad at us. She said they were just angry because we had gotten a better spot than they had. Ms. Shelby told us to ignore them. I tried!

I recall however, locking eyes with a woman who held a small child and seeing her lips move as if she was saying something to me. Although I did not know what she was saying, I knew it could not be good. I began to look down at my clothes to see what it was I could have done wrong. Other kids were also getting the same looks from others in the crowd. Then all of a sudden a very hefty White guy walked over to Ms. Shelby, got in her face, and said something real low, so that we couldn't hear. Whatever he said had to be terrible because tears started to slowly form in her eyes. Ms. Shelby immediately announced in a loud, quick voice to the guy, " Sir, we have got a right to be here just like you." She then pointed toward a police officer who was standing not to far from us and told the man, "If you don't want to go to jail, I suggest you leave us alone sir."

I'm sure the police officer saw and heard what was going on. But, instead of coming over to protect us, he looked right through us as if we weren't there. In any case the man walked away from Ms. Shelby after she said what she said! We all cheered "Yea Ms. Shelby" as the man walked away.

Although some of the kids including myself were growing a little afraid, I think it would be safe to say that we all wanted to stay and watch the parade. Thank God for the little island of space that they had put around us. Although I now know that it was there for the wrong reason, in its own little way though, it seemed to protect us somewhat for at least that brief moment in time.

I guess Ms. Shelby had grown a little concerned and decided to change her mind about staying. She raised her hands to motion to us to leave. But, at that very moment the parade procession was upon us. We had not heard the noise with all that was going on. There it was! As big as life itself! How could we leave without seeing this magnificent sight? We all began to jump up and down and beg Ms. Shelby to let us stay. She hesitated for a moment, glimpsed toward the parade, put her hand up to her chin as if to think about what she should do, then looked around at the crowd, who also now seemed to be focused on the rapidly approaching parade. Then she said the words we all wanted to hear. "O.K. kids, we'll stay a few more minutes".

Man, what a sight! There were horses, clowns, and marching bands playing loud brassy sounding music and floats with beautiful people waving to everyone. Yes, everyone! They were even waving at us. Can you believe that? White people waving at us. I thought to myself, they must have been a different kind of White people from the ones who were standing around us. In my childish thoughts I figured that they must be the good fairy tale White people and the ones around us were obviously the bad wicked witch of the west ones. Yep, that had to be it! That's why they were in the parade and the others weren't!

One thought that kept bouncing in and out of my mind was, "where were all the Black people?" There were none around us and none in the parade. My thoughts were quickly answered. At this point about fifty horses with riders came trotting past us and right behind them were two Black men marching in step with the music. Cleaning up the horse manure as it fell from the horses in big ugly clumps to the ground. The two Black men were smiling as if they were pleased as punch,(happy) to be a part of the show. They were dancing as they stepped and bobbing their heads as if to encourage the laughter. White people obliged them and fed into their nonsense. They began to laugh and point at them in wild hysteria. It was a deafening roar.

Some of the people even began to throw stuff at the men. The men acted like they didn't care. But, when they saw us, they seemed to get ashamed. They both quickly turned towards the other side of the street away from us.

Most of the kids in my class were also laughing, but something deep down inside me screamed that this was not right! I stood motionless looking at the two men trying to figure out what was wrong. I looked around to see how Ms. Shelby was reacting, but she was at the rear of our class. I inched toward her so as to get a better view. I still was unable to see her face because some of the kids blocked my path.

CHAPTER ELEVEN

THE TEARS OF A CHILD

Finally, I was able to see Ms. Shelby's face. She appeared angry and hurt. Tears were streaming down her face as well. A few of the kids, like myself apparently, also sensed something was wrong. They began to cry what we kids in our class called, silent alligator tears. These tears are long lines of water that come from a child eyes who was not making a sound. All of a sudden, someone in the crowd behind us threw a paper coffee cup with coffee in it, directly at us. Most of it missed us. But some drops of coffee did get on some of us. Because I happened to be looking back toward Ms Shelby at the time the coffee was thrown, some of it got on me. I'll never forget the sting of the drops of coffee as they hit my face.

The heat of the coffee didn't bother me as much as how it felt. Until this day I am still at a loss for words to describe it. I can only tell you there was something uniquely different about it. Whether it was my emotions being mixed in with the surprise of what had just happened, I just don't know. But I've never felt anything like it in the rest of my years of existence.

Although several policemen were nearby, and they obviously had seen what had happened, they did nothing. They just laughed along with the rest of the crowd. I remember seeing people inside the Governor's mansion fence, also pointing and laughing at us as well. I assume the people behind the mansion's fence were the governor's staff and family members. There were even little kids with them. The grownups and the kids were pointing at us and laughing uncontrollably. Some of the White people began to move in close to us. Then all of a sudden they started to push against us and curse at us. The invisible space that was around us had now disappeared.

Ms. Shelby was in AN ABSOLUTE FRENZY. She had her arms stretched out over us as if to protect us. We were huddled around her like little chickens. By this time the whole class had realized that we were in big trouble. We were all crying and trying to get as close to Ms. Shelby as possible. In our push to get close to her, she almost fell down. She got her balance and then screamed, "you Mississippi Rednecks. How can you treat innocent kids this way?" This seemed to startle the crowd. They froze for a few seconds. These few seconds really helped us. It enabled Ms. Shelby to push her way through the crowd and move us along with her out stretched arms.

As she moved us from the center of the crowd to the outer edge, a White guy in a cowboy hat pushed Ms. Shelby very hard in the back. She was barely able to keep from falling. She hesitated as if to stop and go back to fight the man, but she looked down at our frightened faces and I guess decided to keep going toward our school. I am so glad that she made that decision. There is no telling what would have happened to all of us if she had gone back.

Ms. Shelby had us almost running back to the school. We were crying and begging her to slow down. She was so angry at what had occurred, that while I'm sure she didn't mean to, it was as if she was taking it out on us. She was crying and pushing us along like we were cattle. We tried to talk to Ms. Shelby, but she wouldn't say a word back to us.

Thank God our school was only a couple of blocks from Capitol Street. I don't think some of us would have been able to make it if it had been any farther. When we got back to the classroom, Ms. Shelby huddled us all together in a corner of the room and tried to explain racism and what had happened to us. She began by saying that all White people were not like the ones we saw that day. One of the kids quickly interrupted her and said "Un Uhn they all bad." We all chimed in, in agreement.

Some of the kids started to scream out some of the things their parents had told them about White people. She quickly told them to be quiet and told us all to listen. She went on to say that these people were very sick with a disease called racism. She said, "racism was created by the devil and it could attack anybody, Black or White. It makes people evil and makes them think that they are better than other people."

Ms. Shelby went on to say that "White people are no better than Black people and Black people are no better than White people. God made us all the same." The point she wanted us to remember was that we were as good as anybody. She emphasized it by making us repeat it after her over and over and telling us never to forget it. Ms. Shelby cried softly the entire time she was talking to us. When she finished she had us lay down and take a nap.

While most of the kids were sleeping, I continued to watch Ms. Shelby. She stood over us like a mother hen with her arms folded until she thought we were all asleep. Although I had my head down, I continued to watch her when she wasn't looking.

Ms. Shelby crept to her desk as if to not wake us. Then slowly eased into her seat as if totally exhausted and stared out of the window and continued to cry. Only now, she cried out loud. Some of the other teachers who had heard her and knew what had happened came in and began to gently pat her on the back. That was one of the saddest moments of my life.

Although I dared not cry out loud, I cried with her.

CHAPTER TWELVE

THE AWAKENING

After my first experience with racism in the first grade, a little light seemed to flick on inside my head. I knew something was not quite right with the world, but I just could not put my finger on what it was. Something deep down inside whispered, "Vernon, beware of this evil beast and hate it with all your being. Those who had done this evil thing to you and your little friends could not be worthy of forgiveness." This thought hung around in the back of my mind and embedded itself like a little seed.

This seed could become more aware and take root and sprout. By this I mean, I could inquire and open my little ears and eyes even wider to find out what this terrible thing was that happened to me and my classmates that day. Or, I would smother it entirely and put it out of my consciousness forever, forget what happened, and trust my grandparents' and mother's belief in the goodness of people. The people I encountered that crazy day at the parade were an anomaly.

This mental confusion however, as to what had happened to me in the first grade stayed with me for years. From that day forward up until I became a young adult, I observed those older than me to see if they all hated children.

I recall one evening after school a few years later in the fifth grade as I played basketball on the grounds of Smith Robinson Elementary, being coaxed by my little friends to go with them to throw rocks at White people who would pass behind our school going toward the capital building. Although I knew what my little bad friends (and just for clarity these were not my regular playmates that I would normally be with) were about to get into was wrong, I found myself driven by the incident in the first grade to at least be a witness to what was about to occur.

I wanted to see how White people would feel and more importantly, react if someone mightier than they did something bad to them. Of course, I now know as an adult that this was indeed wrong, but for that moment in time as a nine year old, I just had to witness this event. I truly don't know if it could be called justice or vengeance or a foolish act of disdain and defiance for what had happened to me in the first grade. But whatever it was, it took control of me that day and made me do something that I knew was wrong. I recall making David Clyde, my normal playmate, who was with me that day when we finished playing basketball, go home. David reluctantly made his way across the little road, looking back and beckoning me to came and go with him with a sweeping arm motion at least ten different times before he finally disappeared between the apartment buildings on the route we normally took each day to get home. David for all of my life had been like a brother to me.

Although we were the same age and size, he always looked out for me because, up until about a year before that point of my life, I had always been sickly. My good friend David seemed to always be there for me, picking me up when I was too weak to get up myself. Or, he would run to get my mom or grandparents when I was having one of the many seizures I seemed to often have while growing up as a small child. David was a great person. I was indeed blessed to have him as my best friend. His family was a lot poorer than mine, but that did not matter, we were like two peas in a pod, inseparable. David's family lived in the alley behind our house, and as a result of being close friends, we were raised together.

David's family practically turned him over to my mom and grandparents to be raised along with my brothers and me. Although we were the same size and age, the big difference between my friend David and me was that he was a lot healthier than I was in my earlier years. As time flew by though, I managed, with the Lord's grace, to grow out of my mysterious illnesses/seizures to the point that not only was I as healthy as David, but was as rugged as he was, and maybe even better in many sports. At the time of the rock throwing event, I'd say I had grown out of my physical weakness and began to exert myself somewhat.

During my sickly years, I would not have had the strength to throw a rock, much less walk that far beyond my school to go throw one.

So here I was, looking back in the direction that my life long friend had gone, wondering if I was crazy not to take off running and catch up with him and let this fool notion, with these seven other bad kids pass from my mind. Their names were Hobo, Dirty Red, Bondonia, Big Baby, Pretty boy Digs, Jamie Ray and Palmer. I would find out later that I made a terrible choice. As we approached Fortification Street, they, for some crazy reason, chose to get on the opposite side of the street away from the school. Even worse for us was the fact that it was in the opposite direction where we all lived.

I guess when you are planning an illegal caper as kids you are living in dumbville, because not only did that positioning make no sense for us, it put us all in greater danger of being caught by the police. Just a few yards from where we were was what would have to be called the main thoroughfare for the police cars that were darting back and forth from the police station that was heading toward capital street in downtown Jackson. Just one little glimpse toward us by any of the passing police officers, believe me, would have spelled total disaster for us all. We would have been dead meat. But still, as the old saying goes, "Foolishness thou name is youth and ignorance."

There we were, throwing rocks at the cars of the White passengers, not being successful up until that point, until razor thin Hobo hit his mark.

A rock he threw hit the oncoming window of a middle-aged White lady and an older lady. The glass broke with a loud crash. They pulled their car over immediately and both got out. They were on the opposite side of the street from us, in the direction I needed to go, if I was to make a beeline to my home. The elderly lady seemed to have either been scared by what had happened or was perhaps hit by flying glass.

They looked SO FRIGHTENED and helpless. I WAS FRIGHTENED TO DEATH AS WELL for them. My mind kept screaming Vernon how could you participate in such a thing? How could you stand by and allow this to be done to someone? I turned to look towards the kids I was with and finally, after a few seconds of shock, realized they had long gone. They had completely disappeared. I can only imagine that they took off running immediately after the car pulled over, while I froze solid in my tracks. After a few sobering seconds, I finally was able to get my feet in gear and run. I TOOK OFF RUNNING FOR HOME. Stupid me!! INSTEAD OF TAKING OFF IN ANOTHER DIRECTION, I RAN RIGHT PAST THEM.

The older lady was sitting on the street next to the car crying and the middle-aged lady was crying and screaming for the police.

If ever there was someone cruising for a bruising, I was it. All that lady had to do was reach out and grab my arm and that would have been it for me. I think I would probably still be in a dark cold correctional institution somewhere to this day, if I would not have been blessed enough to make it to the police station. In those days in Mississippi, just the thought of throwing a rock at a White person, was enough to get you lynched. I don't want to even try to imagine what would have happened to me if the police had gotten their hands on me that day. Man is God merciful.

I think in my mind I wanted to give myself up or go over and help them, but as I got close to their car, something screamed " Run you fool! Run! " Boy, I ran like you wouldn't believe. I ran out of both my shoes that day. I made it home, ran right past my mom and went and got behind the bed in my bedroom.

I tell ya, I was scared to death. There I was lying behind my bed praying to the Lord to forgive me and not let the police get me. In between my prayers, I would think about how helpless the two ladies looked. How could I have done such a stupid and mean thing?" I was not raised like that and I knew better. What had happened to me in the first grade could not justify what we had done to those poor innocent people. It was not right, and no thought of vengeance, justice or turn about is fair play silliness could justify what I had done.

I think my mom, seeing me blazing past her, thought I was probably playing with some of my friends and trying to hide from them. She did not notice I was running in my socks. She went on about her business and continued to work in her sewing room. I just laid on the floor waiting, I think for the Police who certainly had to be going door to door to look for me, to drag me out from my hiding place.

I laid there crouched in a ball behind my bed quivering with fear. The street where I lived was about three blocks from where we had been, so it was probably just my mind suggesting that the police, in full riot gear no less, would be banging our front door, rather than reality setting in. I truly don't know what caused this to happen that day, but I tell you this, that experience did it for me.

I learned a very valuable life long lesson that day. The vengeance or justice business should be left up to the Lord. I had no right to do what I did. The fear I saw in the eyes of those people will forever be with me. I guess if there was true justice, I would have been made to be held accountable for what my little bad friends and I did that day.

After I had been hiding in my room for about an hour, My mom called me out of my room and made me go to the
barber shop at the corner of our street on Farish Street. Boy, you talking about not wanting to go, I think I gave my mom about every excuse I could give for not getting my hair cut that day. She just stood there quietly listening and looking at me, with both arms folded. I put on my best acting job. But, alas it

didn't work. When I finished my own Gettysburg Address, she pointed her finger toward the barber shop and firmly said, " Boy Git Going." I took one step carefully at a time, and made a 360 degree turn with each nervous step, to see if the police were standing right behind me waiting to handcuff me and drag me away.

I wasn't even smart enough to change my clothes. Surely I would have been easy to recognize if I had been stopped that day. But sure enough, I guess the Lord was again with me, because I was able to make it to Mr. Dix's barber shop without seeing the police. Normally when I went to the barbershop, I would be hanging outside playing with my friends or at a minimum standing in his front door killing time waiting for my turn to come in his chair, by talking to my friends who passed along the way. This time was different. I took a seat in the back of the shop, sat quietly and did not say a word or move a muscle. And finally, my time came.

I trembled like a leaf on the tree, the whole time I was in the barber chair. That probably was the worse hair cut my barber had given in his life. I knew that there was no way I could have sat still for him to cut my hair. My head had to look like a piece of Swiss cheese. Holes and uneven spots had to be everywhere, because I was shaking all over the place. Looking towards the door and watching each car as it passed outside the window to see if it was the police.

Man you talking about being glad when the barber finished. I took off running full blast out of his seat and ran a hundred miles an hour to get home that day. Thank God my mom had already made arrangements to pay the bill, because I totally forgot.

What happened that day bothered me for years. Those people I had watched get hurt that day were so innocent and looked so harmless. It made me feel like I had felt in the first grade. Being hurt by someone when you had not done anything to deserve it. It was not right, regardless of the injustice you may have suffered from someone else. You cannot take it out on others. That's the sobering life lesson I learned that day. What happened to me regarding the rock throwing incident as a nine year old child was a hurting, numbing feeling. It was a miserable feeling. I never want to feel that way again. I also never want to see anyone hurt like that again. Never!!!

CHAPTER THIRTEEN

THE WIZARD OF OZ

My older brother Donald probably was the most curious of us four Weakley/Stevens kids. He was a mixture of extreme intelligence and the ultimate in mischief rolled up into one. My little friends and I lovingly called him the Wizard of Oz. No one could make the magic he constantly conjured up and thrived in. His world was truly magical. As a small child, I marveled at Don's many death defying capers. It was like having my own Barnum and Bailey Three Ring Circus, right there in my very own household. All I had to do was sit quietly in an unassuming place, and with the true innocence of a child open my eyes, intensely watch and soak in the wonderment.

My oldest brother was truly a sight to behold a prior to his teenage years. To show you the full range of the Wizard, he was an outstanding honor role student when he was in high school, a first class athlete and probably was the biggest cutup, as far as getting into and staying in mischief, that the world has ever known. As a small child watching him, I must say he kept me totally mystified and spellbound by some of the wild things he constantly got into.

Being light-skinned with slightly reddish hair, he seemed to always be fighting with and having to prove himself to the other kids in our neighborhood. Believe me, Don was no slouch or shrinking violet. He would always rise to the occasion and could hold his own with the best of them in a fight. The biggest bullies in our neighborhood and on our side of town for that matter, only needed to say the words "Dirty Red White Bread" and you'd better believe, the battle was on. My brother Don didn't back down to no one.

I tell ya, that crazy boy was a dirty faced, running and rock throwing, fighting machine. For those kids who got the best of him today, you'd better believe they got the short end of the stick tomorrow. I don't know what it was Don did or could say to the other kids to get them so fired up at him, but whatever it was it should be bottled and sold to the military or better yet hospitals to bring people out of their comas.

As a small child sitting on our porch, I was constantly entertained by my big brother Donald turning the corner of our block at full speed with a mob of kids chasing him. It was a daily routine for me and my playmates to sit and watch his funny escapades. My mom, who was obviously as mystified we all were as to how Don seemed to get into trouble, once told us she went to his elementary school, found a good hiding spot across the street from it in which to watch him, and just watched to see what it was he did or did not do to get into so much trouble.

She said after a while, Don came out of school and with the speed of an African Cheetah ran behind several big kids standing in a row and slapped them on the back of the head as hard as he could as he flew past them. Mom said the noise his hand made popping those kids sounded like rapid fire shot gun blasts. To be expected, the angry kids, in a mad dash took off after him. Ole Don tossed his school books straight up in the air and ran out of his shoes, out running the mob of kids that day. According to her, Don was so caught up in his little caper that he ran right past her without noticing who she was. He never broke stride in his flight home. She said he was laughing and taunting the kids he had just cold cocked all the way!

My mom said she just shook her head, picked up his thrown to the wind books and shoes and headed back to the house after him.

Of course the kids couldn't catch Don. Hey! The Wizard of Oz was just too fast for them. Plus, his fore thought in getting a head start was much more than they could over come. When Mom got home, Don was sitting on the porch, wondering where she was more than likely. Mom said when he spied her coming down the street. He began to do the little happy dance he did when he thought he had successfully pulled off a caper. Mom hid his shoes and books behind her and asked, "Son where are your shoes and books?" Of course the Wizard had his own answer stewing in his mind and quickly offered up that he had already put them in the house. Boy! Boy! Boy, I guess you know it was on then!!! The wizard got smoked that day!

I recall another time when Don was in high school when he got to fighting with some bigger kids and one of them kicked him so hard in his private area that they almost messed him up for life. There I was, sitting on the front porch and a Dottie cab pulls up. My brother Don gets out and just calmly walks past me as I sat on the banister on our front porch. I froze in terror at what I was seeing. The lower half of his body, his clothes, were covered in his blood. This didn't seem to bother Don though. The cab driver was tripping all over his self trying to run up on our porch, and was a bag of raw nerves. He could barely speak.

He tore into our house without knocking on the door. Don was as calm as you please. He looked over at me and said, "Hey ole Water Head Boy, where's mom?" I quickly responded back in a high pitched panicky voice, "She's in the sewing room. What's wrong with you?" Without responding, he slowly strolled into mom's sewing room and began to calmly explain what happened. As he walked towards her sewing room door, I ran in the house behind him.

The cab driver was practically going crazy. He was talking a hundred miles an hour. My mom was talking just as fast back to the cab driver trying to found out what had happened. The cab driver was sputtering and trying to talk, while gasping for breath. The Dottie Cab company was at the end of our street at that time. Apparently the driver knew Don from seeing him at our house on the many trips past our house that he made.

That poor cab driver was in a total panic. His conversation went something like this. "Lola Mae, I saw your son walking down the street coming from Lanier High School. He was bleeding all over. I, I, I stopped and made him get into my cab!!! I tried to take him right to the hospital, but the damn fool refused to go. I caught hell just trying to make him get into the cab!!! What's wrong with that boy Ms. Weakley? He made me bring him over here!! Oh Lord, please don't let this fool die. It will be my fault for not taking him straight to the hospital."

Ole Don sat there as cool as a cucumber, as the cab driver talked. He was practically yawning as if to say, " yeah, yeah, I'm hurt again. Let's get the mending over with so I can start my next adventure." Man what a sight. Mom was moving a hundred miles an hour putting Don back in the cab racing to get him to the hospital. Of course, ole Don lived. And just for the record, he mended perfectly. But for that moment in time, it was truly touch and go! My brother could have easily bled to death that day! I guess the Devil said, Lord don't take him yet. Please don't send that fool down here! He'll just mess up everything! Please, please, please, let his bad butt stay on earth for a while longer!!!"

Of course you know I'm joking, but my oldest brother Don was a riot. Although I was a very small kid to him (Don is six years older than me) and he was constantly putting his foot in my behind or shoving me in the back (lovingly of course) back in the direction of our house to make me not follow him, I loved hanging out in his vicinity just to get a good belly laugh. He always had something crazy going on. I would be walking ten or fifteen paces behind him when he was outside playing when I was a small child of four and five, with one arm and fingers extended out toward him pointing and laughing. He would be shouting back over his shoulder, "Boy, get on away from me. Git on back to the porch and stop following me!!!"

With all of the turmoil that seemed to swirl around my big brother as a child, you can believe it or not, now he is one of the nicest people you'd ever meet today. He has a talent for making people feel at home and good about themselves. He is always the center of the laughs and jokes at our family get togethers He will have you throwing up a kidney from laughing so loud at his hilarious antics and jokes. He in his own way has helped me be the well balanced person I think I am today. He was my example and role model. I learned about courage, resilience, calmness under extreme circumstances, and how to focus and apply my intellect and analytical skills in life circumstances from watching him.

My other brother Stanley was and still is the good guy in our family. As I was growing up, he was always the goody two shoes guy who could find the bright side of any situation. Stanley is only two years older than me, so as it is the case with big brothers, he looked out for me a lot. If ever there was a level headed, good hearted guy, he was it!! He is still that way today. Stan acts as the family's counselor and I would credit him for a lot of our family's success. You can go to him for a clear outlook on any situation or crisis. It is no wonder that as of this writing he is the National Alumni President of Tougaloo College, one of the South's most prestigious independent educational institutions for Black Americans. According to Stan, pound for pound, Tougaloo College graduates more Black doctors and lawyers than most schools in the South. He has also been a great positive influence on me as well.

When my little sister Cheryl, finally came on the scene and broke up our little boys only club, it was like having another mom right there with us all day!! She would follow us boys around the house and tell on us to mom, as if it was a paying job for her. But what can you say. She was our only sister and we loved her dearly. We suffered in silence and managed to shake her off our heels enough to have some good old boys will be boys fun anyway.

Cheryl as a child, was a very beautiful little girl with incredibly long pretty hair and big dimples. Prior to her arrival, I had been the baby in the family. I have to admit that I was pretty much spoiled to the bone!!! Yeah, it was great to be king all right!!

And, I was soaking it all up and playing it for everything it was worth. In addition, my sickly routine took me a long way too. With the honor of being the baby at that moment came money, toys, candy and all the attention you could handle from the neighbors, family friends, mom's sewing customers, church members and family. Man I'm talking about mason jars filled to the brim with money, given to me because I was the cute little baby in the family.

People seemed to come from miles around just to pat me on my head and dig deep into their pockets to hand me a dollar or two or hand me all the change my little hands could hold. My grandmother, for all practical purposes, was like my banker. She kept my jars filled with money in an old locked laundry cabinet in our bathroom and issued it out to me whenever I needed it. She and I made loans to a lot of people from it, with interest of course, and pretty much strutted around like the Godfather. You'd better believe people stayed on our good side. Ah, the good memories. I was the king of the world in those days. Life was indeed sweet for the cute little baby boy of the family. Needless to say, that little so-called bundle of joy called Cheryl totally spoiled it all for me when she come on the scene!!! I am six years older than Cheryl. It was no wonder that we fought like cats and dogs when we were kids.

While I will admit it now, as a child of eight and until I was a young adult, I was jealous of Cheryl and would have gladly paid a hit man then to off her. (just kidding mom) I love my little sister to death now. The big joke in our family in those days was that Cheryl and I were a carbon copy of the old TV characters Fred Sanford and aunt Ester. People see us now and still laugh at how we kept them on the floor splitting a rib with the jokes we cracked on each other!!! Seriously speaking though, my little sister Cheryl is truly a good soul. She has a Masters Degree from Ole Miss University and has dedicated her life to helping people with disabilities.

CHAPTER FOURTEEN

AND THEN THERE WAS LITTLE OLE ME!

In stark contrast to my oldest brother, who was quite the athlete two seconds after jogging out of my mom's womb, I on the other hand was just a sickly little skinny kid who seemed to always have great things happening to and for him. I grew up in a neighborhood full of kids my age who I played with and learned a lot from. They all gathered at my house, I think as a result of the positive environment we were blessed to be raised in. Our family touched a lot of lives in our community in a positive way.

I can truly say that I didn't know we were poor as kids because we were sheltered and cared for so well by our family and friends. The truth of it all, was that we were poor, but extremely rich in the things that really counted like love, family and our belief in God.

My mom was and still is a stanch believer in God!! I believe her laid back nature was due to the fact that she bent her knees and prayed each day, and, as a result, knew that God was going to make it all right for us all. Our church was only a stone's throw from our house. So you better believe we kids were herded up and taken there regularly by our family.

As I mentioned earlier, as a small child I was very sickly. My mother would bundle me up and take me to the hospital on a regular basis because I would have convulsions, seizures and high fevers. It got to the point that the doctors would say, "We don't know what to tell you Ms. Weakley, other than just take him home and keep him comfortable. They simply didn't know what was wrong with me. My illness, and the late night hospital trips were expensive and emotionally draining for my entire family.

Once while I was sitting in front of my food staring at it, as I normally did during this point in my life (I just didn't have an appetite), I overheard Don once tearfully asking my mother in the outer room if I was going to die. He sounded so scared! Hearing what he said and seeing the state he was in made me feel bad. It just kind of made me feel guilty that I was putting my family through so much pain and emotional trauma. I thought to myself, "Maybe it would just be best for everyone if the Lord just took me right now." Of course this mixed up thought that sprung into my mind was not the answer, but that was the way I felt at that time.

I can see as a result of what happened that day why people would take their own lives. Not necessarily from the pain that they are feeling, but for the sake of their family and friends.

I recall my mom's eyes moving back toward the direction I was sitting and catching my head turn away as Don spoke these words. She knew I had heard what Don had said. She quickly walked into the kitchen, put her arms around me and softly whispered, baby it's going to be okay. I'm going to have a serious talk to the Lord about you.

My mom had had enough of the doctors and their lack of knowledge to make me better. She said, " I'm going to put it in the Lord's hand." We humans will often (unintentionally in many instances) get in God's way while we are praying for his help. Sometimes he needs us completely out of his way so that he can manifest his power and get the complete victory. Rather than have us incorrectly thinking, or worse yet, saying when he comes through for us, that we had something to do with the success. We don't mean to, but in many instances we humans will block our own blessings from coming to us. Just get on your knees and pray about the situation whatever it may be, turn it completely over to the Lord, try and stop worrying about it and then get out of the way and let the Lord handle it for you.

People often lean on the old saying, that God helps those who help themselves. This is not in the Bible and it is just an old man made up saying. It's not until we completely get out of the way and turn a problem over to God exclusively, will he get involved full blast and truly intervene for us. We humans are good at muddying up the water. God will not get involved with a bunch of mess, a lie, or worse yet, wallow in the mud with you. He will rescue you from it, once you stop wiggling and finally turn it over to him completely.

In any case, to continue on with the story, my mom took me home that last time from the hospital and prayed and prayed and prayed. She asked the Lord to pull me through the unknown sickness that was slowly draining my life away. And guess what he did. I immediately got better as if by a miracle. Along the way, he sent angels, as far as I'm concerned, to speed my recovery. During this time, two people came into my family's life and for whatever reason, took it upon themselves to always stop in to care about me.

One of the people was a very eccentric little fat lady by the name of Olla Rogers and the other was a lady that I affectionately liked to call aunt Nettie. Once my mom shared with them my plight, they seemed to be there regularly just to ensure she had some more prayers to go along with hers. In addition to their prayers they both were always bringing me homemade cakes they had personally made. For whatever reason, before they intervened, I simply could not seem to eat a morsel of food. Just the thought of putting food in my mouth was enough to make me go into convulsions. This happened when I was three, four and five years old, I'm told. Although I totally refused to eat no more than a teaspoon full of food at a dinner setting, I took an unusual liking to the cakes that aunt Nettie and Ms. Rogers would bring me almost every other day.

Each day I would eat cake only. As time past, I would eat a little bit more each day than the day before. I recall my mom at one point getting alarmed by the fact that I would only eat their cakes. She called our family doctor, Dr. Britton, to see if it was healthy. He quickly said, "Are you kidding Lola? I'm surprised, based on the bad shape he was in when I saw him last, that he would eat anything at all. "By all means" he said, "Let that boy eat as much cake as he wants!" He went on to tell my mom that he knew it sounded crazy, but anything I could get in my system, would help to sustain me. As I said earlier, the Lord does work in mysterious ways. He came through for me and saved my life in the eleventh hour.

To see me now, and for many years beyond my fifth grade years, you wouldn't know me. I'm as healthy as a bull now. But at that time, I was literally on death's door. I am absolutely certain it was God working as a result of my mom's prayers that brought me through.

On another note, it was a good thing for my mom that she had a gift when it came to talking to people, because in my opinion, she was not good at spanking bad kids. Oh, she would make a lot of noise and everyone in the neighborhood would know you were getting it, but in reality, she would not be hitting us very hard. My mom had this ritual type thing she would do when she whipped one of us. She would bring the rest of the kids in to witness whenever any one of the other kids was about to get a whipping. I guess in her mind it was good solid preventive measures for us all.

My mother would make you lie across the bed, talk to you for about an hour and worked herself up pretty good in the process, and from there hit you about twenty licks or so with a good thick belt. She would be talking to you at the top of her lungs the whole time she spanked you. My mother's words hurt far more than the actual lick!! We'd be there looking back at the others in the door thinking, I wish she would start swinging the belt and stop talking.

I remember once bragging to my friends about the fact that

my mom couldn't whip hard. I went so far once that I had my playmates stand outside the window to witness that I didn't cry when I got whippings. Everything was going great that day until one of the ten or so kids outside the windows hollered in after about the tenth lick or so that, " Vernon said you couldn't whip Ms. Weakley, and he wasn't going to cry." Needless to say. I got smoked!! Oh yeah, you guessed it!!! Mrs. Lola Mae Weakley out did herself that day! It took a long time for me to live that one down in my neighborhood. Ouch!!!!

Although for the record, my mom was not normally known as a good whipper, that wasn't the case with my grandmother. You could cry all you wanted and in the end, you were still going to get a whipping. She would hit you with anything she got her hands on, if you looked like you might try to run. Running from a whipping was a bad habit we had picked up in Chicago. Moving to Mississippi to stay with my grandparents put a screeching halt to that nonsense. I think one of my mother's biggest fears when we were growing up was that our dear sweet grandmother would accidentally kill one of us in one of her funny little fits of anger.

Without warning, she would grab something and bean you with it, if she couldn't get her hands on you quickly enough. Although ten minutes later we all, including my grandmother, would be falling out laughing at what had just happened, it definitely would not be funny when it was occurring. So as you probably have already guessed, we were pretty good, AND I MIGHT ADD, PRETTY STILL, when she was around. And guess what, she was always around because we stayed at our grandparent's home!!!

CHAPTER FIFTEEN

MR. SLICK

There always seemed to be some funny stuff going on around my house when we were kids. I recall once, my mom, in order to punish me, made me put on one of her dresses and go outside to parade around in, in front of a bunch of my playmates. She figured, I guess, that I would beg and plead for her not to send me out there, and from there I would promise not to do whatever it was I had done to upset her.

To show you how crazy I was, I thought wearing that dress was a cool joke that was sure to get plenty of belly laughs from my friends. Immediately after hearing her say, "Do I have to take you out there and let your friends see you in this dress? Before she could even get the words out of her mouth good? I had torn loose from her and was high tailing it full blast out of the door. I was screaming to the top of my lungs "Hey everybody look at me. I can really play kickball now that I got my baseball suit on." I had to be about nine years old. The nutty nine days.

I went out and played kickball with my friends and we all laughed and made a big joke out of it. The one thing that my friends knew was that I was no sissy. I had just gotten out of my sick years and was now the epitome of health. I was a ball of fire in my neighborhood and the undisputed leader of all my little playmates. My mom stood there with her mouth wide open unable to say a word at first as I ran a round the bases in her good Sunday-go-to meeting dress, as if to say, "Son you are one crazy fool!" She loudly announced, "Boy, you having too much fun. This was supposed to be a punishment!" She quickly made me come back in and take my new found baseball suit off. It was like taking a play toy from a small child. I kept saying, "Mom please let me keep it on just a little while longer. I'm the hit of our block." I think that was the day I realized that I wanted to be a comedian. The thrill and laughter of the crowd! Boy what a laugh we kids had.

As I grew older I grew healthier and with that new energy and vigor came higher level shenanigans that tried my mom's patience. I recall once when I was about eleven her making a big kettle of peanut brittle for an upcoming family holiday event. For anyone not knowing what peanut brittle is, it's a candy made in irregular shapes made out of peanuts and cane syrup. Boy did I love peanut brittle as a child! My mom had already issued a stern warning for my brothers and me to stay out of the peanut brittle until the next day, which would have been the holiday celebration. Although I knew I would get my share the next day at the event, I decided I couldn't wait, and figured I'd sneak in the kitchen when the coast was clear and get me a few pieces out of the kettle without anyone knowing about it.

My mother was pretty good with her God given intuition, but I figured that night that I could outsmart her. I waited till I thought she was hard at work at her sewing machine and made my move. Sure enough I was able to make it into the kitchen without anyone seeing me and got several big chunks of the candy. After eating the candy I quietly walked into the television room, sat down and went into my side to side head bobbing, I'm the king of the world routine that I would do as a kid whenever I was happy.

There I was sitting in the TV room with a big fat smile on my face figuring I had just pulled one over on ole mom. We're talking the heist of the century! As fate would have it though, mom came into the television room on one of her breaks and sat down right beside me. The one thing I hadn't counted on was the pungent smell of peanut brittle on my breath. In a matter of seconds, my mom was looking me dead in my eyes. She asked me point blank, "Vernon, did you disobey my orders?" Not wanting to make matters worse and risk getting back handed into unconsciousness, I seriously contemplated confessing. After a few more hard stares from my mom, I sang like a bird.

I broke down and confessed like one of the characters on the witness stand when Perry Mason, an old TV lawyer, would cross examine them. To my surprise, my mom didn't whip me for what I had done, but she did give me a punishment I have never forgotten to this very day! Mom got up, grabbed my hand and walked me toward the kitchen. She quickly marched me back to the kitchen. Once we got there she sat me down in front of that big kettle of peanut brittle and told me to eat it. One of my brothers standing in the kitchen door, jealousy said, " but mom that's what he wants. " I looked back at him with a big smirk on my face, as if to say, " yeah you're right sucker!!! Ha, ha, ha, ha. I started to go into my side to side head bobbing victory dance to rub it in just that much deeper with my brother.

After eating a few pieces of the candy I wanted to stop. My mom, who had stayed right by my side the whole time, said, "No! Keep eating son! Since it was important enough to make you steal from your family and disrespect my wishes, we're going to let you eat, 'Mr. Slick.' Eat it all." With that she said, with her voice never getting above a whisper, "keep eating son."

At first I thought I had died and gone to heaven. That peanut brittle just rolled off of my finger tips into my mouth. My brothers told me that I had the biggest smile on my face. There I was doing my little na, na, na, na, na, na dance, shaking and bobbing that little head of mine looking back over my shoulder at my brothers as if to say, " Mr. Slick wins again." Growing up with my brothers, I always had to hear that I got over big time because I could always use being sickly to get what I wanted.
Hey this time I didn't even have to pull out the big artillery, (my sick routine) to get what I wanted. I was in candy eating heaven.

After a few more minutes, I was full and had, had my complete fill. I tried to nonchalantly make my exit from the table, but mom pulled me back and said, "Where you going Mr. Slick? There is plenty of peanut brittle left in that pot. You aren't even one fourth of the way to finishing it." I said, " Oh no thanks mom I want to leave some for Stanley and Don. Mom said, "Don't worry about them. I will make them some more later. But for right now, I want you to finish this whole pot of candy. AND I MEAN FINISH IT RIGHT NOW!!" Her voice went up several octaves and I could feel the heat in the room start to rise. I knew from my mom's tone of voice, she was not playing one bit.

I took one quick look back over my shoulder at my brothers, who were now laughing their guts out and dug back in and kept eating. Before long I could hardly hold myself up to the table. It was tough, but I was able to finish the entire thing. You talking about sick as a dog. I threw up my guts and everything I had probably eaten up until that point in my life. I kid you not. I kept throwing up, off and on, for three days.

My poor mom, was right there by my side, worried to death about me; I don't think she thought it would have that type of effect on me. I think she thought, "Sure, he'll be sick a little while, but the lesson he would learn would be worth its weight in gold. She was definitely right about the lesson I would learn. It has stuck with me for years.

Please don't think my Mom was mean, because she really wasn't. She was just trying to raise us bad kids the best way she knew how.

I tell you this though, to this very day, I still cannot stand the smell of peanut brittle, much less eat it. I kid you not, I have not had peanut brittle since that day. Even as an adult, if I am around it and smell it for any amount of time, I get sick! That was one day that Mr. Slick really got his.

CHAPTER SIXTEEN

THE LEGEND OF BAD BOBBY

Our street had its share of tough bullies as well. My little friends and I were somewhat removed from this but there was one guy in particular, named Bad Bobby, that gave my older brother Stan and his little buddies fits. Stanley was older than me and so the bullies who chased him and his little buddies (Charles Moore, Bobbie Harvey and Gregory Bass) down with a vengeance would just kind of snarl at me and my little friends and leave us alone.

Bad Bobby would completely terrorize MY BROTHER AND HIS FRIENDS! You would think Big Bad Godzilla was heading their way, based on how they would be breaking their necks high tailing it to avoid him! My friends and I would get the biggest kick out of this little show. The hilariously funny thing about this situation was that Bad Bobby was practically a midget compared to them. Although he probably was a year or two older than my brother and his buddies, he couldn't have been no more than three quarters their size.

Now the one thing I do have to admit was that Bad Bobby had muscles bulging from his arms, legs and neck like a fire hydrant. That boy was an animal. He had muscles on top of muscles. But still, you would have thought that Stan, Bobby Harvey, Greg and Charles would have been able to turn the bully tables on this little guy and beat him up. But everyday it seemed Bad Bobby would put on a 'Beat Down Clinic' and wipe up the street with my brother and his friends.

Once I recall Bad Bobby really getting upset with Charles because he laughed a lot and Bobby Harvey, who had asthma. Charles did laugh a lot, but the rest of us in the neighborhood thought his laugh was cool and even entertaining. He would laugh at the drop of the hat at anything, regardless of whether it was funny or not!! Once he started, Charles couldn't stop. It could be a lady falling down on the street or whatever. It made no difference to Charles. He was going to laugh at it. He didn't have a quiet laugh either; it was more like a giant belly laugh that echoed off of every piece of tin and metal in the neighborhood!!

The laughing fit he would burst into, made everything he would laugh at even funnier, because of how funny he looked and sounded laughing at it. Charles had these big buck teeth. They would just vibrate whenever he went into one of his laughing routines. He would practically get down on the floor and roll around on the concrete when he got a good one going. It was totally hilarious.

One day ole Bad Bobby slipped down while chasing after them. And yes, you guessed it, Charles, while still in full flight running, began to laugh at Bad Bobby. Now what did he do that for? Although Bad Bobby didn't catch Charles that day, he made an announcement on the street that he was going to cure Charles of his laughing disease by beating him up so bad that he would never see anything as funny ever again. Bad Bobby, I guess since he was now in the healing business, also added that he was going to do a two for one and cure Bobby Harvey of his asthma as well when he caught up with him.

One day, Charles Moore, knowing that Bad Bobby was serious about beating him up, went and got his BB Gun to shoot Bad Bobby with. Charles, Stan and Bobby Harvey called themselves taking a stand to end Bad Bobby's rein of terror on them. I guess Charles' BB gun gave them courage.

They sat across from Bad Bobby's house and waited for him that day and pointed their little fingers in the air. They kept saying out loud to us, "This is the day! We are going to stop Bad Bobby from messing with us!!!" My little buddies and I retorted back, "Oh yeah, this ought to be good. We are going to stick around and see Bad Bobby finally get his!" We went on to pump them up even more by patting them on the back and telling them stuff like, "man this is so cool. Yawl are going to be world famous for beating up Bad Bobby! Wow!" Me and my little buddies then went and sat under a tree, which was a few houses down from the action, and waited to see the big show.

The big showdown finally came. Bad Bobby finally arrived home. His had apparently been to the store for someone in the house. By the way, with the exception of seeing his sister who was older than he by a couple of years, we never ever saw his family.

In any case, Bad Bobby looked over and saw Stan and his little vigilante group sitting there. All of a sudden this very confused look suddenly came across his face. He stopped, wiped his eyes as if he couldn't believe what he was seeing, and then did a double take to take yet another look back across the street at this unbelievable sight. I guess he thought he was seeing a mirage or something.

Normally these guys (Stan and his little buddies) would be tearing up pavement trying to get out of his sight. But this day, they sat there in total defiance of him. And then, It happened. Bad Bobby saw the BB gun and I guess he figured it all out from there. His shoulders hunched back. He just stood there and stared at them for a moment or two more shaking his head up and down. Tears welled up in his eyes. He then hollered across the street at them and said, "You suckers better not be there when I come out of my house!"

I guess reality finally kicked in. Stan and his buddies

began to shake like leaves on a tree. But to their credit, instead of running like they would have normally done they stood their ground. They all stood up, got in a straight line and faced his house like they were soldiers in a military formation. They looked real stiff too! We all started to holler, "uhh uh now!" Bad Bobby, they said they were going to get you man! Hearing this, Bad Bobby quickly rushed into his house to put the groceries down.

Stan and his boys started to nervously talk out their game plane on how they were going to beat up Bobby. It was obvious that Bobby Harvey (Stan's friend) was a reluctant participant in the plan. At one point he tried to leave but Charles Moore gave him the BB gun and it looked like that caused him to get his courage back. They had been sitting on Reverend Curry's church's wooden shoe shine stand before they stood up and got in their little line of death.

It was like the movie "High Noon." Bad Bobby's door all of a sudden flew open. It almost tore off its hinges. He slowly walked out of his house and started walking toward them.

Bobby Harvey pointed the BB gun and dared Bad Bobby to take another step. You had better believe Bad Bobby did just that!! He kept walking slowly towards them. First Bobby Harvey fired off a shot at Bad Bobby's feet, but still he continued forward. He fired off another shot waist high, I think with the intent to hit Bad Bobby, but he missed. At this point Bad Bobby was only about twenty feet away. You should have seen the sweat pouring off of their faces. My brother Stan was dancing a nervous jig as if he had to use the bathroom. Old Charles was screaming,

" Shoot that sucker Harvey.

"Man Shoot that sucker! Can't you hit him?"

Bad Bobby didn't even break a sweat or stride. He just kept coming in a slow deliberate walk with both of his fists balled as tight as they could get.

Charles in a panic desperately lunged for the BB Gun to

take it away from Bobby Harvey, but it was too late. Bad Bobby had made it to them. Bobby Harvey fired two quick shots into Bad Bobby's mid section. One bounced off and didn't even seem to phase him. The other stuck to ole Bad Bobby's naked stomach. He was wearing only a pair of short pants. Bad Bobby didn't even flinch from being shot. Then all of a sudden he reached out and snatched the BB gun out of Bobby Harvey's hands. Bobby Harvey collapsed on the cold sidewalk in fear. Stan took off running one way and Charles broke loose the other way in a blaze of speed that I haven't ever seen since.

I could swear I saw streaks of light and sparks coming off of their feet as they zipped across the pavement. I'm not talking about any heavy pounding steps either. They were running so fast that their feet barely touched the ground. I'm talking about that bent over in a continuous crouch type running that you only see in the cartoons. Kind of like the Road Runner but amplify that by a factor of ten.

My little friends and I were killing ourselves laughing and pointing at the incredibly funny sight we were seeing. We may have been laughing, but ole Bad Bobby wasn't cracking a smile.

I guess you know it was on from there for poor Bobby Harvey. When he finally was able to get his brains to communicate with his feet to get his feet off the ground to try to run, it was way too late. He tried anyway; it was as if he was running in place in slow motion. Bad Bobby grabbed him by the throat with one hand and held him in place. Harvey's feet were still trying to run, but it was no use. Bad Bobby had him in a death grip. The BB gun fell like a limp noodle into bad Bobby's free hand. All of a sudden bad Bobby went limp as well!! He executed a brand new ultra secret military strategy he called 'The Go Limp Maneuver.' Just in case any of you reading this out there have never heard of it, it's a tactic where you make your body go completely limp when someone is holding and trying to beat you up or do something to you! Its very hard to do something to the person when all their dead weight is put on you. It's a great open field strategy. In any case, if you ever want to know who invented it, it was Bobby Harvey in 1959.

Even still, Bad Bobby was determined to take his anger out on Bobby Harvey. The ole Go Limp Maneuver was working pretty good for a few seconds there though. Bad Bobby, at first just, seemed as if he could not get a good solid lick in on Bobby Harvey. But after a while he figured it out.

He propped Harvey's dead weight up against the shoe shine stand and started to hit Bobby Harvey with the gun as if it was a switch on his back side. I guess Bobby Harvey's feet finally decided they would work again, even though it was too late, he was trying to make a determined effort to get away. Bad Bobby began to really lash into him them.

I don't know if I mentioned this earlier, Bobby Harvey had a very bad case of asthma. He was coughing, still trying to run and pleading with Bobby to let him go. He kept saying, "Time out, time out, please I can't breathe. Time out Bobby, I can't breathe."

And then Bobby Harvey took our laughter to an unbelievable level, if you can believe that it could get any higher, by saying.

"Can you finish giving me my ass whipping tomorrow, please Mr. Bobby can you please finish killing me tomorrow. I can't take no more today, I've already used the bathroom twice on myself, I ain't got no more left. " He then began to beg Bad Bobby to go after Stan and Charles, who had wisely chosen to run in different directions. After a few more minutes of butt kicking, Bad Bobby decided he would quit beating Harvey a little short of death, and take after my brother Stan. By this time though. It was too late. Stan had made it to the safe confides of our house.

My little friends and I, I'm sure took a few years off our life span laughing so hard that day at the incredibly hilarious scene we had just witnessed. WHAT A DAY, WHAT A DAY!

CHAPTER SEVENTEEN

YA'LL PLEASE SAVE MR. HARVEY

After making it home, I laughingly told mom what had happened. Boy, what did I do that for? I don't know what I was thinking about. I guess I thought mom would also get a big laugh out of it like I had, but it didn't even go down like that. Mom turned sour faced, stopped dead in her tracks, and said, "what!!!" Boy, it was on then! Mom walked outside and took one look at the ten feet tall monster that I had told her about and she literally blew a head gasket. She looked back at Stan and screamed, "You mean to tell me that this is the little boy that has been terrorizing you and your friends the last few months? She then announced to the whole world, " I tell you what, you're either going to whip him if he hits you again or whip me. Now you take your choice."

I THINK EVERYONE IN OUR NEIGHBORHOOD went "Woo" at the same time as a result of that loud comment made by my mom on our front porch. You should have seen Bad Bobby. He had made it to the edge of the steps leading up to our porch. He was foaming at the mouth over what my mom had told Stan. Bad Bobby was walking back and forth liked an enraged caged lion, a few feet short of our bottom steps. He was begging

Stan to come off our porch to take him on. Stan didn't budge one inch. He stuck to the floor of our front living room, leaned way over and kind of peaked out the front door. When he saw Bad Bobby's face, he slammed the door, as if to say, "Shoooot, I ain't going out there!" It was obvious he wasn't taking Bad Bobby up on his invitation. Then my brother uttered the words that we have teased him about for years. "You better go on Bobby, and stop being smart to grown folks." Oh man! I don't think I had ever laughed so loud in my life. My mom went ballistic. She dragged Stan to the back of the house by the collar. And, let's just say, what happened next was not a pretty sight! Stan got a killing from mom that day. Whew! I even felt sorry for him.

For the next week or so, my little buddies and I watched old Bad Bobby chase after Stan, Charles and his friends like they were domesticated little lab rats being chased by a mean and hungry Tom Cat.

I know this is going to sound crazy, but one time during this period I even saw Bad Bobby beat up Bobby Harvey's father. Stan and his little friends were huddled together one day on our porch hiding out from Bad Bobby. Each of them had an assigned area to look to try and spot him before he spotted them. And yeah, Mr. Eyewitness News, which was what they jokingly called me, was on the scene, waiting for the next big laugh.

I was right there in my little off to the side favorite spot, straddled the banister on our porch checking it all out. As best as I could tell, they figured if they could spot Bad Bobby before he spotted them, they would have a chance to run inside our house. Mr. Harvey who stayed a couple of houses over to the right of us, had been watching them as well and apparently decided he had had enough of their cowardice. He walked over to our house in his best John Wayne walk, propped his size thirteen shoe on the edge of our lower banister and began to give them a little pep talk. You know how old men will do. He began with his battles in World War II and how he had once had to lay flat in a field and let a German Tank roll over him so that he wouldn't tip it, and another whole battalion of tanks off to the fact that he and his soldier friends were going to blow them up. Ah yeah, it was getting pretty deep on that porch all right.

Of course the old grenade story surfaced again as well. He had already told us a thousand times about how the Germans had once thrown, what he called a German Potato Smasher (which was old men slang for a grenade) into his fox hole, and, he bravely picked it up, threw it back at them and blew up 121 men. Now how one grenade could kill that many men is still probably on the list of miracles in the Vatican? But you know us stupid kids, we would believe anything. Man did we love hearing that story. As a kid I would just visualize that grenade bouncing around, hitting the poor German soldiers on their head. Wow!!!

Anyway, on that particular day, Mr. Harvey ended his story by telling Stan, his son Bobby Harvey and Charles that they had to toughen up, show courage and stand up to the neighborhood bully. Stan and his little buddies were eating it all up too. They were completely mesmerized by Mr. Harvey. Seeing this, I guess in an effort to show the youngsters what real bravery was, he told them he was going to put an end to the terror for them. He went on to say he was going to stop Bad Bobby on the street and demand that he leave them alone. Mr. Harvey obviously intended to have a little man to boy talk with Bad Bobby.

Just a few minutes later, there came Bad Bobby walking down the opposite side of the street as cool as you please. And just as he said he would, Mr. Harvey called out to Bad Bobby. "Just a minute young man, I want to talk to you," he said, in a loud, FIRM voice. Bad Bobby looked around, pointed his finger at his chest and said, "Who me?" Mr. Harvey quickly responded in his most authoritative sounding voice. "Yeah you? And you better not move a muscle until I get OVER there." I don't know where he got it from, but Mr. Harvey had a hell of a lot of bass in his voice when he barked out that command that day. We all stood up and started to go "Uhh uh.

Bad Bobby didn't say another word, he just stood there waiting for Mr. Harvey to get to him with both arms folded. He then walked over to Bad Bobby, with his one hand on his hip and the other pointing toward Bad Bobby and said, "Look, you little bad ass midget, you'd better leave my son ALONE." Bad Bobby slowly looked up at Mr. Harvey with a, 'what did you say kind of look on his face?' And from there it was on!!!

Bad Bobby started going around in circles with his fists balled up. He then said, " I dare you to throw the first lick." Mr. Harvey kind of chuckled. Then he made a back hand motion like he was going to slap Bad Bobby. And what did he do that for? Like a blinding light, Bad Bobby quickly moved in close to Mr. Harvey for the kill and hit him as hard as he could in his nuts. Mr. Harvey bent over and screamed in pain. Old Bad Bobby then quickly reached under and grabbed Mr. Harvey with both of his hands by the crotch and started to swing him around in a circular motion. We all hollered uh, ouch, at the same time!

Ms. Elise, a short stocky lady who used to sit on her front porch all the time, sensing I guess, that Mr. Harvey had, had enough, begin to plead with us little kids to rush to his rescue. She screamed, " Ya'll please help Mr. Harvey. This ain't right! This ain't right!!! " We quickly chimed in, "shoo---t, we ain't getting up in that stuff. " Nooooo, Mam, un uhh, shoo---t , no way, un uhh, no way, no how!!!! "

What made it even worse for Mr. Harvey was that he had a bad heart and he simply was not up to the task. Mr. Harvey was up on his tippy toes, hollering, "whoa now, whoa now son!" I think after a while Mr. Harvey got a little dizzy from going around in circles. Bad Bobby, I guess, sensing it was time to go in for the kill, somehow tangled up his legs when they were tussling and managed to bring Mr. Harvey down.

Mr. Harvey was a tall lanky man. He looked like a giant oak tumbling to the ground when he fell. Bad Bobby stood over Mr. Harvey, grabbed him by the collar and begin to throw rapid fire punches to his face like his hand was a jack hammer. Bad Bobby kept saying in a very low calm voice, " Now how does it feel to be down here with the midgets?

It took several older people in the neighborhood to pull Bad Bobby off of Mr. Harvey. Man what an ugly sight. Mr. Harvey

had used the bathroom on himself. He could barely walk.
I could almost swear that I saw buzzards circling over Mr. Harvey as they carted him back to his house. I guess in a way it could have been a lot worse for him. His heart could have given out and he could have died, plain and simple! So, I guess in a way, he got off lucky. Bad Bobby ruled that day, without question. He virtually floated on a cloud of confidence back to his house, which was in the middle of our block. The crowd of people who had gathered parted like Moses parted the Red Sea to let him pass.

CHAPTER EIGHTEEN

THE SHOWDOWN ON OAKLEY ST.

A few days later after the Mr. Harvey fight, I was playing by myself in front of the neighbor's house in a gigantic stack of bricks that were there. I had made me a little fort out of the bricks. I don't know what Bad Bobby's plans were, but I suspect he figured he could draw Stan out of the house by making him come out to see about me. All of our lives Stan and I have been pretty tight. Bad Bobby's plan on the surface had merit. He kicked in the brick fort and made it fall violently down on top of me, without a shred of remorse. There I was calling out for help from under a four feet tall collapsed wall of bricks. Stan, to his credit, bravely came out once to help me, but after Bad Bobby chased him around that little fort a few times, he took off running like a scared rabbit back to the safety of our house. A crowd started to form.

My mom's sewing room window was at the front of the house and I guess she finally heard me hollering for Stan to come back and help me. Mom heard the commotion and came to the door and saw what was going on. She literally jumped off the porch in one mighty bound to get to me. She carried me in her arms like a little ragged doll (I was limp and almost unconscious) to the porch, laid me in one of the chairs there and took off running after Bad Bobby. Stan stayed on the front porch with me. Needless to say Ole Bad Bobby was too fast for mom. Thank God for mom he was.

My mom was tough alright. But I don't know? If you ever hear her tell this story, you'd hear her say, she would have given Bad Bobby what he needed that day, which was a good old fashioned whipping. But, sad to say, I would have had my doubts. If I was a betting man, I would have already lost a ton of money betting on Mr. Harvey. I hate to admit this, but, I may have had to put my money, (secretly of course) on ole Bad Bobby that day. Bad Bobby was, like the old people say, "really smelling his funk." Remember now, he was fresh off of a victory over Mr. Harvey. And, Mr. Harvey, just in case I failed to mention it earlier, was a tall lanky man.

I wondered if mom could take him. But, it appeared that given the extreme fit of rage my mom was in, Old Bad Bobby wisely chose to stay in his child's role. He kept high tailing it to his house. He made it to his front door and quickly slammed the door behind him. Mom went to his house to talk to his mom, sister or whoever, but no one came to the door. Mom, eventually gave up after nearly pounding down the door of Bad Bobby's house. You'd better know old Stan was in big trouble again.

When mom got back to our house, she got all over him for not protecting me. She immediately started whipping him. She again announced, during his whipping, "This is the day!! This is the day! This is it!!! This is the day!!! You're either going to learn to fight and whip his butt today or you are going to have to whip me."

I guess you know it was on then!!! Stan got up, sucked up as much air as he could get into his chest, tightened his little pants with his belt (I still don't know what that was about) and began to look back and forth at mom, as if he was trying to make a decision.

By this time Bad Bobby had come out of his house, I guess after hearing my mom's comment. He came back to the edge of our porch and kind of stood back a little behind the crowd, waiting I suspect, as we all were, for my brother Stan to make his decision. Bad Bobby slowly pushed through the crowd, moved up to the edge of the steps and then, after a come on down motion with his hand to Stan, he hollered "So who is it going to be punk, me or her? Me or her punk? And you'd better choose her!"

Of course you know all my little friends were there as well as all of Stan's friends. Now my brother Stan was not the fighter in our family. No, No, NO, NO, NO, by no stretch of the imagination! He was a mild mannered guy who wouldn't, even to this day unless he was absolutely cornered, hurt a fly. If I had to pick a famous character that he would be like, just to give you a good idea of how Stan was, it would have to be Andy Griffith, the mild mannered, good guy Sheriff without a gun, in the fictional town of Mayberry on the old TV series " The Andy Griffith Show."

I could probably stop here and leave you in suspense and just let you fill in the blanks. This would be what the famous author John Grisham would probably call a million dollar, leave them on the edge of their seats, moment, but I just won't do that to you. Or better yet, I can't. I have to finish the story and tell you what happened next.

My mild mannered brother Stan, who couldn't have been more than twelve, jumped off of our porch, wedged up pants and all and proceeded to go blow for blow with Bad Bobby. Of course, Charles and the rest of his scary friends kept fronting and acting like they wanted to dive in and help Stan, but my mom would not have it. She kept hollering, "Get Back!!! It's time for Stan to become a man today. Win or lose, I don't care!!!"

I got to admit, Stan took it to old Bad Bobby that day!!! Man what a battle. It had to have lasted a good hour. Standing blow for blow and throwing haymakers eyeball to eyeball, face to face. At one point they were rolling on the ground, still slugging each other, biting and kicking each other with all they had. To be honest, I really have to wonder if old bad Bobby, didn't maybe give in a little bit in the end, because I had seen him flatten kids with one punch. But, MAYBE HE HAD MET HIS MATCH THAT DAY! Man, who cares! Boy what a battle, what a battle. Stan won, and from that day forward, Bad Bobby didn't mess with anybody else in the neighborhood again. For that shining moment, Stan was indeed the man!!! HE WAS MY HERO OF COURSE, BUT MORE IMPORTANTLY, HE WAS THE HERO FOR THE WHOLE NEIGHBORHOOD.

*Just as a side note, I know Bad Bobby is probably out there somewhere reading this book saying, "Yeah, I felt sorry for him and let him win." I say this to you Bad Bobby. You can say you let my brother Stan off the hook if you want to, but we, all of us who were there that day, know my big brother Stan TORE YOUR LITTLE MUSCLE BOUND BUTT UP. AND THAT'S THE BOTTOM LINE OF IT ALL. AND, IF YOU CAN'T ACCEPT THAT, CALL ME AND I WILL GLADLY ARRANGE A REMATCH. HA, HA, HA, HA.

**Bad Bobby is now probably someone famous out there in the world like Colin Powell, or Bill Cosby, Tom Joyner's Jay Anthony Brown, or Steve Harvey and he is rolling on the floor laughing about his old Oakley Street show down. But if I were you Bad Bobby, I'd continue to lay low and keep hiding out too. Because you are the only notch on Stan's belt.

CHAPTER NINETEEN

AHH, FOR THE LOVE OF A PRETTY GIRL!

My aunt Dollie and I have always been tight over the years, but that didn't necessarily mean though that we always saw eye to eye. I recall once when I was about thirteen getting my bell rung big time by aunt Dollie. It all happened because I fell head over hills in love with a beautiful girl by the name of Bernice Harrington from Champagne, Illinois. She completely hypnotized me.

The first time I laid my eyes on Bernice, I couldn't breathe for what seemed to be forever. Bernice was visiting her aunt, Ms. Elise, who was one of our close neighbors. She lived just a couple of houses down from us. From there on, she visited Jackson every summer until we finally lost touch with each other in the tenth grade. Ms. Elise said she brought Bernice to Jackson so that she would be safe from the danger of the gangs and thugs in her neighborhood.

Bernice was a beautiful brown skinned girl of fourteen herself who was from a well-off family. She was very shapely and had the prettiest hazel eyes that sparkled. She was very feminine and talked properly. She also had big, nicely shaped legs and, dig this, the prettiest little feet, I had ever seen. We would spend the summer teaching each other new dances and filling our selves in on the latest slang and fads from our hometowns.

As a young, red blooded American boy of thirteen, I gladly fell head over heels in love with her. Lucky for me, Ms. Elise would not trust her with anyone but me. She constantly would chase off the other little boys in the neighborhood who were trying all types of little tricks to meet Bernice. They would crawl up to the edge of her porch and try to wait for Bernice to come outside by herself, but Ms. Elise seemed to always be a step ahead of them, catch them and make them leave. They would personally bring Mrs. Elise's mail to her door when the paperboy's aim was not as sharp as it should be, just to get a glimpse of Bernice. Their little games were all for nothing though. Mrs. Elise made absolutely certain that no one had a chance to be around Bernice but me. Man, did I thank the Lord for bestowing that wonderful blessing on me.!

If Bernice went somewhere, I had to be the one to take her. And you'd better know, I gladly made myself available at Ms. Elise's every beck and call. As a matter of fact, Mrs. Elise wouldn't even let Bernice venture off of their porch, unless I was at her side. I considered myself the most blessed guy on earth. As you may have already guessed, all of my little running buddies were jealous of my relationship with Bernice. Oh, occasionally, they would try to get their mack on (sneak in a flirt or two) with Bernice if they saw us together, but it was no use. Bernice, only had eyes for me as well.

The Curry boys who were three brothers in my age bracket stayed right next door to Bernice and my best friend David Clyde would always be hitting me hard on my arm when I was alone with them, which was our on little private guy thing that meant, you had gotten one over on someone. They would tell me how blessed I was to have an exclusive relationship with Bernice.

Bernice just barely spoke to them. I don't have to tell you that, although innocent, a boys hormones are just beginning to rage out of control at thirteen. It was the age of innocence for us all. While I had two older brothers who had filled me in on what was going on, I still did not truly understand what my body was going through.

I would have long, wet, erotic flashes and I thought about sex all the time. If my hormones could have fueled a SPACE SHIP, I would have definitely been the first man on the moon.

Puppy love would not even begin to describe the depths of my feelings for ole fine as wine Bernice. Of course, I was a child and even though any serious hanky panky was off limits for both of us, I was in heaven at even the thought of sitting on the porch with her and just holding her hand. Occasionally though, we would manage to sneak a warm moist kiss or two in her home. But for the most part, that was all that was happening.

Our favorite song was "With A Child's Heart" by Stevie Wonder. Bernice and I liked it so much that we put our little money together and bought it at the record store, on one of our many, long casual walks to the grocery store. "With a Child's Heart" was an incredibly beautiful, slow love song that tugged at your heart strings the moment its melodic tones came on. Stevie's incredibly, romantic harmonica solo seemed to always cause Bernice to melt into my arms, like ice cubes on a hot summer's day as we slow danced in the front room of their home. We would dance very close together and hold each other tightly whenever no one was around and whisper to each other like we were the inventors of true love. Both of our hearts seemed to always beat loudly in perfect sync with each other whenever we danced together. The noise from our hearts would be beating so loud, you'd think there was a gigantic base drum softly tapping in the gentle breeze.

Bernice's lips were as sweet as honey and unbelievably soft. I experienced my first French kiss with her. What an unbelievable sensation. It happened while we slow danced to our favorite song. Our tongues would gently meet and intertwine. She tasted mine and I tasted hers for what seemed an eternity. As I dared to continue to hold her ever so tightly before letting her go after a stolen kiss, our bodies would gently throb, as if to say, never let me go! Time stood still as we locked in each other's arms in an embrace of total ecstasy. We were very afraid that someone would catch us.
But we would continue anyway.

It was a good thing that the "Hopper Love Basket" hadn't been invented yet! Because we would have been all up in it! Ump! Ump! Ump! Love is oh so sweet, when two young lovers are stealing away. Ah, those were the days of innocence. Life couldn't have been better for a boy of that age.

Everything was going great in my life until this particular day, when my mother was out of town for the week for a church convention, She left aunt Dollie in charge of us. While aunt Dollie was generally as sweet as she could be and as cool as they come as far as relating to us kids, it was a well-known fact in our household that she did not tolerate any mess from anyone. You would think that being armed with this little bit of knowledge would have helped me to avoid one of the biggest screw-ups of my life. I was about to have a major life shattering event that would stay with me forever.

On this special day, aunt Dollie asked me to come inside the house to eat dinner. I was as usual, swooning all over Bernice. We were sitting on her porch talking and doing what we did for hours at a time, enjoying each other's company. I don't know what came over me. I completely ignored aunt Dollie's call. She had already called me about six times already, but yet she called again, and this time, I yelled back in a proper sounding voice, " Hey, I said, I'll be there in a few minutes! Will you pleeeaaaaasssse stop bothering me." And in a very sophisticated sounding voice, I capped off that little smart remark with, "Gee, what does a guy have to do to get a little piece and quiet around this place?" Boy what did I do that for?

CHAPTER TWENTY

MAN! WHAT WAS I THINKING ABOUT?

Aunt Dollie immediately came to the door and screamed, "Boy, have you lost your mind?" I yelled back, while looking deeply into Bernice's eyes, in an equally loud voice, "I said I'd be there in a minute." Aunt Dollie's head snapped to attention and she then tensed up from head to toe. She quickly responded back to me in the loudest growl I had ever heard, " Oh, I think you will be coming right now mister. " Aunt Dollie quickly broke into a foot pounding walk down our steps coming towards Ms. Elise's house. She had something in her hand behind her, but I couldn't make out what it was. Keep in mind, for most of my life I had been able to dodge a good slap dab whipping with my CHARM OR, if all else failed, my little well rehearsed sick routine. I figured one of my two old standbys would once again save my hide.

Seeing aunt Dollie heading my way, I figured I'd pull my little act out of ear shot of Bernice. Unfortunately for me, I hadn't noticed the wild expression on aunt Dollie's face. Aunt Dollie and I had always been pretty tight. I usually could flash a big smile, turn on the charm, and bam, I had my way with her. Aunt Dollie never had any kids of her own. I seemed to be the one in our family who had filled that void for her. I hung out at her house all the time and soaked in all the spoiling I could handle. As aunt Dollie and

I moved closer to each other, on this particular day, I didn't see any of the big warm smiles she usually reserved for me, her favorite little boy!!

This time something was very different. Aunt Dollie wasn't smiling one bit!! Sensing the odd predicament I was in, I quickly hollered back to Bernice good-bye and slowly continued to walk away from her with my coolest John Wayne walk imitation toward our house, taking my own good time with each step.

I was pretty certain that I could whisper to aunt Dollie as I got close enough to her, to convince her to go along with my little act. I had this obvious scowl on my face as if I was coming to get on Aunt Dollie for embarrassing me in front of Bernice. Aunt Dollie, prior to this little event, had given me a lot of coaching on how to act around Bernice. She seemed generally happy for me that I had a little cute girlfriend. I figured if anyone would understand my need to keep up my act and impress Bernice, aunt Dollie certainly would.

Bernice was still on her porch and watching. There I was slyly motioning to aunt Dollie to let me talk to her on the down low, which meant quietly. I didn't even get one word out of my mouth when I got to her. Aunt Dollie was all over me. She had a board in one hand and was slugging me with all she had with her free hand. When I threw up my hand to protect myself, she connected with a two inch board that dropped me to my knees. Sensing that Bernice was still watching, I somehow found the strength to quickly bounce back up and from there tore up the pavement dodging aunt Dollie to try and make it inside the house. I figured if I was going to get killed, at least I'd retain some shred of dignity by having it done in the privacy of my home. I definitely did not want the love of my life to see me get the living daylights beat out of me on my front porch. Man, was I in big trouble!

Aunt Dollie collared me just as I made it to the door and dragged me back to the front porch. She loudly announced, "Since you wanted to go for bad and play grown in front of Bernice, let's see how you take a butt whipping in front of her! Whew, aunt Dollie was all over me like white on rice. All I could do was crouch and occasionally hold my hands up to keep from getting killed.

My lip was torn open by the first blow of the two feet and several inch wide board she was packing. Blood was spewing every where. I don't think aunt Dollie even noticed though. Man, was I getting blasted. Bernice watching this nightmare, fainted on the porch and had to be carried into her house by Mrs. Elise. She had once shared with me that she had never gotten a whipping and that her family did not believe in putting a hand on their kids. I guess seeing Aunt Dollie open up that can of Mississippi whip ass on me, was more than she could stand. Boy, the Ghetto is something else.

Stanley, finally hearing the loud commotion, came outside, and seeing that that all hell was breaking loose on our front porch, tried to pull aunt Dollie off of me. He finally was able to pry her off, after taking a few licks himself. His intervention was enough of a diversion to allow me to break free and run. It didn't do any good though. I could run but I couldn't hide. I ran to my room and hid behind the bed. Thank God, Aunt Dollie calmed down enough to put that killer board down and revert back to the old-fashioned whipping style.

She came into my room with a thick belt. Man, was I glad to see that she still didn't have that weapon in her hand. It was truly a case of the lesser of the two evils. Plus, I'm pretty certain that my head could not have taken too much more of the ugly stick she was clobbering me with. Thank the Lord for small blessings. Aunt Dollie demanded that I kneel and lean over the bed and not move. Believe me I quickly dived on that bed and did not move an inch. And from there it was on!!!

Aunt Dollie completely went Lash Larue on me (he was a famous cowboy who was very good using a big bull whip) and gave me another good whipping with the belt. Her arm, that was wielding the belt, was going three or four feet above her head in rapid fire succession. That belt was making a double clicking sound and wrapping around my butt like a real bull whip. I think my butt must have had a bull's eye painted on it, because, aunt Dollie didn't miss hitting me not even one time. This whipping was nothing like the light weight stuff I was used to from my mom.

Mom, as it was a well-known fact in my family, pretty much went easy on me, when whipping time came around. My brothers would often tease me about this little perk I had stumbled onto as a result of being sickly as a small child. My older bothers had pretty much made it clear that they wanted to be there when I finally got the real deal! Well, they got their wish. Aunt Dollie had lined them up at the doorway and was beating the living daylights out of me. I guess it was not as much fun as they had thought it would be because they were crying and twitching all over the place with every lash aunt Dollie hurled.

My butt felt like it was on fire! Although I dared not move my butt, I was gripping the covers on the bed and holding on to the mattress for dear life. As I said earlier, Aunt Dollie was a rather big lady. She was putting her full weight into every lick she landed. The impact of her licks had me bouncing up and down on that bed like I was a cowboy riding a wild runaway Brahma bull. For a minute there, I thought I was Bronco Billy!!! I don't know if any of you reading this book can relate to what I am talking about, but suffice it to say that I couldn't sit down for a week. Whew, I can just imagine what I looked like bouncing up and down on that bed.

After finishing with me, aunt Dollie also whipped Stan for getting in the way. After the whippings were over, she cradled me in her arms, cleaned up my busted lip, told me how much she loved me and ended by saying, " boy don't you ever, as long as you are Black, disrespect grown people again. You hear me!" You could have heard me a mile away quickly screaming, "Yes ma'am" back to Aunt Dollie. What a lesson I learned that day!!

Not respect grown people, shoot, there was no way I would disrespect anyone above the age of ten ever in my life. For weeks after that butt whipping I was bowing to every adult I came in contact with. They could be walking across the street, and I would be singing out, "How ya'll doing today." Of course all of the neighbors had heard about my little beat down. They would be saying, especially aunt Dollie's friends, "Oh Yeah, you finally got yours didn't ya. Dollie don't play that stuff Boy!!" Or some of the nicer ones would say, "okay Vernon that's enough, we're not going to give a bad report to aunt Dollie on ya!!"

Although Bernice came over to my house at least fifty times in the next week to see if I was okay, I refused to face her. I hid from her and stayed in the house. Man, was I embarrassed and ashamed. I tell you that was a valuable life lesson I will never forget. As odd as this may seem, I gained a great respect for aunt Dollie. The lesson she taught me is still with me to this very day!! The odd thing is however, for the life of me I can't explain or put my finger on what it is. All I know is that it stuck!!!

I think it has something to do with the hurt I saw in her eyes as she was whipping me and how she cradled me in her arms when the whipping was over and explained to me what I had done wrong. Up until that point my charm and sick routine had pretty much been a big git over for me. But it didn't fly with Aunt Dollie.

Although my mother, when she returned from the convention was upset with aunt Dollie's method on how she disciplined me by hitting me in the face with that big board, she was solidly on Aunt Dollie's side for whipping me. She went on to, in very clear terms, explain to me how wrong I was. I always wondered in the back of my mind if ole mom hadn't planned that hit on me. Hum, well I guess I had it coming, so it really doesn't matter. While I tried to play Mr. Innocent victim when I explained what happened to Mom, I knew in my heart that I was wrong. The only true regret was that Stanley had also gotten a whipping for my foolishness. Well I guess that's what goes along with the job of being my older, caring big brother.

CHAPTER TWENTY ONE

THE WHISKEY HOUSE
(THE LEGEND OF MS. NIGG)

As small children growing up in the mean ghetto streets of Mississippi, my brothers, sister and I grew up with a major known whiskey house not more than a hundred feet from our back door in an adjacent alley. This was one of the many challenges that faced not only our family, but our entire community as well. The proprietor was a tough Black lady by the name of Ms. Nigg. She sold moonshine whiskey out of that old alley to Black people and White people long before I was born and anyone had heard of packaged liquor in Jackson Mississippi. Ms. Nigg's moonshine was said to have been so good that even after cheaper and a lot more safer packaged liquor came on the scene, people still chose her whiskey, rather than buy from the officially sanctioned state stores.

Ms. Nigg ruled her empire (the long rocky alley way and the series of houses she owned in there) behind our house with an iron hand! She often shot and killed or had one of her many henchmen who were always at her side to quickly do it for her, without remorse or reservation to anyone if they threatened her livelihood and/or acted up in her establishment. AND, BELIEVE

ME, I am talking from eyewitness accounts. She did so quite regularly, without any hassle or repercussions from the law.

There were plenty of go for bad, bad asses who made the mistake of challenging Ms. Nigg. Boy did they pay the supreme price! Although they may have thought it was going to be a one on one battle, shootout, cutting spree, fists fight or whatever with Ms. Nigg, because she was doing all the talking, when it went down, everyone of her many henchmen would attack the person simultaneously from all angles, especially from the back.

Her henchmen generally would be all smiles up until the fight began. Their fake smiles seemed to say to the person they would in a few seconds ruthlessly attack, "Hey we are not in this stuff. Your argument is between you and her." Once the battle began though, all hell would break loose. It could easily be one person fighting ten people. No mercy would be given. There was no way Ms. Nigg could lose. I personally, from peeking behind the curtains of one of our back rooms, saw her pistol whip people while her henchmen held them until they were completely covered with blood. In many instances she would continue to beat them long after they were unconscious, and in some instances, in my mind, had to be dead.

The police could be cruising our block when she was in the middle of beating someone down to the ground and they would just laugh and keep on slowly riding by as if it was okay.

While I considered my own grandmother to be a tough lady, she wasn't even in Ms. Nigg's class. Thank God these two never bumped heads! While I think my granny would have had the advantage in speed, Ms. Nigg had the body size, weight, tenacity and ruthlessness as well as speed in an out and out fists fight, to take on anyone. She was a medium height lady with muscles that bulged through the men's clothing she regularly wore.

Often she would wear an old man's fedora style hat broken down and cocked to the side. If it wasn't for her big drooping bra size, it would have been hard to tell Ms. Nigg was a woman at all. Although many of the henchmen who were around her were men, she kept several good-looking ladies around for her sport. It was obvious to the world that she liked women. She didn't hide it not one bit. She was what was called in those days, 'A Bull Dagger.' Just in case you didn't get my drift, I'll break it down to you more plainly! Today they call people like that Lesbians. Ms. Nigg was not ashame either. She would openly feel on and French kiss her girlfriends out in the open without shame.

As small children, my brother and I would sneak and look out our back window at the wild show that would be going on at her house around the clock!! The big shows usually occurred at night, but for all practical purposes Ms. Nigg's establishment was open twenty-four hours a day. She had two big houses on one side of the alley and one even bigger one with several little small outhouses behind it on the other side of the alley. Two big fig trees, a small wire fence and about a hundred feet of space, were all that separated us from her. Ms Nigg also had goats, chickens and everything else you could imagine back in her compound.

I am not joking when I tell you that I don't think Ms. Nigg would have had any problem lasting for years, in her little kingdom there, if a war broke out. She truly had everything she needed to survive.

People, both well respected and dirt poor, would come from near and far to get totally drunk, fall out and hurt themselves at Ms. Nigg's famous whiskey house. She would also have people gambling, playing dice and cards inside her houses and sometimes on her own front porch. She lived in the largest house in her alleyway. With the exception of taking her girlfriends and some of her henchmen fishing occasionally, she was always at home. She would occasionally sit outside on her porch herself and play cards with her customers. She would quickly pistol whip anyone who she thought was questioning her superior gamesmanship or constant streaks of luck. Fights would break out all the time at Ms. Nigg's house. It was nothing to see guns drawn, shots fired and people running out of her houses for their lives at any given time.

Occasionally you would hear Ms. Nigg hollering to her workers, "Cut the water off." That either meant that someone, if you can believe this, she respected, was coming down the alley like Reverend Curry, my grandparents, mom or us kids were walking through and were playing too close to the house. Or, perhaps some new face on the police force was making the rounds. Or, she just thought it was just time to chill out for a bit. That signal caused everyone outside to lay back and be quiet. If you were a not too well-known patron, her people would make you get up and leave when she sung out that signal.

You could hear her screaming "Cut the Water Off. ALRIGHT NOW, CUT THE WATER OFF " a block away. I can just see her now standing on her front porch with her hands on her hips, head twisting slowly back and forth towards the two openings of the alley, as if to get a good look at what was going on. The partying did not begin again until she gave the word for it to start up. As she stood on her porch and stared, her entire compound would be completely silent. It was a surreal feeling.

The things we saw as kids peeking out our windows were totally insane. People who had had one too many would be slobbering, urinating on themselves and acting totally out of their minds. Some of these people were the pillars of our community. I don't know what it was Ms. Nigg put in her moonshine, but whatever it was it had to be incredibly addictive. Whatever the enjoyment those people got out of drinking her moonshine, in my opinion, could not have been worth what I saw. While a lot of the people in our community could not resist this situation and eventually succumbed to alcoholism, our household never budged and was untouched. It truly had to be the hand of God that protected us from what could have easily been our fate as well.

Ms. Nigg was so bold that she would pay off the police in open view of everyone. The police (who were all White at the time) would stop by regularly to get their payoff for not bothering her thriving business and patrons. Ms. Nigg would slowly walk down her brick stairway, and with a stern look on her face, as if to make the White police think that she was upset with them, pay them off. Before giving them the money however, she'd stop at the window of their car, lean in and loudly tell them something like, "You bastards had better keep looking out for me, if you know what's good for ya!" She then would quickly sling them their bundles of cash. She would be giving them several bundles of money. A mass of big bills banded together with rubber bands. The bundles of money would be flying all over the place. It would be hitting them in their faces, stomachs, where ever it landed. They would be quickly diving for the flying bundles to keep them from hitting the floor of the car or worse yet, bouncing back outside on the ground.

In my opinion, it looked as if they were also all afraid not to take Ms. Nigg's money. They would be jittery after stuffing the money away and from there trying to quickly sit up straight in their car seats, as if they did not want to lose their dignity for too long in front of the people who were watching. My brothers and I, as small kids of course, secretly watched from our backroom window. There always was a crowd of people in front of Ms. Nigg's house or sitting on her porch that witnessed these little pay offs. Perhaps she did it for show or for an additional ounce of witness security. Once the police regained their composure, they put back on their game faces and then sped off down the street with their hands propped up in the windows next to their heads, trying I suspect to keep anyone from seeing their faces.

Oh, if only video cameras had been invented in those days; the fun we could have had with these crooked no good cops. Well, but wait a minute, what am I thinking about? My family was so poor in those days that we would not have been able to afford a video camera anyway. A camera was out of the question.

In any case, these guys were obviously scum!! They did our neighborhood a major disservice and they dishonored their badges by not doing their jobs as they were sworn to do! Again, before I go too far, I want to make certain that I don't give the impression that the modern day Jackson police force is like that because they are definitely not. Plus this happened as of the writing of this book, over forty years ago. The current and modern day Jackson police force has proven itself time and time again as a friend to the BLACK COMMUNITY AND THE ENTIRE CITIZENRY OF JACKSON, regardless of race, color or social status. So, I am not talking about the good men and women on the force who have performed their duties with precision, dedication and excellence. But for that day and time, Ms. Nigg had many on her payroll.

Everyone in our community knew Ms. Nigg wasn't anyone to play with. As tough and as bad as Ms. Nigg was, she always treated me and my family nicely. While we definitely didn't associate with her and her illegal enterprise, my family would speak and be cordial whenever we saw her. That's just the way we were raised.

Ms. Nigg also seemed to be compelled to go out of her way to keep the peace with and be very nice to our family as well. In one instance she would be cursing out one of her henchmen or customers, or beating up someone. In the next second, after she had looked over and seen us, her rough, deep masculine sounding voice would quickly change to a pleasant sounding alto. Whenever she spoke to us, she would always be cordial. She'd say, "hey how are you kids doing today?" Or, she'd say something like, "Is everyone doing ok in the family?" Tell your grandparents hello for me, you hear." We'd eagerly respond back, "yes ma'am, we will. How are you doing Ms. Nigg?" She would gleefully respond, Oh, I'm doing okay!

As a youngster in junior high school, I often sat in the backroom with the door open that faced her house and/or sat on our back porch of our house and practiced on my saxophone. I practiced like clockwork each day at a certain hour after school. Ms. Nigg would often make everyone at her house be quiet and civil whenever I played so that I could practice undisturbed. She would sit on her front porch, slowly fan herself and quietly pat her feet to my music. Many of her patrons sat outside with her and listened quietly as well. They seemed to really enjoy it! I guess it is true. Music can calm the savage beast.

Ms. Nigg would often offer encouragement to me, if she perceived that I was having trouble with a piece, or seemed to be getting frustrated because I was unable to play to my satisfaction. She would sing out, "Do Lolly, that was the nickname that she and some of the neighbors called me) that sounds real good son! Just keep practicing, you're going to get even better." Or if I had openly gotten a little upset with myself, she would quickly jump in and say, "It's going to be ok Vernon. Just keep practicing, you're going to be the best saxophone player in the world." My grandmother often teased me that Ms. Nigg was going to ask to adopt me one day, just so I could play for her everyday. Now whether this was the Lord's way of keeping his hands around us and making Ms. Nigg be civil to our family, when she could be so ruthless to others, I don't know. All I do know is, she treated my family very nice.

Based on what I SAW OVER THE YEARS, I SUSPECT MS. NIGG WAS PROBABLY A HARD CORE ATHEIST. In any case, the Lord has supreme power over all things. And that definitely includes all atheists and moonshiners as well. In the final analysis, our family and Ms. Nigg were able to get along in spite of the obvious opposite sides of the religious fence we were on.

My Mom constantly prayed that her family would not be victims and slaves to the sad situations many of our neighbors had sunk to over at Ms. Nigg's business! Her prayers worked!! Not a single member of our household fell prey to this terrible evil that lurked just outside of our doorway. Eventually Ms. Nigg died off and her series of whiskey houses in that old alley way burned to the ground. While I would never talk bad about Ms. Nigg because she is now deceased and she treated me and my family well, I believe that the passing of this era in our community was a blessing in disguise. As a result of the fall of Ms. Nigg's empire, many of our neighbors were able to conquer their alcoholism and get their lives back under control.

CHAPTER TWENTY TWO

THE REAL POWER BEHIND THE WHITE SOUTHERN FAMILY

Before becoming a beautician, aunt Dollie was a housekeeper for many well-to-do White families in Jackson. She put a lot of pride into her work and had a lot of interesting stories to share with us about how her well-off White employers lived. I guess you could say that she opened up a new world for us with her stories. Aunt Dollie is truly something special. Please don't think that because she was a housekeeper that she was an Uncle Tom or meek person where White people were concerned. Nothing could be further from the truth.

While my aunt was as sweet as she could be, she could also get you told and stand her ground when necessary, as you probably have already seen from the previous chapters. She is not afraid to speak out on any subject. Even though she was a housekeeper in White homes, where her employers were most likely racist, you'd be surprised at how much power she wielded in their homes.

Although having disdain for Black people was a way of life in the South, many White families routinely hired them to clean their houses, cook for them and care for their small children during the fifties. On the surface this may not sound totally off the chart. But, given the fact that beyond this domain, Blacks would openly be denounced as dirty, unclean animals who had no place in their society; it made no sense. Nevertheless, in many instances, Black nannies and housekeepers got more respect behind closed doors than they did openly out in society.

Black nannies and housekeepers would often be called on for advice and as a result, wielded enormous power and sayso as to what went on behind closed doors in the homes of their White employers. They shared the most closely guarded family secrets, took care of each family member when they were sick, helped decide how money was to be spent, defined and shaped the family's religious beliefs, decided punishment for not only the kids, but also the male breadwinners when they got out of line. If the nanny was in a good mood, then all was well with the family. If the nanny was not happy, then a blue funk engulfed the household.

The nanny seemed to always develop a close female bond with the mother of the family, regardless of how much power the mother wielded. Working together as a team, the White mother's station was made stronger. This alliance between the mother and Nanny was unshakeable. In many instances it even determined and controlled when the male breadwinner would have sex with his wife. Given this point, you'd better believe the male of the family stayed on the nanny's good side.

Another deep South paradox worthy of examination is the fact that the White man trusted his most prized possessions (his precious family) to the Black housekeepers, even though in public he may have shown total disdain for any member of the Black race. Consider if you will, the White southern male during this period pretending to throw up while he is with his other White male friends at the very thought of being near a Black person, yet getting home and scoffing up food that was just prepared and cooked by his Black maid. This made no sense at all.

Black housekeepers and nannies were in many cases the backbone of a society that would ultimately choke on the contradictory hatred it spewed.

My aunt Dollie was a housekeeper during these crazy

times in Mississippi. She was loved and treated as quite special while in the confines of her White employers' domain. The relationship between her and the White families she worked for over the years was truly unique and worthy of note. I recall many a day when aunt Dollie would come home and share with us the many funny situations she found herself caught up in while she was in the White man's world.

I would sit on our porch and wait until I saw aunt Dollie step off the bus so that she could tell us how the rich White families, and most especially, their beautiful snow White kids lived. I had played with White kids before as a small child when they came to my mom to have their clothes fixed. But, they were not rich ones like Aunt Dollie worked for! Just hearing about the expensive toys and clothes the rich White kids had was enough to make me dream for months of what it would be like to be them. And, why not! They had it all. God's little experiment worked in their favor, or did it?

Now that I have personally experienced the knocks and bruises out in the real world, I think things worked out best for me and my family in the long run. We had to earn our way and pull ourselves up by our boot straps. Looking back now in retrospect, I'd say we were better off. The old saying, "you have to work twice as hard as a well-off White person to get ahead in America" is a truism I have found that rekindled my spirit time and time again as I struggled for success in Mississippi. In an odd sort of way, I guess this axiom helped shape my thinking about success and fueled my desire to always work hard to get to succeed.

My aunt Dollie was a hardworking decent person who was raised to love people, regardless of their race and status. There was no doubt in my mind that she also loved her extended White family.

As a child listening to her stories, I would be afraid when she spoke about how she freely disciplined the White kids in their households. Aunt Dollie could really go off when she was angry.

Believe me, she did not hold back! You could believe her when she said "just because a child's butt was lighter than mine, it deserved no special privileges." She did not spare the rod. I'm sure the White kids in her employer's households got the royal treatment just as we did when we got out of line.

One thing that seemed to bother aunt Dollie was the fact that outside of the White families' four walls, she was considered less than a human being. In one breath the White kids and other family members would hug and shower her with kisses and unbridled affection. In the next instance they would make demeaning racist comments about Black people right in front of her.

Aunt Dollie would say that her White employers "would forget and treat her just like she was one of them." Even to the point of waiting for her to join into their little negative conversation and throw in her two cents worth about Black people. Of course that never happened. Aunt Dollie was not one who would demean her own race for a laugh or acceptance. She would crack us up demonstrating how her White employers necks would be stuck out leaning towards her, as if to be drawn to her like a magnet, waiting in eager anticipation of her remarks. She'd often say "One day they were all going to fall over on the floor at the same time in eager anticipation of her two cents worth."

In the best of times, they truly treated aunt Dollie as if she was a member of their family, while she was within the safe walls of their homes.

It was quite a different story when aunt Dollie and other Black housekeepers transversed the White neighborhoods trying to get to and from work each day. Aunt Dollie jokingly told me that on many a day she thought she was a drum-major, because everyday when she left work to catch a bus home, she'd have ten to twenty little White kids marching in step behind her singing "big fat Nigger, big fat Nigger, big fat Nigger."

The White grown-ups loved this little show, she believed, more than the kids. They would sit or stand out in their yards each day just to get their daily dose of this show. Aunt Dollie would have us screaming when she demonstrated how they, the kids as well as adults looked, especially when, right before she reached her bus stop, she would turn abruptly and chase after them. The kids loved it! The adults who would be watching would be caught up in the action as well. They would be twitching and acting out the excitement and screaming escape directions to the kids to help them get away like "Run little Johnnie run. She is right behind ya." Or, " Quickly run between the bushes Mary. Good Girl! Don't let the Niggar woman get ya." Needless to say, this little daily soap opera was probably the highlight of their day.

My aunt Dollie is one of the sweetest, most big-hearted women you would ever want to meet. I've seen her give a needy person her last dollar! But, as nice as she could be, she did not take anything for too long off of anybody. I can see her gritting her teeth and tolerating these small White kids, because she truly loved kids and deep in her heart knew it was not their fault. The adults, well that was an entirely different story. For the sake of the kids and peace aunt Dollie said she tried to put up with this indignity.

On this one particularly hot summer's day aunt Dollie had had it! Instead of letting the little naughty kid who daily taunted her on her way to her bus stop outrun her, she surprised them and maxed out her 300 pounds and caught several of them. I don't have to tell ya what happened. She tore their asses up! Spanking White kids in your extended family behind closed doors was one thing. But spanking them, especially those of families you did not work for out in public in front of their White neighbors and friends, was going too many steps too far!

She was fired for what her White employer called getting too big for her Nigger britches. Her dismissal letter was dropped in her mail box that night.

CHAPTER TWENTY THREE

THE BLACK POLICE

YOU'D BETTER GIT TO STEPPIN, BECAUSE THE BIG BAD DOGS ARE LOOSE

For many years in the city of Jackson, justice was dispensed by White police officers only. Black police would come on the scene around 1957. Any Black person being picked up by White policemen who was unfortunate enough to be arrested for even the smallest offense, would hardly be recognizable the next day, if he was lucky enough to ever see home again. A lot of Blacks were beaten to death in police custody in the early fifties and prior.

And then, it happened! The rumors began to circulate that there were going to be Black police officers in Mississippi. Just the thought of having Black police to patrol our neighborhoods filled the Black community with glee, and yes, hope. But you know life can be really cruel. And as my old pastor used to say, "Be careful of what you pray for, because you just may get it." Without prolonging the suspense any longer, the joy and hope that we were filled with in our community were quickly dashed and changed into despair. I guess life has always got to hand you a big BUT. There is always a catch when something is being freely given to you!

The first few years that Black policemen hit the scene in Jackson were confusing to our community! We were shocked and totally dumbfounded that the new Black policemen were unbelievably brutal to their own. Add to this the indignity, the fact that they could only arrest Black people.

There were times when the God send the Black community prayed for turned out to be our worst nightmare. I don't want my statement to be taken as a current indictment of the fine and decent Black policemen that are currently on the many police forces in Mississippi and across America for that matter. For many years in Jackson and across Mississippi, Black police have done their jobs extremely well.

They are known for their outstanding dedication to duty and their bravery and commitment to protect and serve all of Mississippi's citizens. So please do not think I am talking about them. But for that time period in Jackson's history, they were what everyone in our neighborhood called "The Big Bad Dogs." This was not meant to be taken in a good sense either. The first Black policemen on the scene in the downtown community of Jackson struck sheer terror in our hearts because of their ruthless deeds.

When you heard the comment, "The Big Bad Dogs have been turned loose and are heading this way," your feet had better had been gitting it. I mean people ran out of their shoes to get out of the vicinity when they heard this comment. Your pulse would quicken, your heart would throb and people would break into a cold sweat at just the mention that the Big Bad Dogs were heading their way.

Sure, the White police were treacherous. Yeah, but they were not the awesome looking figures that the Big Bad Dogs were. Plus they were not as quick, fast and as in shape as the Black officers. Given a few good feet and a turned corner or head, YOU COULD OUTRUN THE WHITE POLICE WITH EASE. It was no contest. This was a big joke in the Black Community. If you got outran and caught by the White policemen, you deserved to be caught! But the Black policemen were a completely different matter altogether. We're talking, big tall, thick lipped brothers with massive arms, bulging and ripping up the edges of their shirts, that could quickly hawk (outrun) you down in a heartbeat, if they had to.

Before, the brothers could at least outrun the White police, given a few inches of daylight and a close corner to turn. But, with the Black Police, forget it, no chance, no chance at all. Black officers with the nicknames of Dirty Red, Charlie Boy, Blue, Mr. Tom, and Black Sambo created heart pounding terror in the Black community. I don't know if it was that they thought they had to prove to their White superiors that they indeed would arrest their own. Or maybe, they thought they had to prove that they were tough enough for the job. I truly don't know. But what I do know is, they were the Devil set free in our community the first few years that they came on the scene in Jackson Mississippi.

The street we stayed on was only a few blocks removed from downtown Capitol Street. You would see the Black police slowly walking in twos in step on either side of the street heading down Farish Street into the Black community. They would be dragging their nightsticks at head high level on both sides of the street against the walls. Occasionally, as they walked, they would bang a beat on the brick walls they passed. That noise made an eerie sound. It was like a death call! Hearing that beat caused people to scurry to get out of their way and stay ahead of them. People would be running for their lives. The Black officers seemed to make a point to stop at each Black frequented location, nightclub, business establishment and raise hell just to let everyone know who was in charge.

On the weekends, my brothers and I, just to make a few dollars, would work at Silver Savers. Silver Savers Grocery store was located in the heart of the Black community on Farish street. It was a short walk from downtown Jackson and the police station. So, growing up my brothers and I saw and experienced it all! Jackson at that time was a free-for-all city. By this I mean, anything was possible, especially in downtown Jackson. You had gambling, drugs, alcohol long before it was legal, and prostitution was so common that it was openly practiced in downtown Jackson.

The owner of Silver Savers at that time was Mr. Norman. He was, for all practical purposes a White man, as far as his looks, and how he spoke. But, if you knew him well, you knew he was of Lebanese origin. His wife, Ms. Bobbie was White through and through. She was slightly on the mean side to her customers and was kind of tight with her money. She kept up with every penny that came through the store and went into Mr. Norman's pocket. Besides that quirk though, she was nice to us kids. Mr. Norman was a super nice man as well. He would give people the shirt off his back if their story was sad enough. He'd be sneaking groceries out the front or back door of his store to people and have us looking out for Ms. Bobbie, because he knew that if she even thought he was giving stuff away free, she'd be all over him.

That dilemma (the fact that Mr. Norman was free hearted and Ms. Bobbie was not) was a constant source of laughter for all of us who worked at the store. Nevertheless, my brothers and I considered ourselves blessed to have been given a job at Mr. Norman's store. As I said earlier, Farish street was like being at the zoo. Eventually you would see it all, if you sat in a good spot for a few hours. That area of Jackson was called Black Heaven. It was where most of the successful Black businesses were at that time!

As a result of all of the actions going on, as kids of nine, ten, eleven on up to fifteen, my brothers Donald, Stan and I and the rest of the employees at Silver Savers (Fred, Luther, Ben Bradley) had a ring side seat to all of the action! We saw some of the funniest stuff you could imagine on Farish street, happen right outside of the three quarter length windows of Mr. Norman's store.

This birds' eye view included seeing the Black police beat down many a person on Farish Street. The festive atmosphere in the area I called Black Heaven, quickly turned to hell for those who were on the receiving end of their nightsticks. Mr. Norman, although he let my older brothers watch these little lessons that the Black police were obviously handing out to the community, if he saw me looking, would quickly send me on an errand or back to the back of the store to do a chore, so that I could miss this sight. Mr. Norman would occasionally walk out of his store and talk the police into not continuing their little show. Although he tried to shield me, I usually was able to sneak and watch anyway. Something in my gut told me that I had to experience this little life lesson, albeit barbaric.

Farish street at that time was the place to be for the (so Called) hip/progressive Black people. It had Black owned night clubs, furniture stores, hotels, the YMCA and YWCA, restaurants (Big Johns, The Home Dinning Room, Peaches Café and the Alamo Theater to name just a few). Big Johns Café is known world wide for its funny little smoke sausage, pig ear, and hot dog sandwiches. I think the guys who invented White Castle and Krystal burgers probably got their idea from Big Johns. Big Johns on Farish street was also famous for melt in your mouth, run and slap your momma hot tamales. They have operated in Jackson, even to this day, in the same little spot for close to a hundred years. Famous people from all over the world would, an even to this day, will still sneak in and get their big greasy brown bags filled with Big John sandwiches. The same is true of former Jacksonians such as myself whenever I am in town.

Additionally, In those days (in the fifties and sixties) at the Alamo theater, all you had to do was present two Hardin's bread wrappers and you could get in free.

To add to all the festivities on the weekend in downtown Jackson, Black Heaven as my little friends and I loved to call, there would be rows and rows of buses bringing Black people into the city from the surrounding country towns so they could shop on Capitol Street and Farish Street. It was a major madhouse on Farish and Capitol Street at that time. It got so crowed at times you could barely walk on the sidewalk. This was before shopping malls came on the scene.

Boy, there were some real country people getting off those buses. I would have to roll grocery carts filled with groceries to their buses and have to listen to all kinds of funny stories just to walk away with a penny or two tip. Just for comparison sake, the going rate for tips when you walked someone's groceries to their house or car was from ten cents to twenty five cents. So, you could imagine after lugging about four or five heavy bags that getting a penny, or in many cases, getting a tip that amounted to just good conversation, was no fun.

I tell you one thing that was plentiful from those country

towns were pretty girls. Man, you'd see and meet some of the prettiest country girls you would ever want to see getting off of those buses. So as you would imagine, the Weakley boys and our little friends looked forward to our little jaunts to the side street of Jackson with our little grocery carts. Farish street was a very festive atmosphere for all concerned. Although Farish Street was jumping pretty good on the weekends, the one thing that quickly killed the fun was the Black Police.

I've seen them completely humiliate Black people and beat them down unmercifully. The sad thing about it was they were our own. You would think that for no other good purpose other than the former reason, (them being black people themselves) that they would lighten up a little bit. But that was not the case with these guys. I personally saw them beat people until they used the bathroom on themselves uncontrollably.

After they finished their public displays, they would drag the person or persons, to a corner and call the Black Mariah (the paddy wagon). The White police, when they arrived or rode by in their shinning police cars, would be practically rolling on the floor laughing at the poor guy that the Black police would have reduced to the lowest possible terms, for nothing more than maybe jay walking or maybe having one too many. Perhaps in their minds they were doing the Black community a favor, because if the White police had gotten to the person, just maybe the arrested person would have had their life taken from them. In any case, even the lesser of the two evils was hard to swallow.

CHAPTER TWENTY FOUR

YEP, PAY BACK IS A MOTHER...

One of the most tense moments I recall in our household for me, was as a child of seven seeing my big brother Don, who was about fifteen at the time, walk past me in our front room with his back practically covered in his own blood. You would think he would have been in a panic, but he wasn't. He strolled down the hall to my grandfather who was sitting in the television room, like it was nothing at all. My grandfather looked at him, paused for a split second and just as calmly as Don, I might add, proceeded to have him sit on the side of the bed, lean forward to its center and from there began to work on his back. I don't think at first granddaddy even asked Don what had happened to him! He just quietly worked to slow the bleeding. He then cleaned the wound and did some type of funny looking, catch as catch can stitch work on Don's back. The bleeding slowed considerably, the more he worked on him.

My mom and grandmother were very excited, and nervous. But Granddaddy was as cool as a cucumber. He kept saying, now everyone stay calm, he'll be okay. This is nothing. It looks a lot worse than it really is.

Apparently, as I came to understand later, Don had accidentally stepped on a grown man's foot while making his way down an aisle in the then Alamo Movie Theater on Farish street. The man, angered, over the fact that my brother Don had accidentally stepped on his foot, pulled a switchblade knife and began to cut him. He cut him several times in the back before Don could run away! Don said he tried to apologize but the man simply would not listen to him. He kept cutting him even as he tried to apologize to him.

Don and I were tight! He was my older brother and my role model! I tried to push my way into the back room to get a closer look at what was going on, but my grandmother and mom just grabbed me by the hand and practically dragged me out of the room. I didn't want anything bad to happen to him. At a couple of points, I could almost swear I heard Don and my grandfather laughing as he was being stitched up. What a man!! What a man!! My brother had nerves of steel. That laugh from my brother and grandfather told me all that I needed to know. I knew all would be okay!

I've never shared this with anyone up until I chose to share this story in this book, but years later I was able to get the man back who had done this terrible thing to my brother. Nothing was never really done to him by the police at the time he cut my brother. He was not arrested nor questioned, even though my family filed a formal report. In those days, where Blacks were concerned, you just kind of lived with the injustices that occurred in your neighborhood, if the law refused to do something about it. Or you chose to take or not take the law into your own hands. It was as simple as that! Even though the police did not act on the report, my family felt blessed that Don had not been killed.

Black on Black crime in those days, in most instances, was not acted on by the police department. It was as if they did not care if Black people killed themselves off. Murderers routinely walked free in our neighborhood. All you had to do was have a good lie to tell as to why you did what you did and said, if even asked by the police, that you would not normally do what you did again, and that was it!! That was just the way it was.

Roughly a year after this incident occurred, my uncle Joe

pointed the man out who had cut Don. I think my uncle Joe was just filling me in for information's sake, he would have never thought I, a fourth grader, would even think about getting revenge in this situation, but I did.

As I mentioned earlier, uncle Joe had pointed out the man who had stabbed my brother Don to me. He was a very familiar face. He was the same man who frequently came by my patrol boy post that I had at the corner of Farish street and Church street.

In those days, patrol boys would be stationed on some of the busy streets near the elementary school. Our job was to report there thirty minutes before school, and we were allowed to leave a few minutes before school was out to help the smaller kids get across the street. We had thick yellow belts that wrapped across one shoulder and then around your waist. The belt had, in big bold letters, " Patrol Boy." Boy, did I have a lot of fun being a patrol boy.

Helping the little kids across the street was a big responsibility. And guess what, I took my job very seriously. This was during the time I had began to be healthy. During my earlier years I was pretty sickly as a child. I could barely help myself much less somebody else! But for that point in time, I stood tall with my little Patrol Boy Belt! It was nothing for me to stand out in the pouring rain, just to make certain no one got hurt at my point.

After uncle Joe pointed the guy out to me, I just kind of watched him and didn't say a word. I would watch the direction he would go just to see if I could figure out where he lived. I must admit, that man probably did not have a clue who I was or what I was doing when I would stretch my neck out to see what direction he went as he passed me each morning. Eventually, I found out that he stayed with a lady in an alley between my street, Oakley and Church Street in a two-story house.

One Saturday, David Clyde and I were playing at the mouth of his alley and to our wonderment, we saw this extremely drunk man, stumbling and half walking, coming down Oakley Street towards us. At that point he stopped to use the bathroom right there in the middle of the street. I guess I don't even have to tell you who it was; it was the man who had cut my brother Don.

I recall telling David Clyde who he was, and David like me, became upset at the man for what he had done to my big brother. Just at that moment, behind the man about half a block, you could see Red, one of the meanest Black Police on the force and his partner Charlie walking past Oakley Street.

David and I ran toward the police and started to scream that there was a drunk man down the street using the bathroom right out in the open. The two Black police took off running in the direction we were pointing. I think they thought something more serious was going on. They took off running towards the man at a break neck speed!

At first I thought the man had gotten away because we didn't see him when we returned with the police. But sure enough, there he was stumbling and trying with all his might to make it to his house. The police spotted him and ran to catch up with him. As fate would have it, the drunk man, half swung at one of the policemen and hit RED in his face. And what did he do that for? Red took out his nightstick and proceeded to pummel the man, beating him down to his knees. The man begin to hold on to Red's legs and plead for mercy. I even felt sorry for him. After a few seconds of Red and the other policeman stomping him, the man's wife, I guess hearing the commotion, came outside and started to plead with the police to let her take him inside to give him first aid. The man was bleeding badly.

They practically pushed the lady down and made her get back inside of her house. As she was being pushed inside the house by the second policeman, one of the lady's neighbors walked up and pointed at David and me and said "it was those two kids who put the police on your husband. They did it!! They are the blame for this." I shouted back at her, "Yeah and that's what he gets for cutting my brother." With that, David and I took off running for my house!!! I did however, feel sorry for the man! I did not expect or want the police officers to beat him like that! I really thought that he would only get arrested. That was the justice I sought for what he had done to my brother. But even still, I also felt in the end, that justice, although delayed, was served!

CHAPTER TWENTY FIVE

BOY, YOU TALKING ABOUT SOME FUN!

Man, did I have some cool playmates while I was growing up. There were the Curry Boys, (David, Sam, Tim, and Rone) Pee Wee, Carolyn, Donald Duck (who had the biggest navel you'd ever want to see) James Earl and David Clyde. David Clyde's sister Carolyn was the biggest, thumb sucking, tomboy in the neighborhood. She could out play any of us guys in any sport. When we began to choose sides to play baseball, kickball, basketball, or any sport, people would practically be tearing ole Carolyn in half trying to pull her over to their side. We all knew that you were a sure winnner if you had Carolyn on your team.

She didn't talk a lot, I guess you could say she was truly a person of few words. But when it came to hitting a ball, tackling guys on the football field, driving fearlessly head on to the goal on the basketball court, there was no match. She was a super athlete. A tomboy plain and simple. And we loved her!!!

The funny thing about old Carolyn was that we all were bigger than she was, but even so, she still was the Michael Jordan of our neighborhood. She had no equal. She could fly through the air on a lay up, it seemed as if for forever, like she had wings. Whether it was in baggy clothes or a dress, she always came to win. My grandfather, uncle Joe and their friends would sit on our front porch and practically throw up laughing at how Carolyn would be dogging us out of our shoes and playing rings around us.

My grandfather and his friends would be laughing at us and cheering Carolyn on big time! After a while we didn't let it bother us though, but it seemed to be a major blow to the egos of many of the visiting kids from other neighborhoods who would frequently come through to challenge us to a good game of kick ball, basketball or football. I guess Carolyn held back on us, because she would go all out to let them know that just because she was a girl, didn't mean she couldn't play. She would be knocking smoke from these guys. They would be so embarrassed. Even we would feel sorry for them. Carolyn would literally be knocking these guys out of their shoes and jock straps when she tackled them on the football field. Or she would be juking them out of their socks and shoes on the basketball court or kickball field. Of course, we never told her this because she would have gotten the "Big Head," but Carolyn was our hero. Better yet, she was our "Shero!" She was truly magnificent. The only real flaw Carolyn had was sucking her thumb. We continually teased her about it. But she didn't care. Between games, or any free moment, you would find her thumb in her mouth. Us guys showed no mercy and had some hilarious laughs sparked around that squeaky clean thumb of hers.

Nevertheless, Man did Carolyn have a sweet three point basketball shot. She'd hit nothing but nets with it each and every time. Carolyn was our ace in the hole when we needed a little cash too. The other unaware teams coming into our neighborhood to play us basketball would quickly run their hands in their pockets and put together a buck or two to bet that they would beat us, when they saw little short Carolyn looking like the weakest link of the litter standing in line with us (she had the worst posture you'd ever want to see) waiting for our down to come on the court. Git this! Some of them would even give us points and beg us to play them for more of their money. When the smoke had cleared, we would be victorious. Carolyn would have spanked these guys thoroughly and have them shaking their heads in disgust. We would be falling all over ourselves laughing at them and happily counting up their money, you'd better know it, as we talked a truck load of trash to them.

There also was another unique young girl who played with us as well. Her name was Debbie Ann Harvey and she was a couple of years younger than me. She was Bobby Harvey's (Stan's friend) little sister. Boy did she have a big crush on me. She would follow me wherever I went, or would just sit on the sidelines and cheer for me the whole time whenever I played with the other kids. You would think it would have been flattering for me but it wasn't; It was the height of embarrassment.

Now, I'm not saying Debbie Ann was ugly, because she really wasn't. She was a very good-looking girl. The problem was that she was so skinny!! Man she could turn side-ways and disappear. She would often follow me around with red roses on the vine in her hand. Next to our house was a row of rose bushes that produced the most beautiful roses you'd ever want to see each year. As a public joke, (since she knew my buddies would tease me about it) she would pull the pedals off of each rose individually and recite the old corny saying, "He loves me, he loves me not" just to frustrate me. I recall once finally giving in to her and humoring her regarding her open display of affection towards me. We were in my backyard and she was singing songs to me while I played marbles with David Clyde, Donald Duck and Pee Wee. My grandmother was also back there with us; she was hanging clothes she had washed on the clothesline. Being used to Debbie Ann's little corny overly dramatic theatrics, we all, including my grandmother ignored her.

Our backyard had several big fig trees that we kids loved to play in. The thing about those fig trees was that the limbs of the tree were not very stout or sturdy. I had finally gotten a little bored with Debbie Ann's bugging me and embarrassing me in front of my friends. Her little antics had begun to cause me to miss my shots when it came my time to shoot at the marbles in the ring, while playing with my intensely serious playmates. I was steadily losing all my marbles. My sack of marbles was dwindling, and my friends' bags were getting fatter and fatter. I blamed this on Debbie Ann. I figured enough was enough!!

I quickly got up, called Debbie Ann over to me, looked her in her eyes, which were opened very wide, I guess at anticipation that I was going to kiss her. Instead of kissing her though, I put my hands on top of my head, looked her in the face and screamed, "I can't take it anymore. I can't take it anymore!!! Please leave me alone. Pleaeeeaaassssse! My grandmother by this time was bent over laughing at my little theatrics. She then turned her back to us and started to make her way into the house. Seeing that my grandmother had left, I tied a rope over one of the nearest limbs of the fig tree and loudly announced that I was going to kill myself, if Debbie Ann didn't go away and leave me alone. David Clyde and Pee Wee practically split a rib laughing. I joined in laughing with them as well. Debbie Ann was wide eyed and appeared scared. Being the little comedian that I was, I figured I'd get a little more mileage out of my little joke. While we laughed, I hurriedly searched the backyard until I found a little stool looking chair that my grandmother often used to pick figs from the lower branches.

I quickly got up in the chair and tied the rope around my neck and kept telling Debbie Ann to leave or I was going to kill myself. She was practically pulling her hair out. As old funny fate would have it, I somehow slipped out of that chair. Whee Man! There I was dangling a foot or two off the ground with my feet occasionally bobbing down to touch the ground. David Clyde, Donald Duck and Pee Wee, I guess, thought it was the funniest thing they had ever seen. They thought I was still putting on an act. The fact of the matter was that I was indeed dying.

The rope had tightened so tight around my neck, I was strangling right there before their eyes. There I was bouncing up and down in that tree, Debbie Ann was pulling her hair out and screaming to the top of her lungs. My boys, Pee Wee, Donald

Duck and David Clyde, who I guess thought I wanted to scare Debbie Ann just a little bit more, and now bored with the show,) went back to concentrating on their game of marbles. Thank God, after a few wild minutes, I'd say, my grandmother heard Debbie Ann and came running to the back door. Once she saw what was happening she practically leaped from our back door steps to the tree. She frantically wrestled to free my neck from the noose while holding me up in the air, around my waist, to keep me from strangling further.

I WAS COUGHING, FARTING AND GASPING FOR AIR AND SHE WAS SHAKING ME UP AND DOWN TRYING TO GET AIR INTO MY LUNGS. It was a good thing for me that fig tree's limbs had a lot of elasticity. The limb I was hanging from dangled occasionally, rather than support my weight completely!! That allowed my feet to occasionally bounce off the ground. This kept my neck from snapping. Once I finally got my composure, and my grandmother realized I was all right she began to tear into my butt with a switch/limb she quickly snatched out of the tree. She had that switch singing like an old Tom cat in heat.

Granny was so upset with David Clyde, PeeWee and Donald Duck that she also started to tear into them as well. Man what a sight! My grandmother started to lash old Debbie Ann a time or two as well for not knowing enough to run and get help. There we all were running around crying in my backyard TRYING TO DODGE A LICK OR TWO FROM MY totally upset GRAND MOTHER.

It was good that there were several of us; granny in all of the confusion, seemed a little confused at first as to who she wanted to pop next. We were darting about and holding our butts, crying and hissing (sucking wind) so that we could be able to suffer through the good old-fashioned butt whipping she was putting on us. My granny wore us out that day. That was one time when my silly antics got us all smoked.

I remember once as a young adult of about 35, having been a way from Jackson for about ten years and not seeing most of my old neighborhood friends for at least fifteen years, going to a parade and being absolutely flabbergasted by a weird sight I came upon. As I walked past the crowd, I spotted this odd looking man. While everyone else's attention was focused on the parade, he had his shirt up and what appeared to be the weirdest thing was poking from his shirt. The man had something long, thick and about five or six inches peeking straight out from under his shirt.

I finally looked up into the grown-up man's face thinking to myself, " What the hell is going on here?" All of a sudden I hear, "I figured you wouldn't recognize my face now that I am old, but I knew you couldn't miss my navel, since you guys used to tease me about it all the time as kids." Boy you talking about laughing; it was ole Donald Duck. My old childhood playmate. Man what a riot! I started pointing at him and everyone in that area, including of course old Duck himself, joined in laughing. People were practically rolling on the street. He's lucky no one reported him for indecent exposure. What a laugh!!

I also recall playing as a child with the Curry Boys (David and Tim) who have now gone on to be internationally famous as the founders and stars of the Mississippi Mass Choir. They were raised a few houses over from my house. Their famous father who was called Elder Curry because he was a nationally known preacher of a sanctified church, would catch us playing popular music in their church in the daytime when no one was around. We would be jamming on the instruments like international rock stars in that little church.

Anyone who knows anything about Sanctified churches know that they go all out where their music is concerned. In those days, they would have guitars and drums, pianos and organs in their Church. And you know us kids; that would lead to a jam session many a day. The bad thing however, was that Elder Curry did not play that mess, not one bit. He was serious about his religion. Man, he would come in there and start chasing and whipping us with his belt. We would be breaking our necks almost trying to get out of his way. I joke, but he was truly a great man with a big heart!!

VERNON STEVE WEAKLEY

A few years prior to the writing of this book I saw a program about his life on PBS. He had an incredible story. His outstanding work as a pastor and church leader was internationally known long before I was born.

Although he would be upset because we were clowning in the Church, occasionally he would have to crack a smile himself at how funny we looked begging him to let us go. In the end, he would corner us in that little church and put the strap to us.

Although my family were Baptist and Elder Curry was Sanctified and very, very strict about materialistic things, (he didn't even believe in watching television) he allowed his kids to play with the rest of us in our neighborhood. Boy did we all appreciate that. The Curry boys were some great kids. Although he graciously let his kids play with us, he didn't like for his kids to buck his beliefs. The fact that my family had a television led to some rather interesting dilemmas for us all.

The Curry boys as well as all of my other playmates would be crammed into my house looking at television, especially on Saturday morning, until of course, Elder Curry got wind of it. He would ease down toward our house, intensely listening as he came to see if he could hear the television, and more importantly, the sound of us noisy kids laughing up a storm in the front room of our house. Then he would start calling out real loud for his boys. I now think he did this to let us know he was coming. You should have seen old David, Sam and Tim running out of our house running home, while trying to dodge Mr. Curry to avoid getting a lick with his belt.

The rest of us kids would be laughing at our buddies running a hundred miles an hour trying to beat Mr. Curry home.

CHAPTER TWENTY SIX

THE CHICAGO CONNECTION

As small children, my brother and I would spend many of our summers back in Chicago. We were born there, and aside from that, our family had always had a strong tie to Chicago because of two special people. As children born in Chicago, but being raised in Mississippi, we were indeed fortunate to have two good as gold relatives there that we could visit each year. Jeff Stevens Jr., my mother's brother and aunt Maxine were pretty much entrenched in Chicago. They both were well-off, as far as my family was concerned, and loved Chicago with a passion. They occasionally came to Jackson for visits, but for the most part, unless there was a funeral to go to or someone was seriously sick, they really didn't like coming back to Mississippi very often.

During the time we made our little visits to Chicago we had to endure a lot of teasing about being two little country boys from Mississippi! Man did we take a lot of verbal abuse while we were up there, simply because we were from Mississippi.

Although it was glaringly obvious that we were living a lot better than most of the kids we played with, they teased us and said we were poor southern trash. The old falling in brick apartment houses and sky high projects they lived in were, let's just say, not in the best of shape. They seemed to always be putting us down about being from the racist and dirt poor deep South.

My aunt Maxine who had moved to Chicago from Mississippi many years earlier, was always defending us and the South. She was thick skinned and kind of on the short side. She had a slow deliberate walk. It was a more hip version of John Wayne's walk that was full of confidence. Old aunt Maxine was nothing to play with either! She was as tough as nails!!Although she is now very old, aunt Maxine has as much energy as most people I know!!! As of the writing of this book, she was eighty-four years old and she still gets around better than most people half her age. Just to give an idea of what I am talking about, I'll share a story with you. A day or two after Thanksgiving day 2000, I took my mom, who was a young seventy-six herself, and aunt Maxine to the movies to see "Men of Honor." As fate would have it, some bad kid, playing a stupid and dangerous joke pulled the theater's fire alarm. He caused the entire stadium style movie house to clear out. You should have seen mom and aunt Maxine leading the pack to get out of the place. I could barely keep up with them. Yep, they still got a lot of energy and spunk, praise the Lord!!!

Aunt Maxine has visited more countries and traveled more places than anyone I have ever known. Most of her excursions occurred in the fifties, sixties, seventies, and the eighties long before integration was an accepted practice in many other countries. No one could accuse her of talking about stuff she didn't know about or not having the courage to look people in the eye and say, "Get the hell out of my way! I'm going to see what I want to see and go where I want to go!' Now aunt Maxine had courage. I personally believe she invented the stuff!!! She can tell stories about Europe and the former Soviet Union Block countries, Hawaii, Jamaica, Puerto Rico, England, Switzerland, Italy and Africa that would have you sitting in awe for hours at a time. She definitely had a thirst for knowledge and adventure you wouldn't believe. Aunt Mack (the name I love to call her) said that in a lot of instances, whenever she walked into a room in many of these countries, all heads would swerve around and focus in on her as if they had never seen a Black person before.

She would be the absolute center of attention in these places until, in her roughneck style, she would get enough of it all and back them up off her with one of her direct, get out of my face Chicago comments, "Look I don't have no time for yawl's ignorance and foolishness, get back off me!" It didn't take a rocket scientist to know from her tone of voice, that she meant business. In any case, aunt Mack is the walking encyclopedia of our family. She knows all there is to know about our family history. Aunt Mack, along with cousin Elisa, who is approaching her nineties herself, as of the writing of this book (and who also looks about 60 and is as spry as you please), at our family gatherings will mesmerize us all with their little known, and often quite shocking hilarious facts about our family that go back as far as the early seventeen hundreds. At the writing of this book, praise the lord, they both are still going strong. They both get around on their own and are always ready to get up and go on a new adventure.

My aunt Maxine is a sterling example of what it takes to succeed in America. She went to Chicago as a young determined woman on her own many, many years ago with only five dollars in her pocket. From there she got up every morning and thoroughly turned Chicago up side down each day to find a job, eventually found a job and worked hard at that job in a very low level position until she retired over thirty six years later.

Now the lesson to be learned here is not in the level she achieved in her position/station in life, it is how she managed, saved, wisely invested her money, and from meager means, she was able to accomplish a lot with the little she had. From her two dollars a week paying job in the fifties, (which was what it was when she started) she managed to save her money, buy stock in the company where she worked (Mid State Paper Company) which eventually became 3M company, and from there conquered the world.

A disciplined, focused person strictly following a well thought out plan can do an awful lot with a little bit of money. My aunt Maxine has bought and completely paid for several houses, raw land and property, cars, helped send other kids, as well as my family to college, helped many a neighbor in trouble with their bills. And, as if that is not enough, with her own saved money traveled many times over, around the world to places most people hadn't even heard in the fifties, sixties and seventies. The list of aunt Maxine's incredible accomplishments could go on and on and on.

For years aunt Maxine would send money and clothes to our family, especially us kids on Easter, Christmas and the start of school like clockwork. When I hear people say that the reason they turned to selling or using drugs, to alcoholism or a life of crime, stealing, robbing, killing, and prostitution, etc. because they were desperate, I say back to them, "Nonsense!" And then tell them about my aunt Maxine. Those excuses are just a crutch for losers. My Aunt will personally bare witness to the fact that A STRONG BELIEF IN GOD, THE INCREDIBLE POWER OF PRAYER, A POSITIVE ATTITUDE, HARD WORK, GOOD COMMON SENSE, KEEPING GOOD HEALTH, A GOOD SENSE OF HUMOR, COURAGE, DEDICATION TO YOUR FAMILY, UNSHAKEABLE DETERMINATION, A GOOD SENSE OF RIGHT AND WRONG, AND A WELL THOUGHT OUT PLAN IS ALL ANYONE NEEDS IN THIS WORLD TO SUCCEED. All one has to do is have faith and tirelessly use these keys to success above and from there quit the crying and feeling sorry for yourself, roll up your sleeves and do it.

The problem with a lot of young people today is that they don't want to start at the bottom and work their way up. They think they should be able to always start at the top. Or, they think they should settle for nothing less that the glamour jobs. That's fine if you can do it. But failing this, you should regroup, pick yourself up, quickly grab what is available and from there stick with it and work your plan to success. The world is truly yours, if you will only put God in your life, put forth some sweat and elbow grease and go out and get it.

Taking an illegal, seemingly easy road as many of our young people seem to choose to do, in the long run, will only lead to death, prison, embarrassment for yourself and your family, loss of dignity, a total life failure and a guaranteed trip to hell. That's what my Aunt Maxine would tell ya.

My Uncle Jeff was the other close Chicago connection that we were blessed to have in our lives. He dressed extremely well like my grandfather and always seemed to have crowds of people breaking their necks to come and hang out with him whenever he came to Jackson. He was very tall and handsome. Not only was he an accomplished athlete (a basketball star) in high school and in college, he also was an incredible trumpet player. As I grew up playing music, people who knew him would always be coming to me to tell me that I was a chip off the old block like my uncle. They claimed he stole a many a girl's heart with that trumpet of his. He could make your heart sing or bring people to melancholy tears with the sexy sounds coming from his horn.

My uncle was the first one in my family to graduate from college. He graduated from Jackson State College when it was little more than five or six small buildings huddled together in what he used to call a cow pasture. He constantly preached to us about getting good grades in school and the extreme importance of a college education. He made a point of stepping in to be our adult male role model and providing guidance to us when our father died. He also loved his mom, which was my grandmother, fervently! He would call his mother Clara, each and every Friday evening like clockwork. In those days, in the early fifties, in order to make a long distance call the operator had to make the connection for you. You'd dial them and they would, after a few minutes, set up the call.

After a long conversation with his mom and my grandfather, he would go down the pecking order and have a hearty discussion with every member of our family. He would want to know how you were doing in school and fussed at you for not getting all As, and everything that mom and grandma, would tell off on you. My uncle married what my brothers and I always like to say was the prettiest woman in Chicago. My aunt Elniva was absolutely beautiful; my brothers and I marveled at her beauty and loved to brag and show off her picture to all of our friends in Mississippi. They have both now passed away. When they left this world, a part of our hearts went with them.

CHAPTER TWENTY SEVEN

IF YOU THINK YOU'VE GOT IT TOUGH, GO TALK TO YOUR GRANDPARENTS

The one thing I treasure the most about growing up in the South is the stories that my grandparents would tell about racism and how hard it was on them in earlier times. These stories really make me appreciate what I have today. While we obviously have a long way to go where racism is concerned, I think we all (Black and White) should take a moment and appreciate, and yes even celebrate just how far we have come in America. As tough as I thought it was when I was growing up, we had it relatively easy compared to our grandparents and earlier generations.

As I share some of the stories in this book that personally relate to my growing up in the South, I can't help but think of an incident that occurred many years ago with my own stepson. I recall sitting with him one day, watching an old documentary on the civil rights movement on television. It was one of the famous scenes where the White police in Alabama were spraying Blacks with high pressure water hoses and beating them, while big German Shepherd dogs were nipping at their heels.

After several of the demeaning police scenes flashed across the screen, I couldn't help but notice that my stepson kept shaking his head. After giving him my, "what's wrong son look," he said, "that stuff really didn't happen now did it?" For a moment I just looked at him in disbelief. But then it came to me that he was reacting just like I did when my grandparents told me the horror stories about the South when I was his age. And why shouldn't he? He had not personally seen any of this type of hatred. And I guess to him it just seemed like a made up story straight out of an old B movie.

After a few seconds of thought, I was able to answer my stepson by saying, "Yep, Rick it did happen. Not only were Black people openly beaten by the police, who were sworn to protect all of its citizens, but Blacks were regularly lynched and killed by them as well." To this he shook his head and said if he had been living in those times he wouldn't have taken that type of abuse. I kind of chuckled. He said, "what's wrong." I told him he reminded me of myself as a youngster when I sat around and listened to the old stories my grandparents would tell me. And with that I went on to share some of the old stories my grandparents told me with him.

My mother and grandparents would share stories with us that would make your toes curl. They talked about the lynching of Black people that occurred when they were growing up and how the police would either turn their backs to keep from having to stop these lynchings, or they openly participated in them with everyone else.

One story in particular that came to mind that I shared with Rick, was the story my grandmother told about how they came to Jackson. The year was approximately 1903. These were tough times indeed for Black people in America. My great grandmother's family used to work for an old rich White Landowner in Bolton, Mississippi. He was one of the biggest racists in that area. While he would allow Blacks to work for him, he also did not hesitate to take a whip to them if they got out of line. Most of the Black people who worked his land, hated his guts, but, tough times demanded that they suck in their pride and get work wherever they could find it.

In those days picking cotton was a primary means to

survive. People would work in the landowner's field and in return he would give you a little bit of money from the crops he sold, and maybe some food so you could survive until the money from the crops came in. The crops were sold once or twice a year by the old landowner. People helping him to get his crop in would get a small portion of the profit. My great grandmother and her two kids had just moved into Bolton from Flora.

My great grandmother and her son, who was about eight years old and my grandmother who was about nine at the time were working the fields picking cotton. They, like every other poor colored person in town, were just working for scraps to survive. They had only been working for the old landowner for a month or so. For whatever reason, on this particular fall day, the Rider who was the designated White person, who in those days would ride up and down the field rows to make certain that the workers worked at a certain pace, decided he would get down off of his horse and beat my great grandmother's son for not working as fast as he thought he should. And beat him he did!

The rider stomped, kicked, beat, and hit him in the face with his balled fists as hard as he could. It was as if he wanted to make an example of the young boy so that everyone watching would know he did not go lightly on Black workers. My great grandmother was working a number of rows away from her son at the time the beatings were going on. Some of the other Blacks, working in the next row from him, ran to tell his mother what was going on. Hearing just a few pieces of the story, she tore out running toward her son.

As she was coming up to the old White Rider, who saw her running up, he jumped back up on his horse. As she got to where they were, he snatched the horse's reins as if he was going to have the old horse rear up and stomp her. Seeing this, she immediately grabbed a metal hoe and started chopping at the horse's legs and hitting the man as well until that old horse threw the rider tumbling practically into her waiting arms. And I guess you know that's when the real ass whipping started!

My great grandmother kept chopping on the old rider with that hoe and hitting him in his head. Every time he would try to throw up his hands and block a lick up high, she would hit him down low. All of a sudden he collapsed into unconsciousness. She finally decided to leave the old rider alone because she was afraid she had killed him. He was sprawled out on the ground, out cold, bleeding from head to toe.

CHAPTER TWENTY EIGHT

CRUISING FOR A BRUISIN

In those days, just speaking back to White folks in anything less than an Uncle Tom, yes sir boss tone, by colored people could mean a lynching. Given this, you could imagine what was going to happen to my great grandmother for hitting the old rider. She did the only thing she could do, she ran. Before running though, she took the ole Riders house and tied him in a good spot a number of rows over, so that if the Rider did come to, he would have to walk to get help.

She grabbed up her son and my grandmother took off running to her old shack. She figured if she could get home, pack and leave town before the old Rider could regain consciousness, walk four or five miles to tell the sharecropper and the other Whites in the town what had happened, she could maybe make it to the train station and get out of town before they caught her. Boy, you talking about quickly packing and throwing stuff in paper bags to leave. My great grandmother could have set a world's record that day.

She was able to pack quickly and indeed make it to the train station within a very short period of time. But, as they were waiting for the train, which was late, to her total dismay, she saw a mob of White people coming their way in a fast walk. She quickly looked around for help. She noticed an old sheriff's deputy standing at the end of the station looking toward her with his arms folded. She took off running down to him and told him, "Sir, I think there is going to be some trouble." He quickly answered her and said, "Nigger, I think you right. I know what you done! Don't expect the law to help your Black ass." My great grandmother dropped her head and walked back with her kids toward the depot waiting room. She figured it was all over for her and her family.

Leading the lynch mob was the old gray headed sharecropper himself, riding a big white horse. The old Rider she had beaten up was right there with him on his own horse. He was bandaged all up and looking like he could fall completely apart at any moment. It was as if everyone of his body parts had caught a lick from my great grandmother's old metal hoe. The old landowner, who had a look that would kill on his face, was dangling a big thick rope off the side of his horse. There my great grandmother and her kids were facing a mob of people who were armed with guns, picks, shovels and sticks. Things looked hopeless. You talking about putting some prayers in the air. My grandmother said that my great grandmother was praying out loud a hundred miles an hour. She kept repeating, "Lord please save me and my children. Please save me and my children!!"

When they made it to her, the old rider hollered out to her to step away from her kids and come over to the crowd, who was off of the side of the train station's old wooden apron. My great grandmother slowly put her bags down, hugged her two kids who were crying to the top of their lungs, and told them to stay back. She slowly walked over to the tall apron side, which made her about eye level to the old White landowner sitting on his horse. You could cut the tension in the air with a knife. He didn't say a word at first. He just looked her in the eyes with an evil stare that seemed as if it could burn holes through her. The steam coming from his horse's nostrils engulfed my great grandmother like a thick fog. My grandmother said that her mother was shaking like a leaf on a tree as she stood before the old landowner and the angry White mob.

The blood thirsty mob of people behind and on the side of him were in an absolute frenzy. They were screaming, spitting at her, cursing her and telling her they were going to hang, kill, and burn her up when they finished. The dust that their feet and horses were kicking up was thick and stifling. The tension in the air was unbelievable. My grandmother said that they had gotten on their knees and were praying because they knew this was it for their mother and maybe even them. All of a sudden, the weirdest thing happened. The uncontrollable, shaking and nervousness that her mother had up until this point, seemed to disappear. Even though the crowd was extremely loud and vocal, she began to talk very softly to the old landowner, who to this point hadn't said a word. Speaking softly seemed to make the mob quiet down so that the old sharecropper could hear her.

She said "Mr. Boss I know you got kids of your own. And I know you wouldn't let anyone beat them like that mean man was beating mines. I know I shouldn't have, but as a mother, I couldn't stand by and let that man kill my child. Surely you can understand that Sir." The crowd let out a deafening roar. They seemed eager for the old White sharecropper to nod his head for them to get her. With just one signal from the old White sharecropper, they would have quickly snatched my great grandmother up, raced her to the nearest tree and stretched her neck as far as they could get it.

The crowd looked up at the landowner who was still on his big horse, as if to plead with him with their eyes and body movements, for him to give the word. They seemed like they could wait no longer for his order. The crowd surged towards the station's raised wooden apron where my great grandmother was standing and slammed into it. The building shook from the impact. Dust and splinters from the crumbling wood jetted skyward. And finally as hands were about to touch her, the old White landowner finally spoke. Everyone stopped in their tracks and looked back toward him. He said in a loud thundering voice, " Got Dammid Nigger you right! I do have children of my own but they White." The mob let out an angry roar of approval of his comment.

The old White landowner paused a few seconds as if to let the crowd noise ease a bit. During the pause he began to grit his teeth. He then crudely spit out a slug of tobacco that went flying by my great grandmother's head, barely missing her. He continued,

"Nigger, you best be glad that I am a family man, because if I wasn't, your Black ass would have already been swinging from the nearest tree."

"Now I am going to give your Black ass a break today! Get your ass on that damn train and don't ever come back round here again, you hear!"

"Consider yourself lucky today Nigger."

With that he jerked his horse's neck hard enough to almost break it and swung around and told the crowd,

"Get y'all asses on away from here and leave these people alone." With that the mob and him quickly went away.

My great grandmother ran back to her two now, scared stiff with fear kids, with tears in her eyes. She was wringing wet with her own sweat. Thank God for her, because at that very moment, the train pulled up. She grabbed them and the little belongings they had and got on the train without breaking stride.

My grandmother said they had no idea where the train was heading. They were just happy to be alive. They quickly got on the train and took the nearest seat. The train just happened to be going to Jackson. That's the story of how my family ended up in Jackson, Mississippi.

CHAPTER TWENTY NINE

THE CHILLING MOMENT OF TRUTH

I also recall my grandparents telling me this story once about the time they went to a wrestling match down on Capitol Street in Jackson. The time was about 1937. My grandparents loved wrestling with a passion. In those days, the wrestling matches were held in the parking lot of a rich car salesman in downtown Jackson. They would rope off the area and the professional wrestlers would have at it.

Even though there were no Black wrestlers participating in these events, Black people would attend in large numbers as well and enjoy themselves nevertheless. People, both Black and White, would go to these events and form a giant circle around the car lot. Whites would get the good spots of course, and the Blacks would have their own little designated area. Although, there was an obvious division between the races, it didn't stop anyone from having fun and enjoying the wild antics of the wrestlers. People would get so caught up in these matches, my mother said, that they would be fighting with each other just because someone cheered for their favorite hero to lose.

On this particular night, my grandparents, Jeff and Clara Stevens, and their three small kids Lola, Dollie and Jeff Jr.

Lola, my mom, was the oldest at fifteen. Dollie was at that time a petite, beautiful, ten year old and Jeff Jr., the youngest, was six. The walk to Capital street was not too demanding, so they had walked. In those days that wasn't unusual. Black people couldn't afford cars so they walked everywhere they needed to go that was close. Buses, which were called 'A Ghetto Chariot' in those days, were used for long distance travel.

Like everyone else they really enjoyed the wild antics of the matches. As they walked home from the wrestling show, a car load of young White men pulled up beside my grandparents and their kids and started to yell obscenities at them. My grandmother said that they had to be in the eighteen, nineteen and perhaps twenty year old range. In those days in Mississippi it was nothing for White people to call Black people "Nigger" out in the open. But, as if that wasn't humiliating enough, on this particularly crazy day, the stakes were taken even higher. The people in the car started to throw empty beer bottles out of the car at them to make them run.

People often say that in a severe crisis, there is a moment of truth that reflects what a person is made of. It is when you see yourself both inwardly as well as outwardly. Many say it is like seeing yourself in a x-ray screen. It is at this point that your sub-consciousness collides with your survival instincts, values, principles, inner strength and what you have represented outwardly to the world. If inside you are truly a coward, but you have represented yourself to the world as brave, it will be crystal clear for you and the world to see and soak in, whether you like what you see are not!! You can either deny what you see and turn away and be haunted all of your life for your lack of courage and faith, or be what your inner being screams that you truly are, and from there live or die (sink or swim) based on the sum of your being. My grandmother decided that night that that was her family's moment of truth.

All that she and her husband had taught her kids about right and wrong, and in particular, right always being victorious over evil, was at stake here. My dear grandmother made a decision that this night she would not run. She would not run!! My Grandmother stopped in her tracks and turned towards the car.

Seeing this, one of the White guys in the old car screamed, "You'd better run Nigger, because if you don't we're going to get out of this car and beat your ass."

After hearing this, my grandmother stopped and told,
(well let's say insisted that) my grandfather and little Jeff, go on and let the women (my wiry old grandmother, my mom and aunt Dollie) fight the White guys by themselves. Wow!

In those days, a Black man getting into a scuffle with a White person meant certain death. Given the fact that they were in downtown Jackson, and the streets were crowded with fired up White people on their way from the wresting matches, it was almost certain that some other Whites would come upon the fight. That scene, if Black men were involved, would have resulted in all five of them swinging from a tree and being burned.

It was obvious that there was no getting around a fight with these guys. So, my grandmother chose the lesser of the two evils. She unilaterally made a decision that the women would stay and fight. She figured at the worst, they would get a few bruises. While White men would certainly go all out to inflict maximum damage to a Black man, most would respect Black women, even in this terrible situation, if it was only to a lesser degree. After a few shoves from my grandmother and assurances that they would be all right and could take the White guys, my grandfather reluctantly walked off with tears in his eyes with little Jeff in tow.

The White guys, seeing that my grandmother had made my grandfather and little Jeff leave, quickly piled out of their car and began to push and shove my grandmother, Mom and Aunt as if they were insulted that they would even dare to think they were any match for them. My grandmother quickly assumed her 'It's time to go to war stance,' and ding, round one was on!

The White boys began to slowly circle them with their balled fists in the air.

To their surprise, grandma got in the first real lick across the head of one of the guys with a coke bottle, that she quickly pulled from her purse, sending him straight to the ground like a ton of bricks. From there on, it was a free for all. Those three, little bitty ladies were kicking, screaming and clawing those guys with everything they had!! What a scene! Dust was kicking up so match that it was hard to see.

My mom told me there were about five of those guys. Here all of them were, fighting tooth and nail in the middle of Capitol Street with people coming from everywhere to see the fight. It would have been great if there were some Black people in the vicinity, but it was not to be!! Those faces eagerly dashing to the scene and letting out blood curdling rebel yells were all lily white. I guess to them it was just an added attraction to the wrestling match!! If you can believe this, my grandmother said that the White on-lookers had some degree of integrity, because no one interfered. It was as if they just wanted to see a good 'knock em down drag em out fight!!'

My Grandmother said that even though she and my mom and aunt were screaming and someone could have easily assumed from their screams that they may have been getting the worst of it, that wasn't the case at all, once your eyes got close enough to behold the sight.

My grandmother told me, it was the easiest fight she had ever been in. She said that she had to pull her punches to keep from killing somebody!! Lucky for them! They definitely did not want to see my grandmother go all out. Wright and Ferguson funeral home, which was the White only funeral home in Jackson at that time, would have been bursting at the seams with White folks that day, if she remotely thought it had to come to that!! And you know what, I believe her. My grandmother was in unbelievably great shape. She was in her late fifties when I was in elementary school and she could outrun all of us kids in the neighborhood, and proved it quite frequently just to let us know that we did not have a chance trying to outrun her, when she was trying to spank us.

She also had blinding speed. I believe that Muhammad Ali had to have gotten his famous quote 'Float like a butterfly sting like a bee' from her! I tell ya something else too, my grandmother was a great dancer. She was poetry in motion! She was so graceful and so feminine with her ballroom movements. As a small child, I loved dancing with her. She had a thin frame that was misleading. It definitely hid a solid steel chassis. She was an unstoppable tank when she got riled up!!!!

My grandmother went on to say that when she started hitting those guys with that coke bottle and mom and aunt Dollie got to kicking, clawing, biting and screaming, those guys never had a chance. I would be spellbound and glued to my seat when my mom or grandmother told these old stories. I would often wet my pants while listening to them from the laughter as well as from not wanting to have to get up, go to the bathroom and miss hearing any portions of her funny stories.

The commotion from the fight, according to my grandmother, eventually caused the police to come up. The police immediately waded in and stopped the fight. When they finally got to the center of the crowd, pushing and pulling the spellbound people to make their way through them, and realized what was going on, the police began to split a rib laughing.

One hollered, "You boys leave these little Niggar girls alone, before they kill ya'll." With that comment the crowd let out a roar of laughter and quickly dispersed.

Oh, I would like to be able to tell you that my mom, aunt and grandmother didn't get a few bruises, but they did. Whenever my grandmother told that story she would say with pride that, "If you think we looked bad after the fight, you should have seen the other guys." Knowing my grandmother like I did, you could easily believe that they were the victors. I certainly believed it.

CHAPTER THIRTY

OUT OF THE MOUTHS OF BABES

After I shared a few of my grandparents' stories with my stepson, he wanted to know why didn't all of the Blacks get together and fight. I told him that some Blacks felt as he did but a good thing for us most didn't. Black people were very afraid of the consequences of fighting back. We would have been out numbered and out gunned. Most Blacks, when I was nine or ten didn't have guns to fight back like the authorities had during those days. Instead we voluntarily chose to follow the example of Martin Luther King who preached non-violence.

My stepson told me he knew about Martin Luther King and the good he stood for. He knew that Martin Luther King was a great man who stood up for Black people and led them in the fifties and sixties. At that moment I was really proud of my stepson. I went on to fill in for him what he didn't know about Mr. King's teachings and the raw courage it took to be non-violent in the face of adverse circumstances and danger.

I went on to tell him that with all of the scenes we were seeing on television in the sixties about Blacks being mistreated, the Black community was divided over being non-violent. Many wanted to follow the non-violent teaching of Martin Luther King, but others wanted to follow the other militant leaders such as Malcolm X. His philosophies were far more violent than Mr. King's. I was frank and honest with him and told him I was kind of in the middle. I probably was lucky that I was a little kid when most of the marches were going on. My mom didn't let me get involved in the marches. I also told Rick about Medger Evers. Martin Luther King showed a lot of bravery but my hero before him was Medger Evers. Rick didn't know about him. I went on to tell him more about my hero, Mr. Evers. He was truly a brave man who was standing up for Blacks in Mississippi and the deep South, long before Mr. King came on the scene.

Telling Rick that he was stalked and gunned down in his own neighborhood by a White man was very confusing to him. He asked how could a White man come into a Black neighborhood, hide behind a tree and wait for someone for hours without someone seeing him and better yet, stopping him? I told him it was a mystery to me as well. That fact has always bothered me over the years. But, it did happen.

I shared with Rick a secret that up unto that day I had not shared with anyone. I often, as a young college student, visited the street where Mr. Evers was shot and spent hours sitting in my car sometimes visualizing what occurred. I painfully pondered how such an awful thing could have happened. I went on to explain to him that our challenge now is to make certain that it never happens in any community Black or White ever again! The concept of freedom that we so greatly cherish in America should not be stolen away by cowards sitting in shadowy darkness eagerly waiting to steal a man's life from him. This ruthless, evil act had many negative far reaching consequences. It took a much needed father from his kids, deprived a wife of her loving husband and denied a struggling nation a valuable son and ideological spark that could have lifted this country to great heights.

I went on to tell Rick that, although initially, my mother didn't let me and my other brothers participate in the marches, after Medger Evers was killed, she changed her mind and decided she would at least let Don get involved. Don was the oldest of us kids. The same decision was obviously being made in a lot of other Black households, because after the Evers murder in Jackson, Black people, especially the high school and college students, came out to what was called mass meetings in droves. I went on to share with Rick some of what I saw in the fifties, sixties and how it affected me.

I began by telling about Don's exploits, as he related them to me, about the marches. My oldest brother Donald made his entry in the civil right marches with a group of students from his college (Toogaloo). They marched because the Whites who owned stores on downtown Capitol Street refused to serve Blacks. At this, my young stepson shouted, "That doesn't make sense. Didn't the White people want to make money?" I told him they wanted the money all right but they hated Black people so much that they didn't want them in their stores, if it meant giving them equal treatment with Whites. Rick said, "that's crazy." I quickly agreed with him. But that was just the way it was in those days.

My brother Donald and many other students participated in sit-ins and marches, and refused to leave when the police ordered them to. The Jackson police, true to form, shot high pressure water hoses on them, arrested and carried thousands of marchers to jail in dirty garbage trucks. But this did not stop the marches. The city of Jackson jails were so crowded that they had to use the old Mississippi Fair Grounds to lock up all the marchers. Eventually they had to let them all go because there were just too many of them. The White downtown store owners crumbled under the weight of the pressure that the marchers were exerting on them. This was one of the biggest triumphs of the Jackson Freedom Marches.

As a young child growing up in Mississippi not far from downtown where most of the marches and demonstrations occurred, I saw a lot. While my mother wouldn't let me participate in the earlier marches because I was too young, I would often, with my playmates, sneak downtown, and at a safe distance, watch what was going on.

I personally remember going to our family church, (Farish Street Baptist) for one of the rallies and seeing our then pastor, Reverend Whitney, begging and pleading with the marchers to give up their weapons before they participated in a non-violent march. As a young child watching him plead with the marchers, I wondered to myself why would he even think that the nice people that I saw in that church, would have weapons. They were passionately singing about nonviolence and even praying together. To my surprise however, Reverend Whitney was right.

His pleading finally paid off. He was able to finally get through to the crowd by posing an odd challenge to them. He asked everyone in the church to pass before the church's altar/pulpit and be truthful with him and more importantly God about their commitment to nonviolence. He asked anyone who had a weapon to pass by the alter and put it in the wicker offering plates he had set up. To my surprise and to the surprise of many of our church members, weapons came from places I didn't know existed on human beings. Reverend Whitney collected baskets of knives, brass knuckles and other lethal weapons from the marchers. These weapons primarily came from the young marchers from all over the city. The older marchers were truly nonviolent. It was obvious that the older marchers were committed to the principle of non-violence as they had said they were.

I remember wondering, sitting there as a child, what would have happened if Reverend Whitney hadn't been persistent and talked the crowd into giving up their weapons that day! That march would have been a total free-for-all as soon as one of these guys had been hit by the police. My mom was so upset over the sight of so many hidden weapons in church that she sent me to the house. My mother, my uncle Joe and Don went on to the march. Nothing out of the ordinary happened that day, if you can call Black people being beaten, dragged and arrested, a normal march. In those days it was indeed normal.

CHAPTER THIRTY ONE

A LITTLE TOO CLOSE TO HOME

    I think the most trying time for me personally during the civil rights period had to be when my little sister Cheryl was being bused to the White schools. Prior to busing, Black kids went to all Black schools and White kids went to their schools. Of course the Black schools were pitifully inferior at all levels. My brothers and I all went to predominately Black schools when we were growing up.

    My sister, who was the youngest child in our family, would be the first in our family to undergo this new experiment. Basically, someone thought it would be a good idea to bus kids, both Black and White, to different schools to ensure the racial make up. This was a nationwide integration strategy. In most instances the experiment resulted in Black kids being bussed way across town to dangerous White schools. Blacks at the beginning of this little experiment were definitely not welcome in formerly all White schools. The violence was fast and furious, up close and personal, and was seen as a result nightly on national television. These horrific scenes of people, mostly White, raising hell was awful and it was very, very scary. The whole nation was in an uproar in the early sixties regarding the new national busing policy. And like everywhere else across the nation, Black kids were being bused across town in Jackson, Mississippi.

They started with the lower grades first. I guess the thought process behind this was that it would give the hard-core die hearts on either side an opportunity to graduate. I was allowed to continue on to graduate from Lanier High school, rather than have to change schools and be bused to God knows where, way across town. The news media was replete with incidents involving little innocent Blacks kids being attacked by much older White kids or angry crowds of adult White people protesting the busing. I secretly feared for my little sister's safety.

Cheryl was in elementary school at the time. Her school was not very far from the Jackson Citizen Council's office. That organization was the embodiment of evil as far as racism in Jackson Mississippi and Black people were concerned. Man did Cheryl, who was only six or seven years old at the time, show a lot of guts and courage. If she was afraid, I never saw it in her face. She, as a result of my mom's prayers and guidance, FEARED NO EVIL. Cheryl packed her little things for school each day and from there went on like there wasn't anything to it.

As it was the case with most Black kids, who were now forced to go to previously all White schools, she got her share of taunting, name calling and slaps like everyone else. I remember being so afraid for my little sister one time that I told my mom that I wanted to play hooky from my school so that I could go over and protect her. My mom quickly said, "Vernon, we're not going to have any of that kind of foolishness out of you son. We've all prayed about this situation. Cheryl has got God on her side. You're not going to get better protection than that! Your little sister's gonna be okay."

While I trusted what my mom said, I couldn't help but think about what happened to me in the first grade. I did not want my sister suffering through what I had gone through because of racism. After a few more tries to take matters into my own hands and being quickly corrected by my mom, I went on and sat down like my mom suggested. Guess what, Cheryl got through busing okay. I remember years later recalling my fears over busing after seeing my sister on national television being interviewed by a well renowned news anchor for receiving a prestigious scholarship to the University of Mississippi. I was so happy for her. In years past, Ole Miss University had been a hard-core stronghold for segregation. I thought to myself as I smiled, "Boy how times have changed!"

My sister went on to get her Masters Degree from Old Miss University. She has made us all proud of her. I can't help sometimes thinking back to those tense moments I went through, worrying about her safety as a young kid integrating the Mississippi school system. I know my grandparents and great grandparents would really be proud of her.

I went on to tell my young stepson that times have certainly changed since then but not to the point that his generation can put down their guard. While he went on to go to school in the late eighties with White kids and definitely got a much better education than I did, a lot of the gains that Martin Luther King, our grandparents and others died for are being lost each day. I told him it was up to him and other bright Black kids like him to roll up their sleeves, get in the system and fight to maintain the gains they have and work hard to get new ones. The future is truly in the hands of our youth. Let's all pray that they are up to the task. I for one believe that they are. I think my grandparents would have said the same thing about us in their day.

CHAPTER THIRTY TWO

OBAAY

Ahh, the foolishness of my youth. I clanged around for years like a dog chasing his tail, DAZED, CONFUSED and still wondering about my first encounter with racism in the first grade. The awful beast that feeds on its young, was it real or was it imagined? I found myself still pondering this mystery in junior high school. Would I act on my anger and bewilderment as a teenager and lash out at those who harmed me as a child, or, would I take the highroad and forgive and forget and go on about my life, seeing the world as a great place filled with new teenage experiences and wonderment? I am happy to say, that with the exception of my little stone throwing incident in elementary school and fearing for my sister, I chose the positive fork in the road.

Of course, my family and the way I was raised played a major role in my decision to be positive rather than negative. Choosing to put away the ghosts and deeply rooted racial pains of my childhood brought about a new dilemma for me known as girls. My mind, all of a sudden, was invaded with thoughts that I could not control. With the exception of being a complete captive of the curiosity of the opposite sex, my junior high days for the most part, were pretty uneventful.

America was a rosy dream land of hypocrisy in those days. The good old sixties. Older Americans could preach to the world about their sins, but could not see the inequity in our system towards our poor and oppressed staring us right in our face. America obviously chose to have tunnel vision, and down right refused to recognize our own sins, particularly where racism was concerned.

Blacks were severely under represented in all phases of America's system in the early sixties. Sure, we as Black Americans had a ray of hope and continued to pray for a better day, but still the problem of racism haunted us and hung around and weakened us like a bad cold. Yes, America was indeed blind in the sixties. It taunted us, the downtrodden, and seemed to mockingly say, " Hey Black America, we got ours (the American dream that is) now you go out and figure out how to get yours the best way you can. All about us was prosperity and happiness for White America, but yet we wallowed in despair and poverty.

The means and opportunities were certainly there for us to improve our lot. There was adequate civil rights legislature in place. Albeit that it was not enforced and/or sometimes purposely misinterpreted. Although I truly feel that most White Americans felt that the inequities facing Black people at that time were wrong, they, in many instances, chose to play the role of the silent majority at that time in America's history. This condition did not speed the pace for Black people to obtain equal rights in America.

So, there you have it!! They threw us a bone and we threw it back and screamed, "We demand more!" Black people were then given several other stages to showcase their worthiness such as sports and the military. But White America knew like we knew that that would not be enough for us. Seeing White Americans revel in the prosperity that was America, only wetted our appetite to get a bigger piece of the American dream. We could not be satisfied with a little taste either. We wanted it all, just like White people. Just being a highly paid, and well liked athlete and/or a highly decorated military man, was not good enough! We wanted to be doctors, lawyers, politicians, scientists and anything else that was high on the ladder of success.

Malcolm X in his brilliance, surfaced a rather interesting challenge to our people at that time. 'By Any Means Necessary,' was what he held up over our heads on a silver platter. Hum, what an intriguing thought! We could stretch and get out of our comfort zones, and see what this bold approach, held head high had to offer, or we could embrace a much slower process that had been humbly laid out at our praying feet by Martin Luther King. Both approaches had merit and both approaches offered danger. The majority of Black Americans, chose the latter.

Since it had become glaringly obvious that the American dream would not be completely made available to us, we (Black America) took to the streets to show that we were not afraid to raise the stakes. NO JUSTICE NO PEACE!!! NO JUSTICE NO PEACE, was the battle cry that militant Black Americans fervently echoed. "We shall overcome!" We shall overcome softly, but adamantly, flowed from the lips of the non-violent majority. We boldly took to the streets, made demands, locked arms, sang songs, went to jail by the truckloads, and yes even died for the God given right that had been so wrongfully denied us.

History, I believe, will record that the Black militant's case was not overwhelmingly supported by Black Americans, and that nonviolence won the day. I say that, that is not correct. I submit that the opposite is true.

I truly believe that it was the fear that Black America would indeed abandon the nonviolent teaching of brother Martin, that caused the White leadership in America to reluctantly find a way to slowly bend and eventually give in to Martin Luther King's method and requests. As a result, Black people slowly gained a semblance of freedom, but over a much longer period of time. This allowed America time to get ready for the great change that was coming, or, if you will allow me the analogy, the train that was barreling down the track heading towards a devastating collision with it.

If this outright collision that Malcolm warned of would have occurred, America would not be the place that it is today.

There would have been a great deal of open, bloody conflict that would have went far beyond the riots that we saw in some American cities. These super state by state riots, if they would have occurred between the races, would have severely hurt and scarred our country forever. And, perhaps this violent, to the death, unrest between races may have weakened us to the point that it allowed Russia or China to take advantage of this golden opportunity and destroy America. How ironic, destroy our magnificent country, while we were busy trying to destroy each other. How incredibly sad. Thank God that Martin Luther King's method was adopted.

After most of the civil rights major battles had been fought and won, my heretofore sleepy since of self-consciousness was awakened and I truly heard the call. Sure I walked the walk and talked the talk in my earlier attempts to find my consciousness. But I was only a robot spouting what I had heard or what someone else had told me. The true meaning of what the struggle was about had not quite dug itself deep enough into my soul.

I awoke out of my deep sleep in high school. I suddenly found myself in a friendly, warming sea of ideologies that were indeed worthy of my time and attention. Stop the war in Vietnam and let's bring the boys back home. Save the whales, well why not! Long live Rock and Roll, sounds like a winner to me. Race to the moon, strap me to a flaming rocket my friend and just point me in the right direction. I would support any cause regardless of how stupid. Then, it hit me like a ton of bricks. All of a sudden my eyes were completely opened.

If I was going to stand up for a cause, then let it be one that was close to home for me. Complete the job that older Black Americans had started and now integrate the universities and march for racial equality. You betcha, what are we waiting on! I truly did not know what this thing called freedom was about. I just knew like everyone else my age, that we too, must have it. There I was a naive, God fearing student at Lanier High School making a conscious decision to join (OBAAY), the Organization for Black Afro American Youth. OBAAY offered a vehicle to feed my growing sense of awareness of the inequities of the struggles that Black people still daily faced in America during this period.

I was not alone in this thirst for fair play and justice, there were many others who were drawn to this organization as well. We were as moths to a brilliant flame. Many of the elite at Lanier High School were members of this student organization as well. OBAAY's purpose was to raise the consciousness of Black students to the injustices that were being unfairly dispensed on Black people in America. Members of OBAAY were the top echelon of a class that was certified as the top Black students academically in the South, mixed in happily with the rowdiest of our class. We were united by a common cause and went about our tasks of demanding justice with energy and fervor. Ah, the passion, unbridled courage and raw energy of our youth.

We took on every cause and rallied our fellow students to march with us. One year we orchestrated the walk out of not only our school but several of our sister schools as well. I wish I could poke out my chest and say that I was a chief, but the reality of it all was, that I was a mere Indian. A happy Indian, because I was involved in a great cause.

We often met at a one of the member's grandmother's little small one room buildings that set apart from their main house, not far from a popular night-club called the Casino. It was in an area of Jackson called Georgetown. Sure we could have met each and every time in the confines of our school, but no, no, no, we thought that what we had to say was so powerful, so earth shattering and revolutionary, that it had to be shrouded in secrecy. And together, like diplomats charting the fate of the entire world, we went about the business of figuring out how to get ours from the racist Mississippi system that was so hell bent on our failure.

You know, although we obviously did not save the world, we were successful in saving ourselves. OBAAY gave us hope.

It also gave us something even more powerful, it gave us a vehicle for expression, awareness, a sense of purpose and yes it even gave us our dignity. There is no greater food for a youthful spirit!

CHAPTER THIRTY THREE

THE BOYS IN THE BAND

After our OBAAY meetings, I often held rehearsals for my R&B band in a little building behind a club called the Casino. My group was called "The Say Lovers" at Lanier High School. Before then, we were "The Bossa Novas." Don't laugh! That was a cool name in those days. Although it definitely rings a little bit corny now, believe me, it was hot back in the day! We took the music skills that Bernard and Kermit Holly, the band directors at Rowan and Lanier, respectively taught us and used them to put together our little band.

There was my lifelong time running buddy, Milton Thomas on trumpet, Leo Mason on the Baritone Sax, my cousin Jimmy Horton on trumpet, Roosevelt Mc Neil on the Baritone horn, Joe Nathan Bracey on Bass Tuba, William Smothers on trombone and me on my Alto Saxophone. We were a well oiled, woman thrilling machine. I can see ole Leo now, laying back in a cool pose grinding his hips while playing the funky bass lines on his big baritone sax. Old Roosevelt McNeil and Big Bad, Super Cool, Joe Bracey would be moving and grooving as well. Those three guys put on an incredible show. The girls would be going crazy at our talent shows over their funky bass lines.

The Funky Bottom Thumping boys, as I liked to call them, weren't the only ones jamming though. My lifelong friend Milton Thomas would have the girls practically fainting in the aisles in Junior High and High school at the cool sound of his hitting incredible high notes and holding them effortlessly for what seemed like forever. Man, my old buddy Milton could make smoke come out of that trumpet of his.

Of course, everyone put on their individual little show when we were on stage. It was as if we all knew our turn would come. So we just relaxed and supported whoever the star of the moment was that the crowd was digging. We were definitely not greedy. We were running buddies who had grown up together in the mean streets of Jackson. Our friendships were true to the bone.

If you let Milton tell it, the first day he and I met in the third grade in elementary school, he jumped on me, bloodied my nose and chased me home. According to him I was wearing a silly looking yellow rain coat. And, since he didn't have one and I was acting all uppity and flashing my cool coat around, he decided he would bring me down a notch or two and bloody my nose. Well, for the record, I don't remember it quite that way. But, I can tell you old Milton was a fighting machine. His father was a Sargent fresh out of the Marines when he moved into our neighborhood. I tell ya, I believe he had taught Milton every karate and Jiu Jitsu move there was.

Milton could take even the biggest, meanest kids down, although he was not a very big kid himself, with just one quick leg sweeping motion or series of quick moves. Milton tried to teach me and the other guys all he knew so that we could protect ourselves, but none of us could ever do it like he could. He was the first Black Bruce Lee in our neighborhood. Oddly enough, this was long before Bruce Lee ever came on the scene. Milton was a butt kicking machine. No one messed with him. So, it was a good thing to have him as my friend. Well, back to my story.

When my saxophone solos kicked in, I would be bobbing my head to the beat and dancing all over the place with my sax. My few moments in the limelight would always seem to bring the house down when I got down on one knee and squeezed every ounce of sex appeal out of my old sax. We seemed to always be asked to give our instrumental rendition of James Brown, the Godfather of Soul's, hit "It's A Man's World! We would rock the house with that one as well as Twine Time, Cold Sweat, Amen and all the other hits of the day. And yes, the Godfather was right. The world wouldn't be nothing without a woman or a girl.

Shoot, I don't think in Junior High school we ever got paid for a gig. Don't laugh, but I don't even think we knew then that musicians were supposed to get paid. We played for the glory and adulation of the ladies. Sad, but true. That was our reward! Yes those were the days. Crazy as they may have been!

All you had to do was get out of the way and turn the stage over to the Bossa Novas, and we rocked the house as long as the law would allow. In Junior high school I remember us being the star attraction off most of the talent shows.

There was this girl who would be in the audience at Rowan Junior High School nicknamed Three Bulls, who would stand at the front of the auditorium cheering for us and swaying to our beat. She was every bit of six foot something and was high yellow with reddish hair. She had muscles on top of muscles. She was the biggest bully in school. When she turned around toward the audience and told them to scream to the top of their lungs for us, you'd better believe that everyone in the place screamed their lungs out. Even though occasionally, we may have truly not been the best competing act on these talent show cases, we knew we could always count on Three Bulls coming through for us.

Now why Three Bulls liked us, I never knew. But I tell ya this, it was a lot better to have her on our side than against us. I had seen her bloody the nose of many a big kid in school and outside of school because they made a bad comment about us. After school sometimes, she would be walking behind us singing our names in melodic tones to the top of her voice. It was like we were rock stars or something. They say flattery comes in a lot of different forms. What Three Bulls did was fun, but it also was the height of embarrassment for us all.

Some days she would make us pull out our horns and we would have to serenade her as she walked along and loudly sounded out our names. Nevertheless, we gladly accepted Three Bulls' adulation and considered her good company as we walked the dangerous three miles home from Rowan Junior High School each day. Most of us stayed in a very tough area of downtown. But, we knew we would be safe as a baby in a mother's arms as long as Three Bulls was in our company.

My cousin Jimmy Horton stayed right across the street from Rowan Junior High. It was nothing for us to steal away from school for a few minutes some days to party at his house, when his mom left for work. Pretty young girls would be drawn to where we were like metal to a magnet. Needless to say, it was good to be one of the boys in the band in those days.

After graduating from Rowan, we kept our band going at Lanier High School. We were fortunate to make acquaintance with Tyrone Bolls at Lanier and have him crooning a smooth tune with his incredible voice. Man did Tyrone add a lot to our group. After him came Eddie Rasberry on the lead guitar, and Billy Brayfied on the bass guitar. We had often competed against them in many of the talent shows we were on.

Eddie was the spitting image of the famous Black Father of Rock And Roll, Chuck Berry. He talked liked him, looked like him and could make his guitar scream and moan while he danced and bobbed his head to the beat just like the great Chuck Berry himself. Eddie Rasberry was a superstar in his own right as far as creating music with that wild guitar of his was concerned. There was no greater lead guitar player in Jackson at that time. Eddie was beyond compare. His side kick Billy Brayfied had his own unique style as well. He would be thumping that bass for all it was worth. I don't think either Eddie or Billy ever had any formal music training. But hey, they didn't need it. They were ahead of their time. Billy didn't say much while he was on stage. Eddie was definitely the agreed on showman of the two. But when Billy began to whip on his bass, it was as if all hell had broken loose. The entire building would bounce to the beat, just from the vibrations of that funky bass guitar of his.

Man, I can just hear our combined groups now wailing on the funky hit songs during our many practice sessions, having everyone in the alley way behind the Casino lounge, and even those who happened to be a couple of blocks over, singing along with us, bobbing their heads, snapping their fingers and dancing to the beat. The practice sessions were extremely long and hard. The little shack we practiced in did not have air conditioning or a heater in the winter time. So we would all strip down to the bare necessities when it was hot and sweat it out for hours, until we got the music right. We poured our hearts and souls into each note.

Our practice location was on the other end of Jackson from where most of us stayed. It was two miles past Lanier in the Georgetown area and most of us stayed downtown. So along with the hard work and Herculean efforts that occurred in our practice sessions, came a long walk to and fro to get there lugging our heavy instruments. Being committed to the band was definitely a tough row to hoe. But when we hit the stage, the hard work and sweat was always worth it though. The thrill of the crowd and the big smiles on ours' and the crowd's faces, made up for it.

CHAPTER THIRTY FOUR

THE MAD DASH

I truly didn't know about the other members, but being a member of OBAAY certainly drew a lot of attention to me. One evening after school in my senior year, while walking home from band practice down old Whitfield Mill Road, the oddest thing happened. I noticed two neatly dressed White men sitting in a car right at the edge of my high school campus. They appeared at first to be watching either something at the school behind me, or me.

Whether they intended to or not, they stuck out like a big fat sore thumb. As I got closer to their car, they seemed to focus in on me even more and got more agitated. They were straining their necks, and their eyes got wider with every step I took towards them. I was now only fifty or sixty yards from their car. I slowed my pace and began to try and put two and two together to get an idea of what was going on!

It was rare that I would go this way home. Normally, I would be heading home down Maple Street towards the railroad tracks which was an off angle from the direction of my home. I routinely took this route because of the many friends that also traveled that way with me each day. But this day was different. Instead of heading directly home after band practice, I decided I would stick around afterwards and hang out with my girlfriend Ernestine. She was a majorette in the high school band. She stayed in the opposite direction from my home in a pretty well to do neighborhood in a Black community called Georgetown.

I was what people called, "An across the track kid." I grew up in downtown Jackson. Integration was in its infancy stage in the South. At that point in time, there was no such thing as integration in Jackson for older kids. Busing had begun for kids in elementary schools. However, older kids, Black and White alike, in Jackson still had to attend separate schools. Black kids had to walk to the nearest Black school, regardless of whether a White school was right across the street from them or if their long walk to school each day, rain or shine, took them past an army of White schools. That was my situation. Lanier High school was at least seven miles from my home.

As I continued my approach toward the mysterious car, my mind began to whisper, "All right Vernon, something is not quite right hear. Why would these two White men be camped out in a Back neighborhood?" As fate would have it, no one was around at that very moment but me.

I thought about what had happened to Medger Evers, who was a famous civil rights leader in Mississippi, who was gunned down in his own driveway that was smack dab in the middle of the Black community. That took a lot of balls. It also meant that no Black person was safe from evil, unscrupulous people if they wanted to cause you harm.

Another terrible thought that popped into my head was, " What if they are Klan members trying to snatch a Black person so that he or she could be the guest of honor at one of their little Klan necktie parties, or 'Picnics' as we Blacks in the deep South called them. The year was 1967. Believe me it was not uncommon for Black people to come up missing and even be found lynched by the Klan in that day in time. It would be just my luck to have stepped head long into this craziness.

The word picnic, as I was told by my grandfather, originated from the phrase, 'Pick A Nigger'. It was common knowledge throughout the South, that whenever the Klan wanted to make their presence known or wanted to intimidate the Black community, that they would sponsor one of these insane "picnics." They were just like a regular picnic, as we know it today. But there was one major difference. That difference was that a Black person at the end of the festivities would be lynched in front of the crowd.

They would spread the word and location of one of these little gatherings, and from there, grab some poor unsuspecting Black person off the street to be the so-called guest of honor. They generally, if you can believe it, occurred brazenly during the daytime!

As my grandfather told me, the next thing the poor unsuspecting Black person would know is that he would be waking up severely beaten, tied and bound with a dark hood over his head. All that he would be able to hear was the sound of a large crowd of people laughing and having a grand time. If you can believe it, little kids and women were a big part of these ungodly gatherings. Many of the people in the audience would be dressed in Klan robes, jeering and throwing partially eaten food at the guest of honor. I guess I don't have to tell what would happen next after his hood was finally snatched off his head.

The poor doomed soul would be face to face with a blood thirsty mob screaming for his life. He or she would be perched a few feet above the ground, usually on the back end of an old pick up. I can just imagine the stark horror and fear that the person would be filled with witnessing this unthinkable sight. Seconds later, it would all be over. He would be pushed from his perch and from there left to dangle like a leaf in the wind and eventually strangle to death or die with a broken neck.

As this horrible imaged danced in my head, while I slowly approached the car, I told myself, "I can either be brave, put this nonsense out of my head, ignore these two men and continue on past them, or I could show them why most track and field events were dominated by Black people. Of course you know I chose the latter.

Man, I took off running like a madman possessed. There was no shame in my game. I quickly veered from their car down Scott Street in a mere two or three steps. I made it across the street from where they were parked, ducked between a couple of houses and from there dropped it into overdrive and tore up all kinds of dirt and gravel on Ash street putting distance between me and them. I then purposely stayed on the back streets, and to the extent possible, stayed within a step or two of a back yard. I figured that way I could spot them quickly and from there disappear out of sight through someone's property. The crazy thing about all of this madness was that my paranoia was right. These guys, for whatever reason, were after me. It was very obvious from how they reacted when I took off running.

In my first couple of steps, as I began to run, I noticed that their heads snapped to attention and seemed to almost fall off their necks trying to turn in the direction I was running to keep up with my blinding speed. I obviously had surprised them. There wasn't a doubt in my mind that at the least, these two guys would have a severe case of whip lash from jerking their heads so fast around to try and keep up with my blinding streak. Another thing I noticed that bothered me in my first few steps to get me beyond the view of their car, was that they had indeed cranked up their car and were making an attempt to either cut me off or follow after me.

Man, I don't know what they were thinking about, because they didn't have a snowball's chance in hell of catching me. Just like the ole Road Runner, it was Beep Beep and I was gone!!! In those days, although I was as skinny as a rail, I was in excellent shape. Even though I was pretty sure I had put three of four blocks between me and them, I didn't let up. I kept trucking!

CHAPTER THIRTY FIVE

A SHORT DETOUR DOWN MEMORY LANE

As I continued my mad sprint to 131 W. Oakley Street, keeping a vigilant eye out for the two men and their car as I ran, a weird irony came across my mind. At the very spot where the two men had been parked was where I had gotten knocked out cold by a bunch of kids who had hit me in the head with a Barq Root Beer bottle, roughly a year earlier.

As I ran full out home making my getaway from the two White men, my mind traveled back a year earlier to the circumstances that led up to that crazy event.

It was shortly after I had started to date Ernestine Alford. She was a majorette in the band and had the prettiest brown eyes and hair I had ever seen. She also had an incredible body!! I was a junior in high school when I met her. Ernestine was a very popular senior at our high school. We were both on the rebound when we began dating.

I had just broken up with Hazel Barrymore, an incredibly beautiful, light brown skinned girl herself. She was as sweet and as innocent as they come. The only problem with our relationship though, was that her mom was unbelievably strict on her.

This was probably a good thing now that I think about it. Poor Hazel couldn't go anywhere or do anything.

Our relationship was limited to a few minutes on the telephone occasionally, walking her home from her choir practice or my getting up early in the morning heading to a predetermined spot, hiding out till the coast was clear and from there walking her to school each day. And maybe, if we could manage it, sneak an occasional kiss or two. While that was probably all I deserved as a jerk water geek eleventh grade band guy, suffice it to say, I wanted a little bit more.

It's tough being a young man with your hormones raging out of control, having to sit and listen to your running buddies talk about what they had done or not done on their dates, and not having anything to add. It took me twenty years after I had graduated from Lanier to realize that most of the stories these guys told about their conquests were enhanced, (you know boys will be boys). I bought it all at that time though, hook, line and sinker.

I would be sitting there listening to all the cool guys, like Lynn McQuarter, who was like the Fonzie of our class. He was the coolest guy I had ever met. There was also Milton Thomas, John Mason, Willie Batman Johnson, Tyrone Bolls, Melvin Lott, Harold Kennedy, Super Cool Nate Mayberry, Everest Smith, James Studaway, Perry Wilder and the rest of the straight up players. They described their conquests while my mouth watered profusely. Boy, was Vernon Steve Weakley ready for some real action!

Ernestine had recently broken up with one of the most popular senior guys at Lanier High School. His name was Larry Hayes. I kid you not, that guy was a basketball superstar. It wasn't anything for Larry to save the day at our high school basketball games by pumping in thirty to forty points a game. And to top it all off, Larry was guaranteed to hit the game winning shot at the buzzer on any given night. Lanier High School basketball players in years past were legendary. Players like Titty Boon had set the bar for excellence very high. But even still, incredible athletes like Larry Hayes on the men's team and Nellie Hartfield on the women's team kept the heroics alive at Lanier. It was no wonder that other teams feared stepping into the DOG PIT, (our gymnasium) as we loved to call it in that day and time.

Opposing teams would be more upset over the fact that old nonchalant Larry, who had a real easy going nature, would tease them into thinking they were going to win, up until the fourth quarter, and from there whip the basketball game going crowd (the opposing team's fans and ours) into an absolute frenzy with his sweat wringing show boating. Now, after hearing all of this, you've got to be asking yourself, "what was it that made Ernestine fall madly in love with and pick little ole me over this super cool guy. I don't know? All I knew was, I was in heaven! My ego was through the roof.

Even the cool guys in the school would be saying, "How did you pull that off?" Since Ernestine was a popular senior, we were frequently invited to the A class parties. In most instances, I would be passing my eleventh grade running buddies at the door, who were trying to beg or sneak their way into these senior parties. I would hold my head back, stick out my chest and high step it past them, of course I'd give them a wink, as I walked into the place, with Ernestine smiling on my arm. What a rush!!

Although Ernestine was incredibly good-looking and sexy, she was also as sweet and as nice as they come. I think out of all the great qualities Stine had, (that was my pet nickname for her) that was the thing I liked about her most. She had a great personality. Everyone at Lanier liked her. She sang in the school choir and her church's choir and would break into tears at the sound of a sentimental, romantic love song. Or would cry her eyes out watching a sad movie. She also loved kids with a passion. I never knew what a real daydream was about until I met Ernestine. For that day in time, she completed me. Everyone at Lanier seemed to be excited for us when we started dating. While Stine and I was were definitely a perfect match, in those days, there were a few people who didn't care for our little love thing.

The word had quickly spread to me, not necessarily from Larry, (who by the way was a pretty good guy), that some of his friends, fans, running buddies or whatever, didn't like the fact that I stood in the way of his happiness. Which meant, him and Ernestine getting back together again. I guess they thought that a happy basketball star meant a good winning record for our school. They intended to do whatever it took to keep the golden goose happy!

The word was constantly coming to me by way of my boys, Milton Thomas, Roosevelt McNeil, Lee Bernard, Willie Pinkston, Nathaniel Mayberry, Robert McClure, Lynn McQuarter, Leo Mason, Harold Kennedy, William Smothers, and my cousin Jimmy Horton, that I would pay dearly if I continued to date Ernestine. I just kind of ignored their obvious concern for me and dismissed it as needless worry.

Milton had just recently moved out of my neighborhood to the Brinkley High School area of town. He and I had known each other since the third grade. He stayed a street over from my house, but oddly, in a bee line directly in front of my house. We often zipped between the houses separating our streets as kids and played together. As kids we had gotten pretty tight! Milton was a super cool guy who also played trumpet in Lanier's High School band with me, as well as in our little "Get Down Band, The Say Lovers" We went way back. I had eaten at his kitchen table a many a day. He and I learned a lot of valuable life lessons listening to his sweet, beautiful mother and his cool father, who we lovingly called "Sarg".

My old friend Milton personally validated the rumor for me. He abruptly stopped me coming out of band rehearsal one day, pulled me off to the side, and said, "Vernon, man, this thing with you and Ernestine has gotten into the danger zone." Milton went on to say that I was a regular focus of the conversation at the Casino with some of the local thugs, which was a local nightclub and hang out in Georgetown not too far from Ernestine's home.

Milton continued by saying, "You know I will do my part to help ya my brother, but I can't be there with ya all the time now that I stay out this way. They say they're going to carve "Don't mess with Larry Hayes Girl" into your butt, if you don't leave Ernestine alone!" I quickly responded, "Those guys are not serious. Sounds like a bunch of fools trying to get a laugh or two to me. I'm not giving Ernestine up over some foolishness." He said, "Okay, I hear ya. And I knew you would say that!! Just promise me you will take me seriously and watch your back. Watch your back my brother, because the word is the Casino Boys are coming after you."

He and some of my other tight buddies (McClure, Lynn and Nate), who also stayed on that part of town, said that they had also tried to cool down the tension for me, but were unsuccessful. Although my mom and the rest of my family loved Ernestine dearly, my mother was not too happy about my many trips into her dangerous neighborhood given the tension to see her. Of course my mom, Stine's mom and our families did the best they could to keep us two love birds together.

They all constantly volunteered to give us both rides to and from each other's house and pleaded with us both to be careful. Even still, it was inevitable sometimes that I found myself happily trotting back and forth from Stine's house late at night. That trek back and forth was indeed a long walk. But hey, Ernestine was well worth it. SHE WAS THE SWEETEST THING THIS SIDE OF HEAVEN, AS FAR AS I WAS CONCERNED.

CHAPTER THIRTY SIX

GROOVIN, ON A SUNDAY AFTERNOON

One Friday night after band rehearsal, I decided to walk Stine home and hang out with her for awhile. Her mother, who everyone called Ms. Lou Emma, was a very nice lady. I could see where Ernestine got her great personality from. Ms. Lou Emma had a contagious laugh that would make you burst into laughter yourself. You didn't have to know what the joke was or what she was laughing at, but when you heard her laugh, a giant grin automatically came across your face. Regardless of how hard you tried to contain yourself, there was no way you would be able to hold back.

I don't know why Ms. Lou Emma liked me, but for some strange reason, she and I seemed to just hit it off. When I wasn't cuddled up with Stine, I would be sitting next to Ms. Lou Emma on their front porch or in their television room listening to one of her great stories about life. She had incredible insight on human nature.

I recall her once, while we swung slowly back and forth in her front porch swing, saying to me in her soft voice, "Vernon, Black kids have been given a big opportunity by being able to go to school and college. Kids didn't get chances to have schooling when I was growing up!! We had to drop out of school, if we were lucky enough to have ever started, to help our families survive. Basic survival was the best that a Black person could even hope for in my day and time. Yawl, (young people) are our future. Don't dare let us down, because our race is counting on you to lift us up."

Ms. Lou Emma continued, "I want you and Stine to work hard and both make something out of yourselves, you hear! You are both very intelligent, hard working good kids. Being in love is great. But don't let that get in the way of yawl continuing your education. You have got to keep getting your education and learn all you can. Education is the key to success for the Black race!! Soak in all you can son!"

Of course, I respectfully listened intensely and quietly responded, "Yes ma'am" now and then during her conversations to let her know I was indeed listening. She was right and I knew she was right!! Over the years, my life experiences validated Ms. Lou Emma's kind words of wisdom. She is now, at the writing of this book deceased, but when she graced this earth, she was something special!

She trusted me pretty much with Stine and didn't seem to mind if we sneaked a long tender kiss or two, if she wasn't looking. Stine and I would cuddle on her front porch in the dark on their old creaky swing or sit in their front room where their old piano was. Stine was an excellent piano player by the way.

In our romantic moments, and believe me there was a lot of them, she and I would melt away into each other's arms in the big lounge chair in their front living room.

We often ate ice cream and listened to music. For the record, our favorite song was "Groovin." I can just hear it now! "Groovin! On a Sunday afternoon." Life could not be better for two young people in love. The toughest thing Stine and I had to handle in the confines of their home was having to dodge and look out for her little sister Laura. She would be constantly barging into the room where we were, at an unbelievable rate of speed, just hoping that she could catch us fooling around so that she could tell Stine's mom.

She caught us in the middle of long, juicy passionate

kisses all the time. Stine and I were always having to pay bribe money to old Laura to keep her from ratting on us. Occasionally though, our best efforts were just not good enough, and she told on us anyway.

The next thing I know, I would be hearing "Alright Vernon it's time to go! You two lovebirds have got five minutes to say your good-bys and that's it. Stine and I would close the door to the front living room, if we could get away with it, and start kissing each other a mile a minute. We would be trying to squeeze all the loving we could into that five minutes.

On one particular night, Mrs. Alford asked if she could call my mom to come pick me up or pay for a cab to take me home. I think that night she was concerned for my safety, based on some of the rumors that obviously had made their way to her. Oddly enough that night, I said no, gave Stine a big kiss good bye and headed out walking for home. Stine's house had to be a good ten, twelve miles from my home. Ah, but you know how it is when you are young and dating a very special person. I planned to float home on the wings of love. At the end of Stine's street, which was Flora street, I ran into her cousin, Jimmy Roy Catchings.

He always jokingly called me, "Bump Buster" because he claimed that I would someday have to deal with the big bumps, knots and bruises I was going to get when the guys in the neighborhood finally caught up with me for dating his cousin. As usual, Jimmy Roy started up with his teasing as I walked past him. I didn't even break stride. I just gave him one of my famous "Yeah, Yeah, I know comments " and kept on trucking down the street. At the end of Flora Street, I noticed a car filled with thugs parked on the side of the curb. I kept walking toward them and had really planned to ignore them. As I walked past them, the driver said, "YEP! EVERY DOG HAS HIS DAY!! We told ya we were going to get ya, didn't we? Ernestine belongs to our neighborhood. "

I kept walking, but boldly said back to the guy, " Come on man, ya'll have got to have better things to do! Ernestine ain't thinking about you shit heads. " What did I say that for!!! All four doors of the old broken down car they were riding in, quickly opened at once. That was all I needed to see. You talking about breaking the sound barrier running. Shoooot! It was definitely on! I was running for my life!

The next thing I know there are five guys chasing me down Dale street, which was a small side street off of Flora, heading toward the main intersection called Woodrow Wilson. I figured I only had about fifty steps separating me from meeting my maker!! If I didn't come up with something fast, in just a few seconds, I would be playing a harp in front of St. Peter's gate.

There was no way I was going to be able to outrun these guys. I knew it and they knew it too! My feet were hitting the pavement as hard and as fast as I could make them. But theirs were sounding off louder and at a much faster pace. In just a few seconds someone's hands would be gripping my throat or shoulders to haul me to the ground. There was an old auto garage called McElroy's a few paces ahead of me, at the corner of Woodrow Wilson and Dale, across from an old Glorioso Grocery store. I faked like I was going in the other direction and quickly darted into a row of bushes, back across the narrow little street to a house, jumped under it, came out the other side, and then quickly snaked my way back to the old closed auto garage.

With one push from a supporting hand on the top of the fence, I jumped the six feet fence surrounding the garage compound there as if it was nothing at all. I guess it was time for someone up above to get a good laugh at my expense, because I missed clearing the fence entirely by less that a quarter inch. To my dismay, my old tattered jeans caught at the cuff on the top of the fence as I was coming down the other side. Here I was hanging upside down by one leg on the fence on the inside of it praying that they (the thugs who were chasing me) didn't see me.

Don't tell me that the Big Guy upstairs doesn't have a sense of humor because this little hilarious situation, certainly in my mind, proved it beyond a shadow of a doubt. I know he does because what I am going to tell you next completely boggles the mind. Through the fence openings (between the spaces in the fence) through my legs I could see the thugs franticly looking under the house across the street from me. Apparently I had thrown them off by going under the house on that side of the street and quickly coming out the other side. Here I was, wiping sweat from my forehead, breathing hard like a madman, but as quietly as possible, and thanking God for getting these guys off my tail nevertheless.

The next big challenge, as I saw it, was how to quietly get myself out of my predicament, which was hanging upside down, caught by my pants leg on the inside of the fence, without being heard. I decided I would just freeze and hang quietly until the knuckle heads left. So here I was, still hanging upside down on the inside of the fence mind you, but believe me, that was a much better place to be than where those guys were.

The one thing I learned growing up in the ghetto is that you do not want to make a bully or group of bullies work too hard to catch ya to give you a beat down. The harder they work to catch ya, the worse the butt whipping etc. you are going to get, because you made them work for it!! So the stakes had gone up tremendously! There was no way I was going to get off with a few bruises now. I began to try to figure out how to quietly get myself down from the fence so I could make a clean getaway.

CHAPTER THIRTY SEVEN

OH, DON'T WORRY ABOUT THE DOG, HE'S MY DRINKING BUDDY

The next thing I know, I'm looking into the face of a big red bone guard dog who is only a few feet away. He's laying on the ground, head twisted in an odd sort of angle looking up at me as if he was mystified at the weird scene he was seeing. So there I was, praying that the dog didn't bark, or attack me. I began to smile away at him. Don't ask me why, but I did it!!! I figured it would also be good to throw in a very quiet, " Ti Ti, good doggy, Ti, Ti good doggy, Ti, Ti nice doggy, out under my breath, hoping he would see me as a friend or maybe think he was dreaming this crazy scene.

At the same time, I was also hoping and praying that the Casino Boys didn't look across the street and see the big juicy Thanksgiving turkey that was hanging on the fence just waiting for them to come and carve their names into.

I closed my eyes and started to quietly pray for the Lord to get me out of this mess or let my end come not too painfully, because I knew my life was definitely over if those guys caught me.

Man, I was blessed that day!! The next thing I knew, I felt this gentle nudge on my leg. It was Willie the wino. He had been laying on the ground a few feet from me all the time. I guess in all the excitement, I didn't see him. He quietly moved closer to me and whispered, "Don't worry about that old dog, he's my drinking buddy. He ain't gonna do nothing He ain't barked since the owner kicked him in the throat a few years back for stealing his fried chicken." The funny thing is, ole Buster didn't steal the chicken, I did. He kind of chuckled quietly and leaned back on the fence and then stuck out a greasy, dirty hand to pet the guard dog on his head.

While he was talking and was now petting the dog, who had rolled over on his stomach, I'm looking at this guy as if to say, "Man are you crazy. Pleeeaaase get me the fuck down from here." Instead of helping me though, Ole Willie continued by pointing back through my legs. He whispered with a big grin on his face, "Ole Buster and I are pretty much harmless. Now I can't say the same for those assholes across the street."

At that moment, I looked through my legs and sure enough the thugs were slowly inching towards where I was hanging. Lucky for me, they still had not looked across the street in my direction and seen me though. They were still frantically searching the bushes and under the house across the street looking for me. I quietly said, "Okay, okay, Willie, what do you want? I could really use your help man!" He says, "how much money you got in your pocket young blood. I said, " shit Willie as many times as I have passed through here and given you money to get wine, you ought to give me this one for free." He quickly said in a low firm voice, " Un unh, life don't work like that young blood!"

I sheepishly said, "okay, okay, I got a few bucks in my pocket. Help me back over the fence." He said, "back over the fence. Hell that's going to cost you double, that's twice the work!!" Ole Willie grinned and said, "besides, if I was you, I would come on in and go out the other side of the yard to throw those boys off your trail." He definitely had a good point.

Willie punctuated his remark, by saying. "Those boys aren't too smart!! They ain't got no 'Edu-ma-cation' like me and you." Ole Willie continued by saying, "you have always done me right. Those boys over there are always disrespecting me. They are no good!"

After a few tense moments of quietly struggling, Willie was able to get me loose from the fence and help me get into the compound. While looking back over my shoulder to watch the movements of the guys, I emptied my pockets, which was only a few bucks or so, and gave it to Willie. I crouched down inside the fence and asked Willie to do the same to keep from being seen by the jar heads who were still wandering up and down Dale street looking for me, inching ever closer to the spot where we were. Willie stared at the little money I had given him like it was a pot of gold. I guess those few dollars would feed him for a few days and maybe even get him a swig of wine or two. In any case, I moved deeper inside the compound and hid out there for another few seconds until the Neanderthal brothers finally gave up looking for me.

Man, what a relief. After quickly surveying the area to make certain the coast was clear, I high tailed it to Whitfield Mill and Woodrow Wilson intersection in front of Stine's church (New Hope) which was also a popular hitchhiking point for kids. After a few minutes, I was able to get a ride with an elderly gentleman. As we are taking off, I thought to myself, "I know there is a God. There is no other way to explain why I am still alive at this moment." The next thing I know, after only going a few blocks, the little elderly gentlemen who had so graciously given me a ride, announced, " Well son, this is it! This is as far as I am going toward downtown." The old gentlemen then made a big wide turn onto Maple street and put me off at Lanier High School.

I'm thinking as I exit the car, "Boy, I really was hoping he would have gotten me closer to downtown Jackson." Oh Well, I guess it could have been a lot worse."

CHAPTER THIRTY EIGHT

WE TOLD YA WE WERE GOING TO GIT YA!!!!

So here I am trucking it past Lanier down Whitfield Mills, right beyond the little bend in the road, across from Cherry Grove Baptist Church, when all of a sudden, I hear a car's tires screeching. Then I hear what I had been running from all night. "We told ya, we were going to git ya mother fucker." It was the same bullies who had been chasing me earlier. I'm thinking, "Man these guys just don't quit and Lord please get me out of this one!" I crouched to run and before I could make a step, something hard clunked me upside my head.

The next thing I know I'm waking up. I'm lying to the right of the sidewalk with a big knot on the left side of my head. My head is hurting big time and I'm groggy and still reeling from the blow. I slowly look around, while still laying on the ground to see if there is anyone there, and lo and behold, there is no one there except me. I guess those idiots thought they had killed me and decided to high tail it out of there before some witness saw them. The spot where I gotten hit was right at the beginning point of a large apartment complex. As I pulled myself to my feet, I began to think, " Man, what a night! What a night" And, the hilariously funny part was, it wasn't even over with yet. I still had roughly seven miles to go to get home. By this time it was about twelve o'clock. I quickly began to run towards home in a fast trot.

Finally, I could see the nightclub lights at the end of my street. The little juke joint was called Oakley Street Café. It was jumping as usual as I made it past it. I hid my face slightly to keep any of my neighbors from recognizing me. In those days, everyone knew your business. At least half the people in that place knew that my family did not allow me to be out that late. Good for me, no one was outside. I was able to get by the front of the place without notice, I guess. Thank God, a few more hundred feet and I would be home.

Then all of a sudden, it hit me like a ton of bricks. My mom was going to kill me. It had to be at least after 12:30 AM. As I walked up to the front porch of my house, I caught a break; my oldest brother Donald was walking out our front door. The house was quiet as if he had been visiting, but now everyone had gone to bed. It was not unusual for Don to come over and watch television until the wee hours on Friday night. He said, "Vernon what are you doing out this late? Mom's going to kill your butt."

Keep in mind that I'm only barely sixteen years old. I quickly put my finger up to my mouth and motioned to Don to keep quiet. I pleadingly asked in a very low voice, "where is mom?"

He said, "ah, she couldn't hang. She went to bed a little while ago, around eleven." He followed up by saying,

" Damn you look bad little brother.

"What happened to your head? " I guess the knot on my head was saluting big time!! I said, "ah it's nothing." I slapped his hand five and said, " if mom asks, I got in around eleven fifteen."

Don laughed, shook his head and said, "You better hope she doesn't ask." I kind of followed him for a few steps out to his car asking, " What does that mean? Come on big brother. I could sure use your help!" He laughed, jiggled his car keys in his hand and kept walking to his car.

Don and I were real tight. I knew he would look out for me!

All I had to do now was make it just a few feet more to my room without getting caught. Could I do it? I really had to wonder, after all the mishaps I had experienced that night. Now wouldn't that be the irony of all ironies. Make it through all the hell I had managed to get myself out of that night and then get beaned by my mom a mere few feet from my bed!

By now it had to be approaching 1:00am. Good for me, my brother Don was walking out the door. My mom did not play that stuff. My curfew was 11:30pm on Friday nights. Normally my mom's super hearing would have detected me by now, but apparently she was pretty tired. I took off my shoes, and tiptoed like a thief in the night. Being careful to dodge all the known creaking spots that my two older brothers before me had discovered in their little capers and had warned me about.

I held my breath and put a few seconds between each step before taking another. Step by step, inch by painful inch. Holding yourself rigid and taunt is really tough on your muscles and nervous system. I slowly moved forward. Being careful not to make even the slightest sound. I was able to make it past her door, apparently without her waking up. That was a miracle in itself. Although my mom's ears were certifiably super human, my little sister, Cheryl's, were even more powerful. That little girl would sell me out just for the fun of it all. She enjoyed seeing me squirm and be in trouble as a kid. She would love to be the one to catch me sneaking into the house after my curfew. Boy, sibling rivalries are something else.

Throughout our lives as we grew up, she had been a thorn in the side of us boys. Cheryl was like having a second mom around. As kids, she followed us around, made mental notes of our every move and quickly turned us in to mom at the slightest hint of an infraction. So now, as I crept down the hall, I slowly turned toward her room, which was opposite from mom's, to better focus my ears her way. I probably looked like a little mouse creeping low to the ground, trying to go undetected.

Then, all of a sudden, I heard a noise and saw her light go on. I'm thinking to myself, how do I get out of this one? Cheryl was on the scary side. So it would take her a few good seconds to gain her coherence and get up the nerve to look outside her doorway. So I quickly got out of my pants, and shirt and along with my tennis, quickly stuffed them in the draw of the cabinet in the hallway.

Her door then opened slightly. Cheryl said in a very low scary voice, "Who is that?" There I was stripped to my underwear, caught in the high beams of the light shining through her doorway. I turned around in the direction I was coming from to make it look like I was coming from my room, gave a big dumb looking stretch, being careful to keep one hand over the knot on my head and then gave out a quiet yawn and said, "ahh it's just me going to the bathroom. Go back to sleep girl!" She buys it.

I tiptoed into the bathroom, walking like a person who had just gotten out of bed and waited for her light to go off, which it did in just a few nerve racking seconds. I walked out of the bathroom, reached back and grabbed my clothes and crept to my room. My sister Cheryl may have bought that little act, but mom would not have. My mother had raised two super slicksters, Don and Stan, before me, and I am sure she would recognize the old play like you've been there all the time trick!!

I could now see the edge of my bed. I had been able to successfully, I guess, sneak into the house undetected. In any case, my bed felt like heaven as I eased into it. My old tired bones and muscles just seemed to sink as deep as they could go into that soft bed of mine. Ah, the joys of the little pleasures in life. Of course, I quickly got back out of bed, got on my knees and said my prayers. I concluded my prayers with, "Thank you Lord for saving my butt once again."

The next morning I was able to talk my brother Stanley into covering for me. I stayed in bed, deep under the sheets, to keep anyone from seeing the knot on my head. I told Stan initially that I was skipping breakfast because I had to go back over to Lanier for a special band practice. I had to find a way to get out of the house without mom and Cheryl seeing me. I knew that once mom saw that knot on my head that it would not be long before she used those special powers of hers to wring the truth out of my butt. My little confession would surely have put a big fizzle on my going over to Stine's house for awhile, if not forever. I definitely didn't want that to happen. So I hid out and kept my big knot under the covers for the morning. My mom religiously got up early and cooked breakfast for us all. No one was exempt from eating breakfast in our house. It was a family rule. When the chickens got up, the Weakley/Stevens got up with them as well, regardless of what day of the week it was. That morning was Saturday, so you could go back to bed once you got up, but you at least had to show your face at the table.

Mom made her routine run by our rooms to wake us up for breakfast. Without getting out from under the covers, I said "okay mom, put my breakfast out for me and I will be there in a few moments." I sat on the side of the bed when she had passed and wondered how I would explain the new growth on my head. Lucky for me, there was an emergency with one of our neighbors. Like clockwork, my mom quickly took off like she always had many times before, to see if she could help out. That little blessing saved my life. That was the break I needed to get up and out of the house without her seeing me. I dodged Ms. big mouth Cheryl and made it to Stan's car without anyone seeing the knot on my head.

I had been able to corner Stan in the bathroom, tell him the real story and get him to meet me in his car to take me back to the scene of the crime where I had gotten clobbered. It had to be around eight in the morning. As I walked towards his car, I realized that I had lost my wallet and my keys to get in the house. I had remembered having them when I got out the elderly gentlemen's car. I had to get back over to the spot where I had gotten beaned to see if any of my stuff was over there. Sure enough, as we pulled up, just as pretty as you please, there was all of my stuff laying in a neat pile where I had fallen.

There was also something else lying a few feet away from the pile as well. It was a Barq Root Beer bottle. It wasn't broken.

It wasn't even cracked. My brother Stanley practically threw up a kidney laughing at me. He said, "At least you got something out of the deal." I responded in a slow voice, " what are you talking about Stan?" He reached down, picked up the root beer bottle and said, "looks like they left you a present behind." I said what is it? He responded, "It's the bottle that probably hit you in the head. It didn't even break either! Wow! That's got to be a record in itself. Man, those Barq Root Beer people make good products, don't they?" I just kind of stood there with a don't make me dump you on the ground look on my face and didn't say a word.

    My brother continued with his little joke, "Hey if I was you, I would cash this baby in for two cents or, maybe, even better yet, frame it. Yep, that's it! You should frame this sucker!!" With that comment, he started laughing at me out loud again. Of course, my crazy brother was being funny. But he just didn't know that I almost took him up on his framing suggestion.

CHAPTER THIRTY NINE

YOU CAN RUN, BUT YOU CAN'T HIDE!

Now, to get back to my mad sprint home running from the two White guys story. *I know, as a reader, going through the story, you're probably thinking, it's about time! You've held us in suspense long enough! But oddly enough, that's a good tool of the trade for a writer. Suspense creates anticipation and in doing so enhances the story line. If you recall, I encountered the two suspicious White men sitting in the car outside my high school, and took out running like a scarred rabbit for home fearing for my life.

As I ran, my mind drifted back to how I had gotten beaned by the Barq Root Beer bottle at precisely the spot where the two White guys were parked. Anyway, to get back to the story. It had taken me no more than about fifteen minutes tops to make it to the corner of my street.

As I turned the corner of my street, I eased back on the throttle a little bit and decided I was out of danger. It was about 6:30 pm and there was still some daylight left. I could see my brother Stanley standing in front of our house as I got closer. He was looking towards the corner of our street. This was nothing new. He would normally sit outside with Charles Moore and a couple of his running buddies and shoot the breeze, (which meant talk about nothing in particular). He was the person that I wanted to talk to about what had just happened to me. I figured Mr. Cool,

Calm and Collected, as we liked to call him in those days, would know exactly what to do! He would definitely get mom involved and she would call the police or the news media just for starters.

As I got closer to our house, I could make out several images on our front porch. To my surprise, as I got within a hundred feet of our steps, I realized that among the people on the porch were the two White men who had been sitting in the car. Mom was on the front porch as well. They all were laughing and seemed to be having a lot of fun with whatever the subject was they were discussing. This was puzzling to say the least. As I got within a couple of houses from our house, I stopped completely, tucked my thumbs in the far corners of my back pocket jeans and quietly asked Stan, who was still standing out in front of the house, " What's going on?" He said, "Come on up here Vernon. You're going to love this!"

I had to have a look of total confusion on my face. All of this made no sense at all to me. I had just broken the sound barrier getting away from these guys and here they were laughing and having a grand ole time with my family. Why would the Klan be sitting on my front porch partying with my family? Stan quickly broke the ice and said, "You'll never guess who these guys are?" I quickly said, "The Klan right??" With that comment, everyone on the front porch begin to laugh. You had to have been able to hear them laughing a block away. Mom said, "come hear son. This is FBI agent James Black and his partner Mr. Hilliard, I believe," as she looked back toward him. Mr. Hilliard responded, "Yes Mam, you got it right." She continued, "they want to talk with you a little bit about Lanier High School."

I slowly responded, "Lanier High School? Why would they want to know about Lanier." She said, "they'll fill you in son." At that moment, Agent Black stood up. Cleared his voice and began to speak. His voice was very official sounding but yet, very courteous as well. He began by asking basic questions like "what grade are you son? How many students go to the school? Are there any White kids at your school? And then, he asked a rather odd question. "Are there any disturbances going on over there at the school?" Before I could speak, he continued by saying, "I understand that you kids had a little walkout over there a few weeks ago, something about the food, right!" I said "yes, but it really was no big deal."

He suspiciously responded, "Hum, I see!!" His hand immediately went up to his face and rested on his chin. He looked as if he did not believe me. He paused for a few seconds, looked over at his partner and continued. "Vernon, we are really worried about you students at Lanier." I quickly said, "why are you worried about us?" He said, "well, before I tell you that, you tell me about some of the student organizations at Lanier that you are involved in." Before I responded, I paused for a long few seconds. My mind raced a hundred miles an hour.

CHAPTER FORTY

OBAAY POPS UP AGAIN

During that long pause, before answering the FBI agent's question, my mind kind of wandered to a Black student organization I had joined called OBAAY (which was an acronym for Organization for Black Afro American Youth.) I thought to myself, "could he be interested in OBAAY?" I quickly made a decision in my mind not to bring it up at all. I began to answer his question by talking about the band, choir, football team, and the Corridor Patrol. In mid flight, he cut me off and said, " Yeah, Yeah, I know about those son, now tell me about OBAAY." I replied back, "OBAAY," as if I didn't know quite what he was talking about? He said, "Yeah OBAAY. And don't even try to play like you don't know what I am talking about!"

Up until this point my brother and mom had sat quietly and basically were inattentive. But now my mom stood up out of her seat and was hanging on every word coming out of the FBI agent's mouth.

Agent Black continued, "We understand that many of the kids at Lanier are joining OBAAY and getting ready to start a lot of trouble" I slowly responded back, "Ah, Mr. Black, OBAAY is just a small school sanctioned club. I think you may have your information mixed up! He looked down at the ground, slowly folded his arm across his chest, looked over to my mom, who looked like she was going to explode with anticipation, and said, "Vernon, my facts are straight son. There is no mix-up here. Sure OBAAY's membership is filled with the elite of the school, but something is not quite right there son. What type of activities are you kids involved in?"

My mom, after hearing that comment almost hit the ceiling. She quickly responds, "I know my son is not involved in any illegal organization." Agent Black jumped in quickly and said, "Ms. Weakley, I didn't say it was illegal. But I do maintain that it has ulterior motives." At this, I tersely responded, "what do you mean by that?" Agent Black said, "Son I know for a fact you are a member of this organization. And what I mean is that you guys are planning some major disruptions in the city."

He continued by saying, "Didn't OBAAY lead students out of the school a few weeks ago in that walkout you had at Lanier?" Didn't OBAAY talk kids from other schools out of their school and had them march with you. There are also rumors that OBAAY members were fire bombing White businesses. My mom, with her voice filled with anger, said, to me "You're not part of OBAAY, are you?" I paused for a few seconds, looked slowly around at everyone on the porch, which included the two agents, my mom, my brother Stan and his friend Charles, whose bottom jaw was almost hitting the floor, and then said. " yeah. I am a member!"

I went on from there to explain what OBAAY was. "OBAAY is a school organization started in our government class to raise the consciousness of students and get them to be aware of politics and the world. I don't see anything wrong with that. And yep, you're right we did take a lead role in the walk out the other day. That walk out had more to do with the lousy quality of food in our cafeteria, than anything." Agent Black began to speak again, but my mom stopped him before he could get another complete word out of his mouth. She said, "I think it's time to get our lawyer involved. She quickly took off in a fast walk inside the house.

Agent Black seemed totally off guard by what had just happened, as we all were. As mom dialed our family lawyer super quick, she stopped long enough to ask, "Are you arresting Vernon?" Agent Black quickly responded, "Whoa now ma'am! No one's being arrested here." My mom, standing just inside the doorway continued to dial to get our family lawyer on the phone. While the phone continued to ring, she quickly came back to the door and with the phone up to her head, again, in an angry voice, "said, " I asked you if Vernon is being arrested?" Agent Black said in a very firm voice, "no ma'am he is not!"

He continued by saying, "as I said earlier Mam, we were just asking him some questions," and again, before he could get all the syllables out on the word questions, My mom said, "I think you need to get off my property!!!" With that, rather hotly put comment, Agent Black motioned to the other agent with a sweeping hand motion, who hadn't said a word during the exchange, "let's go!"

With that, I began to laugh. Agent Black looked back over his shoulder and said, "we will be seeing you later son!! This isn't the end of this!" Before I could get a snazzy remark fired back off at the agent, I found myself being dragged into the house by the back of my shirt by my mom. And from there, I guess you know the real interrogation began.

My mom, quickly asked "Boy, what is this mess you've gotten yourself into?" I quickly responded. " mom, OBAAY is just what I said it was, nothing more! Sure we have had meetings, but what's the big deal with that. We are just concerned with school issues. I say the FBI is just playing games. They don't have anything on me because I haven't done anything. If they did have something on me, I would be on my way to jail right now. They are just fishing to see what they can dig up." Mom gives me a hard look and an even longer, maybe you're right sigh, and from there says I'll talk to you more about this later.

While my mom was calming down and regaining her composure, I walked back to the front porch where Stan and Charles were still sitting. Stan jokingly said, You probably shouldn't have laughed at those guys as they walked off. They are now going to make a career out of riding your butt. You had better get used to bread and water man." After that meant to be funny comment, Charles throws in his two cents worth and says, "Your next girlfriend may just be a six foot guy in a jail cell named Bubba." Of course, true to form, old Charles finished that funny verbal hand grenade off with one of his notorious belly laughs.

Before they can get another one of their wisecracks off, I fire off with, "Hey you two guys lay off the jokes. And you had better be careful not to make any of your stupid wisecracks around mom, the kids at school or the FBI for that matter. Because you just may be sitting in a jail cell right there next to me! This stuff ain't funny man! A lot of innocent people are in jail today because someone jokingly said the wrong thing at the wrong time in front of the wrong stupid person. Sure OBAAY members meet and talk a lot of stuff, but that's basically it. It's just a bunch of students talking about issues of the day and what's going on at the school. This is nothing. End of story."

The next thing I know, I'm being bronco busted and dragged back into the house by my mom for another fresh round of questions. After a few tense moments, I was able to get her to calm down to a roar. I basically told mom what I told my brother. My mom ended the conversation with, "This will not be the end of this mess. I want you to tell me if they (the FBI) contact you again." Of course, I responded back with a hardy military sounding, "Yes ma'am!" and a stiff salute that made a loud slapping sound as it bounced off my forehead. True to form once again, ole crazy Charles Moore almost falls out of his chair laughing at my funny antics.

CHAPTER FORTY ONE

THE SNEAKY, SNEAKY FBI

A few days later, very suspiciously I might add, on a Saturday when no one is at home but Stan and me sitting on the porch, the same FBI car pulled up to our house. Again, it is agent Black with a big fat sneaky grin on his face. The first thing he says in a rather sarcastic voice, is " Son I hope we didn't get you into any trouble with your mommy the other day! We really didn't mean to! Is your Mom home" he asked? I said "no!" He followed up by saying, "We just need to ask you a couple of other questions." They never got out of their car. They just spoke from the curb.

Agent Black then began to quickly read through a list of names of everyone in OBAAY. I said, "How did you get your list?" He responds again in a sarcastic voice, "Its no big deal. We're the FBI." They then looked at each other and laughed in a real sneaky tone. Then agent Black continued in a more serious tone, "Just like you said the other day, the club is pretty basic. We were able to verify that!" He went on to ask, "Vernon are all the meetings with OBAAY at school?" I really didn't want him to ask that question. But since I had already gotten blindsided once before, I figured I would be forthright. He probably already knew the answer anyway. I said, "no, sometimes we hold them immediately after school at a little place off of Whitfield Mill in the Georgetown area."

He quickly retorts, "Now why would you do that son?" I said, "Do what?" He says, "meet after school like that, if you guys were so innocent and all." Before I can say a word, he goes on to say, "we know about the meetings at Tyrone's grandmother's little utility house behind the Casino." I quickly responded by saying, "It's really no big deal. Our school meeting time is only forty-five minutes. Sometimes our meetings need to go longer. I am also in a band called the Say Lovers. We practice immediately after band rehearsal. We sometimes have our OBAAY meetings when something causes us to miss our scheduled time in school. That place is the only real place we can practice. It's also the only place we have found to have the meetings. They won't let us hook up guitars and stay late in the band room at school. Plus, a lot of the guys in OBAAY live in or near Georgetown. It's no secret."

Agent Black quickly jumped in and said, "Are there ever any other persons at the meetings other than students?" I said, "for the most part no. But occasionally people in the neighborhood who are sitting around to hear us rehearse may be there. But that doesn't happen very often." With that, he asked me to take a look at something. He then slowly got out of his car, as if he had a bad case of arthritis that day and thrust a picture up close to my face. After giving me a few moments to study the picture, he said, "Have you ever seen this guy before?" After closely examining the picture, I quickly, in an excited voice, said "yeah, "We had some problems with this guy!"

"The last time we rehearsed, he mysteriously appeared outside the building, as if he was waiting for us to either finish our rehearsal or have our OBAAY meeting." On that particular night though, we didn't have an OBAAY meeting scheduled. To all of our surprised, he angrily burst into our rehearsal. It was as if he was waiting for us all to get inside. He started spouting off a bunch of militant stuff like, it's time for the revolution, are you young brothers ready to die with me for the cause?" We all looked at him as if he was a raving lunatic. When we didn't respond back to him, he stuck his hands deep into both of his front pockets and just stood there and looked back at us. The silence between us was very weird. It lasted a few long seconds. Then he began to laugh. He then said, "Hey, hey, hey, lighten up guys, I'm just kidding! "How you young Black warriors doing" tonight" he said. Agent Black quickly jumped in at this point and asked, "Did he say any other type of militant stuff to you guys? Now tell us exactly what he said." I told them I couldn't remember everything word for word, but it went something like, "We should be joining the struggle rather than wasting our time playing in a band." I kind of laughed and told agent Black, "that comment was all he needed to say to get him thrown out the place." And that was basically it!

As he started to walk out, he made a few more comments. Agent Black quickly in an excited voice said, "What did he say?" I continued, He commented loudly that "the struggle is going on out there and you guys owe it to your Black heritage to be out there in it." With that comment, we all kind of laughed. One of the guys in the band told him "The struggle ain't only out there man, it's everywhere. We are in it, whether we want to be or not." After hearing this comment he seemed to get a little more upset with us and speeded up his pace out of the door.

I went on to tell agent Black that, "Being the leader of our band, I asked him to leave." The other agent excitedly chimed in, "did he say anything else to anyone else outside?" I responded by saying, I truly don't know. I stayed inside and continued practicing. Agent Black asked, "How did he take you asking him to leave" Did he act like it was no big deal? Or did he say something to let you know he was upset about leaving, or what? I told Agent Black that although he left within a few seconds after I asked him to, it was very obvious from the look on his face and how he bolted out the door that he was very angry.

Agent Hilliard quickly followed up by asking, "Do you know his name? I quickly said, "No, I never heard his name and never asked!" agent Black asked, "Has he been back?" I told him not to my knowledge. With that question my brother Stan quickly jumped into the conversation. "Hey, I thought you guys only had a few questions for Vernon?" Agent Black said, "Sorry, we got a little carried away; that's it, no more questions." Agent Black, then hobbled back to his car. As he pulled off, he said "Vernon, please tell ya mom that we came by today and may need to ask you a few more questions. Tell her its nothing serious." I did tell my mom as she had asked me to do.

Over the next few months, off and on, I would find myself running into agent Black and his partner. After a while, it became obvious that they were just waiting for an opportune time to talk with me. It was as if they really didn't want my mom or another grown-up around. I told my Mom and she called our family lawyer. He told her, "Well, they are FBI agents. They have the right to ask questions if they want to, that's their job." My mom told me after her discussion with our lawyer, to try and avoid talking to the FBI agents if possible, until she was around. mom said, "I don't know if I like them talking to you without someone else present! It's just too sneaky!" I promised her that I would not talk to them again by myself. She did say it was okay however to talk to them if Stan was present.

Everything went pretty smooth there for a little while. By this I mean that I didn't have any pop up, oh we just happen to be in the neighborhood, run-ins with ole sneaky agent Black and his partner. One day after school this would all change, agent Black and his quiet partner stopped me as I was leaving school and tried to ask me some more questions. I was truly in a hurry and really didn't have the time for their foolishness that particular day. Besides, I didn't like the fact that they were asking me questions this time, in front of my schoolmates. I told them point blank to, "Leave me alone, get lost, buzz off." They apparently thought I was joking. I wasn't. They were slowly driving behind me as I walked with my friends home from school down Whitfield Mill Road. It really pissed me off that day that they were bothering me out in the open like that!

I finally had enough and exploded on them!! I let them have it!! I told them that I hadn't done anything wrong and I knew my rights. I repeated what my government class instructor had told me when I asked him for advice on what to do about the situation, which was, "If you bother me one more time, I am going to have my mother and our lawyer call the main FBI headquarters in Washington and complain to the head man in charge. And if that doesn't work, we will go to the media." Man, you should have seen those guys speeding away after that comment. Arriving home, I told mom what had happened. She called our lawyer and he agreed with me and said enough is enough! Before we could hang up the phone good, guess whose car was coming around the corner.

Mom stood on the porch with her hands on her hips waiting for the FBI agents to get to our house. I could almost swear I saw steam pouring out of the top of her head. As agent Black pulled up to our porch, my mom began to rip into them. She began with, " I hope you two have got some other jobs lined up because I intend to get your jobs. How dare you stop my son out on the street and question him. Before she could go further, old agent Black said, "Ms. Weakley I truly apologize. We were just trying to keep Vernon out of harm's way." My mom and I, at the same time said "harms way, what do you mean?"

Agent Black responded in a matter of fact tone, "Remember that guy we asked about before? The one who tried to push his way into your band rehearsal." She said, " yeah, Vernon told me about that!" He is a member of the Communist party. He has put together a crazy plan to either personally kill off some of the students in OBAAY and make everyone think the KLAN did it to cause a race riot, or fool some of the students to put themselves in harm's way so that they can be killed by some of the racist Mississippi police. Agent Black went on to say in a weird sounding voice, "This guy is a bad dude Mrs. Weakley! Either way, his plan is to start up a lot of mess so that a major riot can start here in Jackson. We have BEEN WORKING TO TRY TO STOP THAT.

We have been told that Vernon is one of the people on his list to kill. That's why we have been hanging around here so much. We have been trying to protect Vernon, not harass him."

mom almost fainted after hearing this. My knees almost buckled a little bit themselves. Agent Black continued by saying, "we think we may have ran this guy off because we can't seem to find him. We do know this though, that he is no longer in Jackson. Generally when suspects vanish into thin air like that, they have gotten wind that we are on to them, and they stop what they are doing and leave town. Let's all hope and pray that this is the end of this mess!

After hearing this absolutely fantastic story, whether true or fabricated, our attitudes softened toward agent Black significantly. He went on to give us some things to look out for and ask me to stay away from the Casino area for awhile. My mom wanted to call the police but agent Black talked her out of it. He gave me his number and asked me to call him immediately if I saw the guy again. We thanked agent Black and he went on his way.

I guess a couple of months passed before I saw or heard from agent Black and his silent blond partner again. I thought for sure that nightmare was over with until, again one Sunday when my mom was away at church, guess who showed up? It was the two FBI agents. My brother Stan just happened to be there with me. I recall thinking to myself, as they pulled their car over and walked toward our front porch. "Man. I wish my grandfather was here; he would definitely know how to handle this situation."

My grandfather died when I was in the eighth grade and my grandmother had died the year before my eleventh grade year. If they were still with us, they certainly would have been able to tell us how to handle this difficult situation. But, as it stood, they were not here. It would be Stan and me facing this crisis alone. Agent Black walked up on the porch, and with the first words coming out of his mouth, offered an apology for what had happened the times before. He then asked if my mother was home. Stan quickly jumped in and said, "You already know she is not here! You know she is at church. What do you want with my brother this time?" Agent Black began by saying, 'Well, we wanted to ask if Vernon was interested in a career with the FBI, the Bureau." I kind of smiled and excitedly looked over at my brother Stan with a look of "Hey, I am all for that on my face." Stan quickly said, Vernon, that's nonsense, that's not the way the FBI works. You need a law degree to get in the FBI.

My brother Stanley has always been my protector. He has always been by my side to make certain things go right for me. He is two years older than me. All my life we have been tight and have had a special bond between each other. When I was a small child of four growing up afraid of the dark, being afraid to go to sleep at night, because I thought I would die in my sleep, my big brother Stan had indeed been the one there with me, right by my side comforting me and letting me know everything would be alright. So, it was no wonder that my hero, my cool as a cucumber big brother Stan, would be standing there fighting for me once again in this odd circumstance.

Agent Black said back to Stan, "Well that's not necessarily true now. There are other ways to get into the FBI. Do I look like a guy who has a law degree? Agent Black had a point there. He was kind of on the rough looking side. He kind of looked like a bum in a suit! He went on to say that, he had gotten into the FBI after doing undercover work for them.

He continued by saying, "Now if Vernon wants to go off and get his law degree, he is certainly free to take that route, but, quite frankly that would take years." He looked over at me and said, there is another quicker way. He can do some fairly safe, high level, under cover work with us for a few years, and he would get my recommendation to be certified into the bureau's new recruit training program." There I was with my naïve self, looking all excited and my brother Stan, on the other hand, was shaking his head no. Stan finally said out loud, " No Way Man! I don't think so! I'd appreciate it if you leave." Stan began to escort agent Black by the arm off the porch. Agent Black, gently pulled his arm away and turned back around and said, "Just hear me out for a second, if you will.

The assignment we are talking about has to do with Jackson

State College. There are a few student radicals over there who have a newspaper called the GAD Fly. All Vernon would have to do is enroll at Jackson State, get involved with the GAD Fly and occasionally report back to us. That's it." Stan looked over at me. I excitedly chimed in, "That's all?" Again keep in mind, I was only 16 years old, and I might add to that, a very naïve 16 year old at that! Agent Black, says in an equally excited child like voice, "That's right Vernon! And from there we will pay your tuition and give you some spending money to boot. If you do a good job, I will personally prepare your recommendation to be accepted into the bureau on experience."

And finally, the silence from my older brother Stan was broken. I guess he just couldn't take it anymore!!! He said, "Sorry, you can forget it! My little brother ain't doing no mess like that!" After that loud comment by my big brother, dead silence and boiling hot air filled the foot or two of empty space between Stan and agent Black. They stood for a few tension filled seconds staring each other in the eyes. Damn! THE POWER OF SILENCE IS AWESOME! Agent Black, after a few seconds, got the message! All of a sudden he turned and walked off our porch along with his fellow FBI agent in hasty tow!

That decision by my big brother Stan probably changed my life to the good forever. You know, I never saw agent Black again, until one tragic day in college when the Mississippi Highway patrol brutally shot two students to death and wounded many more. Years later, while I was watching the national news on television, a special report came on. It talked about a congressional report on how, during the Nixon years at the direction of the White House, the FBI had hired college students at thousands of colleges across America to be paid informants. Their job, according to this special report, was to keep a lid on the often explosive situations on campuses across America that led to violent race riots and protests against the war in Vietnam.

As I sat and listened to this story, I thought to myself silently, how glad I was that I had not taken the FBI's offer. And then as soon as that thought exited my head, I wondered if some of my classmates, who were true to the bone members of OBAAY as I had been, had taken ole Agent Black up on his little undercover assignment? I'm pretty sure that I wasn't the only one that the FBI had approached with their little sneaky offer. Hum! Well, anyway, I can only account for myself. I definitely did not take them up on their offer primarily as a result of my big brother Stan's intervention. Man, it is good to have a big brother who loves you and will stand up for you when the stuff hit the fan!

CHAPTER FORTY TWO

THE HURT

Billy Brayfied, as I said in an earlier chapter, was the bass guitar player in my band in High School. He and I became pretty tight and ran together after our two little bands merged. I had known Billy for years. He was from my old neighborhood in downtown Jackson. He stayed a block or two over from my house. I don't know why, but up until the time we started to play together in the band, I hadn't really ever hung out too much with Billy. He and his family seemed like good people. But for whatever reason he stayed on his end of Farish street, across from the cleaner, and I stayed on my end which was directly in front of the Dottie cab station.

Eddie and Billy asked if I would play with them some nights in some of the juke joints in downtown Jackson. Although I already was the leader of the Say Lovers, and they occasionally played with us, it wasn't practical to have guys packing a bass tuba and baritone horn into these types of clubs, so we decided a few of us would make a little extra money on the side and occasionally play the chittling circuit. At first I was reluctant, but old Eddie and Billy eventually persuaded me to give it a try.
It was Billy who also persuaded my reluctant mom to let me go to these types of places. He assured her he would look out for me. After playing sleazy nightclubs together in downtown Jackson in a very poor area called Doodyville, I came to realize that most of the poor people who frequented these little hole in the wall

joints were just plain good people too! They just wanted to be able to relax with a cold beer and enjoy some good music just like everyone else in America, rich or poor. Hanging with Eddie and Billy and gigging in this environment opened up a new world to me that I never knew existed.

Walking home late hours at night with Billy and Eddie after playing these gigs, I can say, I got to know my buddy Billy quite well. He was a nice guy, who also had a slight temper. Mind you, he never messed with anyone, but if someone rubbed ole Billy the wrong way, (or even accidentally bumped into that precious guitar of his that he absolutely adored) they were going to hear about it in no short order. Being the eternal peace loving guy that I was, I learned how to get along and blend into their after hours world.

Some nights, we would be playing in these little hole in the wall places while the people were up fighting in full brawl. You would think that would have been it for us playing once a fight broke out, but I found out that the real world didn't work like that. We couldn't just pack our little instruments (our axes as we called them in those days) and scadattle because of a temporary disturbance, as one nightclub manager we played for put it. Once the fight was over, the band had to play on. That was the house rule in many of these places.

I remember one owner named Joe Sweet, who owned and ran a place called "Funky Mary's" telling me once that nothing healed a few bruised feelings and busted heads quicker than some good music. So, as you can see, we had to keep playing, even during some of these free-for-alls, because if we didn't, we didn't get paid. And while I wanted to take off running a few times or so with my old sax safely tucked under my arm, ole Billy and Eddie would settle me down and say, "Hey man we've seen it before. It ain't time to start running until the actual shooting starts.

Boy these were some funny times for me. I was the undisputed king of the drunks. My buddy Billy called me a drunk person magnet. It was just something about the sound of a crying sax that will bring tears to a drunk person's eyes every time. I would have drunks crying in their beer, slobbering all over me during my breaks telling me their sad stories. During the gig, my new found friends would often stand no more than a foot away from me while I was performing. They either would be dancing and encouraging me to play some melancholy tune that had just touched their heartstrings or pointing to my sax and bragging about how good I was on my horn. They would be hollering, "Play that Saxophone Boy. Play it! Damn that skinny boy can play the hell out of that horn!"

Thank God for the club owners. They seemed to always be saving me from these funny situations. They would be saying stuff like, "Man go sit down and let Mr. Saxophone man finish his show." I was like a duck out of water. My mom did not allow me to go into places like that at that age, never. So, this was truly a life education for me!

Sometimes these situations would get a little bit out of hand. Eddie and the drummer would be practically rolling on the floor laughing. But ole Billy would be right there going to the mat for me if necessary. When it was over, my buddy Billy would be making funny announcements on the microphone that went something like, "Okay everybody, that little ruckus scared the living ba gee bees out of our sax man here. Aw, he ain't used to this kind of fun like we are. Let's see if we can keep the fights down to a dozen or so tonight. We got to keep the sax man happy, or he's gonna take off running on us. Now what's a blues and R&B band without a good saxophone player? Huh? We brought him down with us tonight to class up the joint!" Billie's sense of humor would have the entire club laughing in full roar.

These were some extremely hilarious funny, but dangerous times for me. Thank God, the sax man always made it out of the juke joint alive.

Probably one of the saddest memories I have from high school was of having to be the one to tell my good friend Billy

Brayfied that his high school sweetheart, Linda Jenkins, who everyone lovingly called Tootsie, had been killed along with some of our other classmates in a bad car wreck. Boy did Billy take it hard.

If ever there was an angel on this earth, Linda Jenkins was it. She was as innocent, polite, God-fearing and as nice as they come. She was also incredibly beautiful. She was one of the most popular girls in her class at Lanier. Billy and she were juniors. I was a senior. Ernestine, my girlfriend, was now a freshman at Jackson State University. Everyone in the school adored Tootsie. She was also a Rangerette in the Lanier band.

For those of you who are not familiar with the pecking order in bands in the old days, it was the Drum Major, then the super sexy majorettes, who were the more voluptuous and usually older senior level girls. And then, there were the band of course, and from there, there were girls at Lanier that they called Rangerettes. There would usually be an army of them. They were generally the younger girls in school. What the guys nowadays call the Tender Ronnies or Jail Bait! They were good-looking, but more or less for looks and show more than touch. They were the real sweet, naïve and innocent little girls that no one really wanted to hang around with during the football games or at band practice, because their parents would usually be right there in the immediate vicinity hovering over them like nosy mother hens.

Simply stated you could forget trying to rap to them or put what we guys in those days used to call a bug in their ear. You would either get your lips slapped off by them or get collared by their overly protective parents. Or, you would either get a blank stare from them because they had no clue what it was you were trying to talk them into doing. The bottom line was, you could forget it. They were not going anywhere. If you were going to get your "Mack On," you had better be trying to get next to the fine and generally more worldly majorettes or some of the wild girls in the band.

My exclusive duty while I was at band practice, according to my best friend Billy, was to closely watch Tootsie for him and inform all the guys in the band who dared to try to flirt with her, to keep their hands off. Tootsie was an absolute knockout. She had beautifully shaped legs, a perfectly formed little round butt, and the biggest round eyes you'd ever want to see. Tootsie, Billy, and myself often laughed about my funny antics in the band room, chasing the smooth talking, so-called players away from my best buddy's girl. Believe me it was quite a chore. Tootsie was just that good-looking!

Billy usually would be perched at the edge of the band room door each day waiting for Tootsie to get out of band rehearsal. They were together all of the time. I jokingly called them, "Two Peas in a Pod" Whenever they walked into the lunchroom they would be hand in hand. I would sometimes jokingly stand up and announce, "Here they come everybody. Make way for Romeo and Juliet," It was obvious to everyone that they were madly in love.

Although Billy, sometimes had a rough exterior when he was hanging out with the guys, with Tootsie, he was as gentle as a lamb. It is true. A good woman can really change a man! And, I guess the same thing is true for a woman. These two good people were great for each other. Where Tootsie was shy and not very outgoing, Billy was what she needed to bring her out. Where Billy was a little rough around the edges; Tootsie mellowed him out and made him shine like a new penny!!!

My most vivid memory of these two would be Billy gently holding her little hand and pulling her along as they walked with Stine and me wherever it was we were going. We hung out together often. Tootsie was younger than Stine and me, but her mom allowed her to hang with us anyway. Ernestine and Tootsie attended the same church and stayed right around the corner from each other. I think her mom liked Ernestine because of her church work and great personality. She knew Ernestine would take care of her. Where Billy could sometimes get a little loud and carried away in the moment, Tootsie's little soft angelic voice would be all that was needed to immediately calm him down and make him stop whatever it was that Tootsie felt that he should not be doing.

Tootsie was a tiny little thing compared to Billy. She just seemed to fit like a hand in a glove in his big massive arms. Billy was a very handsome, brown skinned brother with a super physique. He could have easily had any girl he wanted, but he wanted Tootsie. End of story. They were the perfect couple.

The funny thing I recall about their relationship, was that as tough and as rough as Billy Brayfied was, I don't think he ever won an argument with Tootsie. I teased him about this all the time. He would be stomping around mad, kicking up dirt at the beginning of one of their little arguments.

Tootsie would just stand there not saying a word, with her arms folded, and let him finish his little so-called tantrum. Then, when she had had enough, She would softly call his name, "Billy." He would stop in mid flight and turn towards her and from there she would slowly walk over, put her little arms gently around his neck, whisper in his ear "I Love You Billy! " and then she would softly kiss him on his lips and that would be it. And guess what, nothing else mattered.

Billy would grab her little hand and they would passionately hug and all the problems in their little world would magically disappear. Of course, all of the guys and I would tease my good friend about his little surrender. But you know something, I think every man secretly wants a soft tender plea from a good woman to bring him back to earth, once he has hit the boundary of reason and logic. I was always telling Billy, when he appeared to be embarrassed over giving in to Tootsie, "Hey man you just don't know how truly blessed you are." You and Tootsie really have a good thing going." Tootsie never steered him wrong and she was always looking out for his best interest. Tootsie was very good for my friend Billy.

Tootsie also stayed in the Georgetown area, a few blocks over from my girlfriend Stine, rather than downtown like Billy and me. It was good to have company via my, 'I will stomp a mud hole in somebody's butt if they mess with us friend Billy,' on our little treks back and forth to Georgetown and Downtown

Jackson. We truly had the best of times in High School.

Occasionally, Lanier would have a tragedy or two where the students were concerned. Although it didn't happen very often, it was inevitable that tragedy would sometimes strike. For the most part though, these incidents occurred over the summer. I recall a very popular guy who was nicknamed Grand Son, getting high on wine one day and jokingly playing Russian Roulette in front of some fellow students, with what he thought was an unloaded pistol. HE THOUGHT WRONG! The gun was loaded and it cost him his life. There were other incidents where students were involved in tragedies. The one that will forever be burned in my memory as old cruel fate demanded it, involved my two good friends Billy and Tootsie.

Early one Sunday morning, I received a call that would be my first experience with sorrow and hurt, other than the death of my grandparents, I had ever come in contact with. Up until this point in my rather young life, I incorrectly thought that death was for older people. Kids never died. In my mind, it just didn't happen. Why would God snatch away something so pure and innocent as a child. I could kind of see an adult being called away, since they would have lived their life, either good or bad. But a young child or kid, I wondered what would be the sense of it all. Why not take them before they are born? Why even let them come into the world, if they are going to be snatched back to heaven before they have truly experienced life. Whether it made sense to me or not, I was on the verge of tasting the depths of true pain.

Like a bolt out of the blue that morning, I received a surprise phone call from Ernestine. The first words out of her mouth were, " Vernon, Tootsie was killed in a car accident last night." Ernestine didn't prepare me. She just hit me across the head with this terrible news. My emotions and insides seemed to completely twist into painful little knots that day in a matter of seconds while listening to Ernestine's voice. I had never felt this type of pain before. I kept saying over and over, 'this can't be true. Who told you this nonsense!" I was in total denial. Stine, fighting through the tears herself, finally was able to convince me that it was true. Once I had kind of come back to my senses, she told me that I needed to quickly get to Billy and be the one to tell him. She thought that I was the one who needed to do this because of our great relationship. Although I knew she was right, I really was not up to the task. I tried to talk my way out of it but I knew it was the right thing to do! I quickly threw on some clothes, told my mom what had happened and where I was going and took off running to Billy's house.

As I ran, I put my arms and legs on total automatic while my mind fell deep into thought! How would I break this terrible news to my friend? What could I say to take some of the sting out of this terrible situation. I didn't have a clue. Giving my dear friend Billy this terrible, terrible news would be the toughest thing, up until that point in my life, I had ever done. Man, what pain and agony. My entire body trembled with each crash of my running feet on the pavement. It was a hazy overcast day.

Billy stayed not too far from my house. As I approached his house, still not having an idea what I would say, I slowed down a few feet from his door, put my hands on my head and struggled to find the right words to say! They never came!

I recall standing outside Billy's doorway for a few more minutes to try and get my composure. I still had tears in my eyes. I tried to thoroughly wipe them away. I did not want the fact that I had been crying or my tears to be the first thing Billy noticed. It was still pretty early in the morning. I finally got up the courage to knock on his door. After only getting two knocks in, Billy opened the door and appeared surprised, but was smiling as he usually did whenever we hooked up. Standing in his open doorway he said. "What's up man!" In a sad voice, I said, "hey has anyone called you or anything, He said, "Nope! Eddie and I were out on a gig last night until about three this morning. I crashed and have been sleeping like a dead man since I hit the bed." After finishing this comment, he quickly walked outside to me. As his feet hit the bottom step and reached me, I kind of hesitated for a moment, then put my arm around his shoulder. Billy, I guess, at this point sensed something bad had happened. He said in a very firm, but concerned voice, "What's wrong Vernon?" He looked me straight in my eyes, as if to soak in my every emotional response. I paused for a few more seconds and with uncontrollable tears slowly forming in my eyes, gripped his shoulder tight with one hand and said, "Billy prepare yourself for bad news."

Billy quickly snatched loose from me and said, "Now look you scaring me man. What the hell is wrong." From there I began to slowly tell him what had happened. With each painful syllable that poured from my lips, he screamed to the top of his lungs "No," in excruciating agony. He also began to hit me as hard as he could with his fists to make me stop saying what I was saying. At that point, we were both wringing wet with our tears.

Although he was hitting me as hard as he could, it didn't hurt nearly as much as the pain and pure hell we both were going through. After a few minutes, I recall his sort of giving out of gas emotionally and falling to his knees on the ground. I sat down next to him. We just sat there for what seemed like hours, from that point, not saying a word.

At one point Billy began to laugh. I wondered to myself if my dear friend had lost his mind. And then, he told me the strangest thing. He said, "You know we live down here in the ghetto, scratching and fighting to survive. Nothing good seems to ever happen to us. But just this one time, God was merciful. He sent Tootsie to me. And now, he has taken his Angel back!! I'm just grateful to have had her here on earth with me for this short time. I'm not mad at God, I am mad at myself for not being there by her side to go with her."

Billy and I both openly sobbed and held each other for what appeared to be an eternity! Oh what pain! What tremendous, numbing pain!! It took me years to get my good friend Billy's tear stains out of the shirt I had on that day. We were completely drained of our strength and our emotions. That was, without a doubt, one of the worst days of my life. My mind often revisits this terrible moment in time. Why, I don't know? Is there some lesson for me to be gleaned from that dreadful day in time?

Perhaps not! I do believe however, that there are some pains and hurts that a child must go through in order to toughen and prepare itself for the many trials and tribulations that God has written into his master plan for it. This awful pain that Billy and I experienced that day will certainly be our rock on which to lean on throughout the storms of our lives.

CHAPTER FORTY THREE

THE EVIL POWERS THAT BE

My second year at Jackson State College, I experienced something that would totally change my life forever. It would be a terrible weight on my subconscious and a dark foreboding cloud that would hang over me for many years. It was only by the grace of God that I would recover from this unwanted intrusion into my life. On the night of May 14, 1970, I, along with many other students at Jackson State, witnessed the unthinkable. Two innocent students were brutally murdered. Scores of horrified others were shot by gunfire and/or severely wounded by flying glass as a result of merciless heavily armed members of the Mississippi Highway Patrol. Call me 'Mr. Wrong Place at the Right Time,' but I was also one of the many students who was shot down on this hideous, unforgettable night.

This brutal atrocity, I believe, was done under the direction of the 'Evil, Greedy, and Power Hungry, Powers That Be' that were in control of Mississippi at that point in its history.

There is one very important point I hope that people get from reading this chapter. If nothing else, I want people to clearly understand that the murders at Jackson State University on May 14, 1970, were not only about blind racism.

They also, more than anything, were about the strategic use of racism as a tool to achieve monetary goals and gain absolute power over others.

The city of Jackson along with Jackson state was enjoying a boom period in 1969 and 70. Many new businesses and nationally known industries were beginning to move their companies to Jackson. And with them and their new industries (and suitcases filled with money I might add to buy influence and favors) came additional opportunities for the corrupt powers that be in Mississippi to grow even more filthy rich and drunk with greed and power. This period of new seemingly unlimited prosperity, was made to order for the powers that be in Mississippi, if the students at Jackson state didn't mess it up for them.

It was also a well-known fact that in the early 60s that Jackson State students had been a major support factor for many of the sit in marches in downtown Jackson. It was the countless waves of students from Jackson State, that helped to bring the city of Jackson to its knees and force the White citizen's council and powerful business men into humbling concessions during these demonstrations. Additionally, In the latter 60s, Jackson State began to grow by leaps and bounds. It went from roughly two thousand students to eight thousand, as if overnight. This large concentration of educated Black students would now also surely become aware of the knowledge of the power of the vote. And, with that, it's enormous political clout within the city of Jackson.

One of the benefits of getting a better education is that it broadens the intellect of whoever its recipients are, regardless of race, social status or color. In Jackson State's case, with enhanced intellect, would also come a true knowledge of the power of the vote, an intolerance for racism and some rather hard questions thrown in the direction of the all White Mississippi leadership by its Black citizens.

Black people wanted to know why was a state so rich in

resources always on the bottom of the nation economically? Mississippi at that time was the laughing stock of the nation. Where was all the money disappearing too? Maybe it was time for a change in leadership. Maybe it was time for Black leadership in Mississippi!!!

Add to this, the fact that college educated kids were certainly not going to be satisfied with the old jobs and careers that their parents eagerly worked! There is an old saying that goes, "How are you going to keep them down on the farm, once they have seen Paris." That was an understatement in Mississippi's case. The thriving atmosphere that was Jackson State was calling these kids away from the cotton fields of Mississippi, like the pied piper of old.

There would be no more generations of Blacks picking cotton, loving it and looking forward to it when they were of age, as their parents had before them. This in itself was a serious threat to a major source of historically reliable income for the state. The powers that be would much rather that this cheap labor be sweating away out in a Mississippi cotton field, rather than sitting leisurely in an air conditioned Jackson State college classroom.

Although Jackson State had quieted down significantly in 1970, it was now once again seen as a potential new threat to the 'Evil Powers That Be.' This factor alone was enough of a threat to cause the White 'Powers That Be' to take extraordinary measures to protect their new found wealth and their old racist way of life.

So there you have it! There was indeed a perception of emerging power at Jackson State. The evil 'Powers That Be' probably thought that it was only a matter of time before. this sleeping giant awaken again. Of course, I can only speculate. But this perception of emerging power made it necessary for a much greater power to feel threatened by the new power. The evil 'Powers That Be' felt it had to move to exert itself and show the new power that it was the supreme power in the state of Mississippi. The clock was now ticking toward disaster! The final explosive ingredient, which was White fear, had now been thrown into the power keg. The rest is history.

The one thing I did learn from what happened to me at Jackson State was that even though racism in itself is truly a terrible thing, its negative effects are greatly amplified when it's used by unscrupulous people to keep the masses confused, in fear, hopelessly poverty stricken and at each other's throats, so that their own selfish goals can be accomplished.

You know, every good story has a villain, a bad guy! In the case of the Jackson State Murders, the Mississippi Highway patrol and the "Evil Powers That Be" fit the criteria all too well. The Mississippi Highway Patrol, acting blindly as willing pawns, were more than eager to carry out the hideous and cowardly act at Jackson State. The Evil Powers that Be were more than willing to wield them like a tool to achieve their purpose.

Prior to the murders at Jackson State, I was just a naive, God-fearing student. But something deep down inside of me snapped after I got shot at Jackson State. This incident caused me for a period in my life, to turn my back on God, my family, my up-bringing and everything I knew that was right. The shootings and murders at Jackson State gave birth to my wild and crazy years.

What happened to me at Jackson State manifested itself in destructive behavior directed inwardly at myself as well as outwardly at the racist system in Mississippi that had done this terrible thing to me and my friends and fellow students. Whether right or wrong, as a young kid reacting to the blind hatred, racism and violence that was being thrust upon me, I made a decision to act on my own raw impulses and eagerly chose to fight fire with fire. I lashed out violently at those who were trying to hurt me and/or who stood in the way of whatever I wanted. Where racism is concerned, I quickly found out that that was not the way to fight it in the deep South, especially in the bloody sixties and seventies. I foolishly put my life in danger many times without forethought. God protected me though, and shielded me from harm.

For years after witnessing the murders at Jackson State, I held the source of my anger, bitterness and pain inside. My family members and friends wondered what was wrong with me. Up until 1990, I acted out my anger and plain refused to talk about its genesis with anyone until God stepped in and relieved me of my burden. He forgave me my sins and let me come back to him. I am living proof that if he will allow me to return to his grace, there is hope for every sinner who has fallen, regardless of how low he thinks he may be! God is truly merciful

On May 14, 1970, the night the murders occurred, I was hanging as usual with a bunch of my frat brothers, the Qs of Omega Psi Phi Fraternity. Several of the Deltas (our sister sorority) were also hanging out with us that night. We were doing what college kids all across America did, partying and having a good time! Sitting out on the grass listening to music at the girls' dorm was pretty normal for the Qs (the Omegas) and the Deltas on a hot spring weekday night. It was not unusual for large numbers of students to hang out in front of either the men's or women's dormitories at Jackson State College. These dorms were at opposite ends of the campus. Lynch Street, a major thoroughfare at that time, ran through the heart of Jackson State.

The evening began as just a regular quiet night on what we students called, 'The Yard.' Then all of a sudden, a truck came speeding down the street past the girls' dorm where we were, heading in the direction of the men's dorm. In the truck was a White man who was screaming racial slurs and obscenities out of his window at the students. I personally don't think anyone had done anything to this guy. we figured he probably was drunk and just wanted to get off on harassing some Black people.

Although what the White man had done was highly unusual, no one on our end of the campus got too alarmed by what had just happened. I guess it happened so fast that we really didn't have time to react to this insult. Keep in mind however, that we were at the girls' dorm. He had entered the campus at the beginning point of the street on which he was traveling.

You would think if you were going to pull a stupid stunt like that you would wait until you were almost off the campus, and not as you were entering it. In any case, the people on the front end of the campus, where I was, basically ignored this fool. That was where the lovers were. He would not be as lucky at the boys' dorm, which was in the direction he was heading.

I truly don't know what happened to the guy in the truck, but I can probably guess. He got bricked! By this I mean every hard leg who was pissed off because he didn't have a girl to be with that night picked up whatever he could get his hands on and threw it at the guy. It doesn't take a rocket scientist to figure out what happened next. The guy called the police and made it sound like he was the innocent victim. Or, who knows, maybe a more sinister plot was being set in motion.

At the time of the murders at Jackson State I wondered if the guy in the truck could have been a plant. A setup? I now am convinced that he was just that! As history sadly recorded on the night of May 14th, 1970 two innocent students were brutally shot to death and many, many more were wounded. I was just one of the students who was wounded in this terrible tragedy.

It is through my eyes that I have tried to let the world see what I saw and experienced emotionally that night in my writings. I felt it necessary to take people back to the scene of this crime. The state of Mississippi said the Highway Patrolmen were sufficiently trained and were provoked into the shootings that occurred that night by a sniper. Of course, the world now knows that there was no sniper at Jackson State. The fact that the city police, who were also out there in the ranks with the Highway patrolmen on this terrible night, did not fire their weapons is a clear indication that there was indeed a conspiracy to commit murder and therefore an illegal effort to deprive American citizens of their constitutional rights. As an up close and personal witness of this event, I know the truth. I also know that one day the truth will prevail.

CHAPTER FORTY FOUR
NO GREATER LOVE

The year before the murders occurred at Jackson State I pledged Omega Psi Phi Fraternity and went over on the Q Pledge line. The night of the shootings, if it weren't for Howard Levite (Dolemite, my frat brother) risking his life to come to me seconds after the shootings ceased, and taking care of me during the night, I truly believe I would have died. Dolemite bravely faced guns pointed at him by hard-core racists who had already killed and wounded scores of students. Without a doubt, he willingly risked his life to save me! He was the first person I saw stand up and face the Highway Patrol mere seconds after the barrage ceased.

Clearly, without hesitation, these evil, cold-blooded murderers could have easily killed Levite, given the heat of the moment, without further explanation. It would not have been anything for them to go a step farther and blow him to bits. Howard Levite would have been just another dead NIGGER to them, added to the list. I'm sure he knew this before he took one step! But still, he came anyway! As far as I'm concerned, Dolemite has the stuff that real heroes are made of. The tremendous courage that he showed that night is what this book ("Fear No Evil") is all about.

For many years through the 80s, 90s and up until 2001, I lost complete touch with Dolemite, this soul mate of mine, who my life was so intertwined as a result of what happened that hideous night. I can offer no explanation as to how this could have occurred. All I know is that after the untimely death of a close frat brother of ours, (Johnnie BB Byrd) Dolemite left us to go into the military, and from there, he seemed to just get lost in time and the universe. Oh sure, my frat brothers and I constantly inquired as to his whereabouts, without a shred of a reply, until a caring frat brother by the name of Mandrick Williams in Leavenworth Ks. heard some frat brothers and I talking about our many failed attempts to locate Dolemite. He stepped into the conversation and told us, he could find my long lost savior from May 14th. Sure enough, he was successful. Thanks to brother Mandrick, we were reunited with our OLE friend Dolemite.

Now back to the story. After being shot and violently knocked to the ground by the bullet's impact on the night of may 14th, 1970,, I knew that I was lucky to still be alive. I was in a state of shock, cold and trembling violently as I lay on the ground, not necessarily from the gunshot wound I had received, but from the horrible sight I was witnessing. Although I knew I had been shot, it did not hurt as much as I had expected!

I could feel my pants' leg wet with blood. I kept whispering to myself in slow soothing tones that everything would be okay. Then all of a sudden my leg seemed to explode with pain! My breathing began to get very heavy. As this was happening, I looked up and saw Howard (Dolemite) Levite, peering out from behind the west wing doorway. Dolemite was a super cool, Mad Dog 20/20, wine drinking rough neck who was very popular on campus.

Everyone called him Dolemite from the Rudy Ray Moore character because of his well-known reputation with the ladies. In spite of his hell raising, hard-core gangster exterior though, I knew Dolemite as a great friend who had a heart of gold.

I screamed out to him to help me! How Dolemite was able to distinguish my voice from the many others that were out there screaming, moaning and crying that night, I don't know! Along with hundreds of students that were out there that night, there had to be at least fifteen to twenty fallen bodies within five or six feet of me. It was as if I was in the middle of a pile of bodies. Another fifty or so lay injured and/or motionless in the grass in front of the girls' dorm.

I could tell from the look on Dolemite's face that he was also in a state of shock. His face was twisted and contorted. It was obvious that the sight of the bloody bodies sprawled on the ground repulsed him. Although I am sure Dolemite was also afraid, he was the first person to stand up after the barrage of gunfire.

He had somehow managed to get just inside the building doorway before he had to fall to the floor to avoid being shot in the back. He slowly began to move towards me, stepping over people who lay in what used to be a full glass doorway. Most of the people were still too frightened to move. All of a sudden, as Dolemite began to inch his way towards me half crouched over, a policeman on a bull horn announced that "anyone not obeying their order to stay in the building would be shot." Even with this deadly threat ringing in the air, Dolemite came anyway. With a loud defiant comment, he told the highway patrol and police who were still pointing their weapons at him, that " You're just going to have to kill me then, because I'm not leaving my wounded frat brother on the ground to die." Without any regard for his life, Howard Dolemite Levite boldly put our brotherhood and my well being above his own life and stepped out from the fallen terrified crowd and boldly walked back to pick me up. Without fear, he bravely moved forward toward the murderous officers with their gun barrels still smoking and menacingly pointing at him to get me. To this very day I have admired Dolemite for the raw courage he showed that night.

Dolemite and I pledged Omega Psi Phi fraternity together our freshman and sophomore year at Jackson State. During that time we pledged to give our lives for each other while on line, like all Omega men had done who had painfully pledged and went over before us. When you're making promises in a fraternity ceremony, in the back of your mind, you never really think that a time will actually come when your promise will be put to the test. But here

Dolemite was, putting our fraternity creed in practice.

The friendship, everlasting bonds, principles, perseverance, and brotherhood I learned while in Omega Psi Phi fraternity helped me to survive the severe psychological trauma that I experienced as a result of the murders, and gunshot wound I received on May 14, 1970. Without the frat, my frat brothers, and more importantly God, I don't believe I would have survived. I would have bled to death, or passed away from shock out there on the cold ground as a result of my gunshot wound the night of the shootings. Or, I certainly would have been murdered by the racist 'White Powers That Be' prior to or after the trial in the name of vengeance, if I hadn't had God and my frats standing next to me each step of the way, protecting me.

It is also my opinion that if it wasn't for the Qs positioning themselves between the Highway Patrol and the girls' dorm that night, many more students would have been killed the night of the shootings at Jackson State University. As a result of seeing us, a large group of male students, the Highway patrol could not set their evil plan completely in motion.

The girls' dorm at that time was shaped like an opened ended square box. The opened end of the box, if you can visualize it, was facing the street where the officers were standing. The girl's dorm was lined from top to bottom, end to end with dormitory windows. I believe that their purpose was to get directly in front of that opening and cut loose on the students. If they had been successful in doing this, hundreds of bullets would have gone directly into the girl's dorm, instead of hitting the brick wall on the right edge of the box(the west wing wall) where we were standing.

I am not saying that the Qs positioned themselves there purposely; that would not be true. It just happened to be mere fate that it was our normal partying spot. The point to be made is that many, and I do mean many, more students would have been killed that night had the officers gotten fully into position. They were not able to shoot directly into the dorm because the crowd which was made up of many Qs, as well as other students, I believe spoiled their evil plan. The fact that the Highway Patrol and police ignored the male students at the men's dorm end of the campus, strongly indicates that a more calculated, sinister plot was being put in motion. It is obvious to me that the Highway Patrol knew they would face little if any resistance at the girls' dorm.

The men's dormitory was situated at the very edge of Jackson State College on one end of Lynch Street where the officers had entered the campus. By coming in quickly at that end, they had saved themselves a lot of hardship, knots and headaches. If the male students had had just a little bit of warning/notice that they were coming through, THEY WOULD HAVE DEFINITELY GOTTEN BRICKED TO THE UTMOST! There would have been no way they would have gotten off with a little verbal abuse. And they knew it!!! And perhaps that's what they, the Highway Patrol and the 'White Powers That Be', had figured on.

Armed intrusion into a college campus by the police or military was considered a slap in the face for any American college campus, (Black or White) especially in that day and time. Our campus should have been off limits to the authorities, unless there was a major crisis occurring. And, that night, there simply was not one, other than the one that they themselves were creating. The crazy truck driver had gotten what he deserved, a few broken windows and perhaps a few bruises as well. That should have been the simple end of the matter.

No, that would not be the end of the matter, because they (The Evil Powers That Be) had already decided to make their big gaping, dramatic example at the girls' dorm.

The Qs (my frat brothers and I) were standing shoulder to shoulder at the front of the crowd, directly in front of the west wing dorm when the shooting began. We could not have been more than fifteen or twenty feet from the officers, inside a small chain link fence that separated the sidewalk from the campus grounds. We were on our campus, they were the ones out on the city street intruding and forcing their way on to it, without authorization.

A last minute decision to come through the campus was made because it looked peaceful, since their cars were parked on that end of Lynch street, just off campus beyond the girl's dorm. Of course, any logical thinking person can see the holes in that lie. There was no way they could have thought, or should have thought, that they would be able to walk through a college campus, armed to the teeth in full riot gear, and not cause a response from the students as they did.

They knew exactly what they were doing and why! They knew we students would respond as we did and scream at them to leave our campus. That's what they banked on, and that is exactly what happened. This evil angle served their purpose and allowed them a flimsy excuse, but an excuse nevertheless, to cut loose on the students. Thank God, they were not standing directly in front of the girl's dorm opening when they unleashed their barrage. If they had positioned themselves in this manner, many, many more students, primarily women, would have been killed that night!!

As a result, most of the gunshots, automatic fire and shotgun blasts were centered on the west wing wall side of the building. Although over thirty years have now passed, you can still see the many bullet holes and shrapnel pock marks caused by the Highway Patrolmen's gunfire.

Another extremely damning piece of evidence that came out of the court trial in Mississippi was that no city policeman fired his weapon that night. The savage barrage was fired exclusively by the Highway patrol. This single point in itself, strongly supports the evil presence of a organized plan on the part of the Highway Patrol.

We have recently seen justice served, although severely delayed, in the case of the Birmingham murders as well as other racially motivated cases that occurred in the 50s, 60s and 70s. I truly pray to God that the rogue Highway Patrolmen, who rained absolute terror down on us that night and The Evil Powers That Be who sent them out there, killing two innocent students and wounding countless others, will be brought to justice eventually as well.

CHAPTER FORTY FIVE

MAN, JUST HOW DID WE SURVIVE THE 60s &70s?

People often ask me how the murders at Jackson State College could have occurred. I often find myself surrounded by well wishers asking me how America could have stood by and not brought the full weight of its judicial might down on the state of Mississippi for letting the 'Evil Racist Powers That Be', PULL SUCH A BOLD STUNT. It would be nice to equate being evil and racist with stupidity, but in this case it doesn't apply. The 'Evil Powers That Be' in Mississippi at that time knew exactly what they were doing. They had an air tight master plan.

They were cold and calculating, and, whether I like it or not, were right in their prediction that they could indeed get away with the murders at Jackson State College. I know it all sounds crazy, but sadly enough it's true. Not a single state official was sentenced for the murders at Jackson State. I personally believe that they were able to get away with the evil they did because of the many bad things that were going on in this country at the time. America was on the verge of ruin at this point in its history. This chaos was an excellent smoke screen for them. America simply did not have time to stop and give adequate thought to, and right the wrong done to such a few on a small southern campus. This country was more concerned with saving itself.

Add to this powerful mix the fact that the Kent State incident occurred just ten days prior to the murders at Jackson State. If America could be so engrossed in other things that it could care less over the ruthless murders of rich White kids at Kent State, it certainly was not going to stop dead in its tracks and give a hoot to protect poor Black kids in the deep South. I personally believe that this was the final deciding variable that caused the evil 'Powers That Be' in Mississippi to feel that the time was right to pull off their evil plan.

For those of you who may not be familiar with the Kent State incident, it was where four White students were shot to death during an all out demonstration opposing the war at Vietnam. Please allow me to make a very clear distinction here. There were no similarities between Kent State and Jackson State.

The Kent State shootings occurred, unfortunately, during a major demonstration. There was no demonstration at Jackson State when the shootings and outright murders occurred. Although the evil 'Powers That Be' often like to confuse this issue and try and make people think that the two events occurred for the same reason, we must not let them get away with this big lie!

The pathetic truth of the matter is that the Highway Patrol just showed up on campus on a quiet night, marched up to the girls' dormitory, and to everyone's surprise, began shooting people. They, in my opinion, were carrying out a plan that would allow them to protect and therefore maintain their racist power in Mississippi by taking a proactive attack on what they perceived to be a new, threatening power, which in this case was Jackson State. They were betting all the marbles that they would get away with it. And guess what, they were right!! THIS TIME THE BAD GUYS WON!

Please also allow me to paint a picture of the era/climate in America at that time. I think it will help to explain a little bit more how something as tragic as the murders at Jackson State could have occurred. In 1956-1970 there were three majors issues facing America. One was the war in Vietnam. Another was integration. And the third, was the threat of our outright nuclear destruction from Russia.

Across the country, hundred of colleges were experiencing massive demonstration by mostly White students against the draft and the war in Vietnam. The demonstrators wanted to know why American kids were being sent to die in a little known country called Vietnam. Many of these kids were being sent to Vietnam by way of the draft against their will I might add.

In those days, during the Vietnam war, you got a draft notice in the mail telling you to show up at one of the many Draft Inductee Stations. And guess what! After a very brief physical and a hilariously laughable IQ test, you were sent directly to the military. In many instances, you didn't get a chance to go back home and say good-bye to your family. YOU WERE QUICKLY HERDED ON TO A BUS AFTER YOUR PHYSICAL AND SENT DIRECTLY TO THE MILITARY.

The Vietnam war was not like the war we saw in Iraq or the Balkans. No, No, No, No, No! Vietnam was the real deal my friend! The North Vietnamese were not throwing their hands up and surrendering as Iraq's soldiers did. They were fighting tooth and nail and to the absolute death my friend. They were not giving in one bit and were not afraid of us at all. The Viet Cong as the North Vietnam soldiers were called, killed our guys by the thousands. American soldiers, in their defense, for all practical purposes had their hands tied. They had what were called crazy rules of engagement. Get this!! They couldn't fire their weapons unless they were fired upon. At the beginning of the war, the Viet Cong could be walking right in front of our soldiers with their guns and we couldn't do anything about it.

We supposedly went to Vietnam to help the South Vietnamese not be taken over by the communist North. So unless one of them took an action against us, it was assumed that they were friendly. As a result of this stupid approach to war, American kids were being killed by the thousands. The painful, heart breaking funerals of American kids were taking place all across America. If you were young, you probably knew someone in the war and/or someone who had been killed in it. So the question was why was, the United States, a world super power, sending its kids to a tiny Asian country to die where there was no clear national interest, purpose or a will to win it. America's leaders could have easily won that war as they did in modern day Iraq, the Balkans and Afghanistan. But our leaders at that time, not our military mind you, simply did not have the will to fight all out and do what it takes to win that war.

It was obvious to everyone who had eyes here in the states and across the world for that matter, that our kids were dying needlessly and being used as pawns inappropriately by our leaders. As a result, many of the remaining students in the state openly protested the war and simply refused to go. Violent demonstrations occurred daily throughout America on college campuses. This issue by itself, almost ripped America apart.

I have a good friend of mine by the name of Maurice Cournoyer, who is a Bronze Medal Of Honor recipient. He received his medal for bravery under fire in extreme battle circumstances in the Vietnam war. He was rewarded this prestigious medal that few men can only dream of, less on actually receive, for bravely manning a 50 caliber machine gun and wiping out an attacking Viet-Cong force that had completely over ran his base. The 2002 Mel Gibson hit movie, "We Were Soldiers" is about Maurice's old unit. I once asked my friend what was it like to take the lives of the many men he killed for the day he received his medal. He said, "Weakley, it was either them or me. They had just killed many of my friends and quite frankly, given the circumstance, it was easy." He went on to share some gut wrenching stories with me of how you can become numb and devalue life in general when you are constantly seeing death around you everyday.

My friend Maurice went on to tell me that while he was in the bush in Vietnam, he lost friends so routinely to death that he and his remaining friends became desensitized to life in general. My brother-in-law, Joseph Peychaud, has often told me similar stories about his exploits in Vietnam in Reconnaissance.

Everyday that he took point and went out to find and determine the strength of the enemy, he laughed at death as well because he knew he might not return. Most men would not have the courage to go out in the dark of night and do what he did on these death-defying missions. But Joe went bravely, many many times, because he knew his country was counting on him. And more importantly, because he knew his friends' very lives depended on it. That's why he willingly risked his life. He did not want to feel the hurt of seeing his best friends lose their. But needless to say, many of his friends were killed in spite of his heroic efforts in the dark of night, crawling through dangerous underground tunnels and the open bush in Vietnam.

My old friend Maurice once told me that the biggest hurt he felt in his life was on returning to the United States from Vietnam and having protesters in the airport get up and refuse to take a seat next to him because he was a Vietnam Veteran. This broke his heart. He hid this for years until he was able to share it with me. The hurt, he painfully told me, that he experienced that day from those thoughtless people will be forever with him to his dying day. Our soldiers who fought bravely and died for this country did not deserve this type of disrespect and mis-treatment. But nevertheless, that was the climate in America at that time. We were truly a nation divided against itself.

The second burning issue of the day, if you can even believe that the war in Vietnam wasn't enough, was segregation. By 1969 and 1970, at the time of the murders at Jackson State, this issue had basically been decided, but the EXTREME TENSION FROM THE EARLY 60s WAS STILL IN THE AIR. From 1960 to 1966, thousands of Black Americans were taking to the streets and marching across the country, protesting over the fact that they wanted to have true equal rights in America.

Blacks could not shop at, eat at, or use the bathroom in many of the stores in this country. This was especially true in the deep South. SADLY, Blacks in the South were considered far less than second class citizens. It made no sense to go and die in Vietnam, when we as Blacks were openly being mistreated in this country. So along with White kids, we not only protested the war in Vietnam along side them, we also demanded our rights. Call it a sign of the times, but these two issues fed off each other and in my opinion, thrived as a result.

For many years, Black Americans were not allowed to vote in this country. And even after this privilege was extended to Blacks, many Black Americans in the South, especially in small country towns, were openly threatened, severely beaten and killed, if they even tried to exercise this privilege.

Although the great Martin Luther King, who was alive at that time, embraced nonviolence in his marches, which meant that all of his participants were not to fight with the police or the many violent White bystanders, nonviolence was not the case where the police were concerned. Blacks were openly beaten during these marches. Billy clubs often were used as well as high powered water hoses and vicious German shepherd dogs, to break up marches and intimidate participants. This was indeed a terrible, terrible time in our country.

Now add to all of this violent, internal madness, the fact that America was also at odds with Russia. Russia was a first class super power at that time who openly preached the total destruction of America via their nuclear weapons. It was none of this stuff we see nowadays in Russia, where they are begging for loans/ handouts and whatever from the world. They were a proud, fierce, and arrogant country then that preached total world domination via any means necessary.

I vividly recall one of the leaders of Russia who was named Khrushchev taking his shoe off and wildly pounding his desk in a speech he was giving in the United Nations. As he hysterically pounded his desk like a raving madman, he screamed to the top of his lungs that the Russian people were going to completely destroy America and personally bury the dead bodies of the American people. This was a frightening scene that set the stage for the terrible relations that would fester between our two countries for years.

I recall one deadly serious standoff we had with Russia over the blockade of Cuba, that almost brought on the end of the world.

We had an eyeball to eyeball standoff with Russia because they were sending nuclear weapons to Cuba. They were boldly making these weapons operational and pointing them right down our throats, only a few miles off our coast line. Putting missiles a few miles off our coast would definitely even things up for them greatly and make the concept of mutually assured destruction possibly obsolete. This was of course good for them and terribly bad for us. Our country would have been in grave danger, if we would have allowed this. Their leader Khrushchev, would have been able to easily make his threat of totally destroying America, as he screamed he would at the UN come true. We simply could not afford to have nuclear weapons pointing at us so close to our shores. There were no ifs, ands and buts about it.

As this crisis unfolded before the world's eyes, people all around the globe were either rushing to their churches to pray and/or were looking for some type of underground shelter to hide to try and protect themselves from the nuclear fallout that was inevitable. I vividly recall my brothers and I as small kids being huddled together in our little family hallway (as if this was going to protect us) by our grandparents, because they and everyone else in the world thought that this was it! America and Russia were getting ready to destroy the world.

Man, America was dead serious! The end of the world was indeed upon us. The entire world was on the edge of its seat. You could see fear in everyone's eyes. No one knew if any of us would see the next sunset. That's just how bad it was!

Thank God, Russia blinked and gave in to us. But not until the very last second. They struck a deal and quickly agreed to move their weapons out of Cuba.

So as you can see, America at this point in time in its history, was a very scary place. It's truly amazing that the country was able to get through these chilling times. But the country survived. That alone, I think, is a testament to America's greatness.

These times were especially scary if you were a Black

American living in the deep South. It was no wonder that the evil 'Powers That Be" in Mississippi thought they could get away with what they did, given the major events that were occurring! Blacks were being lynched and killed fairly routinely during this period in Mississippi. Going a few steps further and setting their evil plan in motion by pulling off the evil murders and shootings of innocent students at Jackson State was, in their sick minds, a good calculated risk.

Of course, the rest is history. On the night of May 14, 1970, two students were brutally shot to death and many more were seriously wounded by gunfire and or flying glass. As history would sadly record, I was one of the students who was shot down that night. I stood only a few feet from one of the students who was killed. This experience changed my life forever and I am sure the lives of many, many more that night. As they say, time heals things. It did for me, but oh so painfully!

Jackson State, as well, recovered from what happened that terrible night in May 1970. It is now one of the most prominent Black Colleges in America. It is prospering and growing by leaps and bounds once again. While it is now not under the leadership of the highly thought of, legendary administrator, John A. People, who was there at the time of the shootings, it is in great hands in that the new President as of this writing, Ronald Mason, is doing incredible work there and has set Jackson State on a course that will ensure its continued dominance as an outstanding educational institution, for all races, for many years to come.

While many other predominately Black colleges throughout the nation are collapsing in on themselves from disrepair and neglect, Jackson State's campus is growing unbelievably and is truly a thing of beauty. Many new buildings and dormitories dot the campus and are constantly being built, even as we speak.

It's good to see that the terrible wrong that was done to Jackson State and the Black community in general in Mississippi on May 14th 1970, is in some ways being rectified. But for that point in time on the night of May 1970, there is no doubt that the evil 'Powers That Be' had their way with us.

CHAPTER FORTY SIX

THE AWESOME POWER OF A MOTHER'S PRAYERS

One of the most powerful forces on earth is the prayers of a God fearing mother. My mom, Lola Mae Weakley, is no exception to this rule. Her sweet, sweet prayers have protected me and my family through the years. Her tear stained, airborne prayers have brought me through a lot of troubled times in my life. I don't know what it is, but I tell you this, and I tell you sincerely, " My mom has got a direct line to God's ear." When she gets on her knees and pray, as far as I'm concerned, miracles happen!

My mom has prayed members of my family back into immediate good health from illness and is the one all of the neighbors have called on through the years when they were ill or had seemingly insurmountable problems.

While I will of course, argue you down that my mom is indeed special. The truth probably is, my mom, while as sweet as she can be and certainly special to me, is probably no different from any other God-fearing, praying mom. I'm certain that my mom would also probably be the first one to admit this as well.

I'm sure that everyone has a story or two to tell about how their mom got them or their family through some hard times. So, rather than argue with you that my mom is more special than yours, or better yet, sing out an even more childish position like "My Mom Is Better Than Your Mom.' I think it best for us all to just respectfully agree that mothers in general must truly have a soft spot in Gods heart, because he will listen to them, and answer their prayers when all seems lost and nobody else's prayers can get through.

Exodus Chapter 22 verses 22 through 24 goes a step further to say that widows and fatherless kids are especially protected by God. He warns all that if they mistreat them, his wrath will be kindled against the perpetrators. I often wonder if this was the source of my mom's success in her prayers, because we were indeed fatherless and she was a widow as a result of my father's untimely death when I was a very small child. In any case, the point I want to make is that there is no need for a mother to have to do anything other than have faith and call on the Heavenly Father's name for whatever she wants. There is no need for mothers to turn to the dark side to solutions like prostitution, stealing, selling drugs or whatever for their needs. They simply need to turn their heads upward, bend their knees and pray for what they want. God promises that he will come through for them, each and every time, when they ask in sincerity.

As you may have already guessed, my mother is a stanch believer in God and the awesome power of the gift of prayer he has so graciously given us here on earth. Although my mom is well-known for being happy to help anyone when they come to her and ask her for her prayers, one of the first questions she will ask when you come to her is, "have you prayed about your problem?" If not, she'd say "take it to the Lord in prayer and state your case. If you are true in heart, love him as you should, and be sincere, he will listen. No one is too good to get on their knees to ask God for help, the Lord will at least listen to even the worst among us. That's not to say that he will grant their prayers all the time, but he will listen.

I truly believe that God looks out especially for kids, fools and baby Christians. If you are a baby Christian, (by this I mean someone who had executed his God-given free will to accept him, but is not very knowledgeable about his/her faith and religion, regardless of what it is) that God will hear your sincere prayers and in most instances grant each and every one of them. The dilemma is that most people don't know how to pray! My mom could truly hold a clinic in this area. She, I truly believe, has got it down pat.

As baby Christians grow in their faith, and in doing so ultimately come to the shining conclusion, that whatever happens, is God's will, and everything, as bad as it may seem to us humans here on earth, will in the end be okay and therefore is all right. Then they come into the realization that everything is perfect and according to God's master plan. God does not make mistakes and believe me he is in total control of all things. And I do mean all things, which also includes Satan. Sometimes bad things are allowed to occur so that God's magnificent glory, in the long-run, can be manifested and magnified.

My mom, although she is well beyond the baby Christian stage and knows whatever happens is okay, will still bend her knees and ask God to intervene because she knows, like I know, that God is also very merciful and in some cases will change his master plan, as crazy as this sounds just for you. He loves us all just that much! He is God and he can change his mind, if he wants to. This was soundly demonstrated in the Bible in Exodus Chapter 32, verses 9 thru 14.

This is where Moses was on the mountaintop receiving the ten commandments from God and the children of Israel were disrespecting God by turning to idols. After all he had done for them in freeing them from Egypt, they still chose idols over him this particular time. God, as a result, became very angry and had made a clear decision to destroy the children of Israel who he had led out of bondage, but Moses was able to plead with him and convince him to turn from his anger. As a result of Moses' pleading, God changed his mind. So, while God's master plan (or destiny as we humans often perceive it) is constantly running its course, we as humans via God's mercy and grace can plead our case and can sometimes change things. God will listen to the pure in heart and/or the righteous or a sincere plea, even from a repentant sinner. He is just that merciful and good. Although the fact that God will also be merciful and answer the prayers of a truly repentant sinner, has often puzzled many who feel that his grace and mercy should only be for the longtime faithful Christian, I think beyond him just being bountifully merciful, that the answer lies somewhere in the bible parable, 'the first may be made last and the last may be made first.'

Instead of humbling ourselves to God and coming to him in prayer to have him help us, I have often heard people talk about being lucky and/or making wishes for their needs. I have come to believe that both (making wishes and hoping for luck or incorrectly justifying God's gifts and blessings to you as luck or good fortune) are a perpetuation of Satan's trick to try and steal the Heavenly Father's glory. While it is tough, a lot of times, for even me to remember this and not use these terms because of my longtime habit, I believe that God's people should be constantly trying to rid themselves of these terms and talking in terms of BEING BLESSED instead of saying they are lucky. Or, saying that they are going to pray for what they want and ask God to give it to them, rather than wish for what they want and possibly be granted it by Satan. We (God-fearing people) should all strive to purge the use of the word luck, or being lucky and the word wish from our vocabulary. I believe that God, not Satan, would be well pleased with his people doing so. By using these terms, we unknowingly work for Satan, rather than the Heavenly Father.

When it comes to my mom obtaining God's blessings, my experience was once your sincere prayers were in the air for yourself, and hers kicked in with yours, good things were sure to happen. God rescued me, forgave me my sins and let me come back to him. I am living proof that if he will allow me to return to his grace, there is hope for every sinner who has fallen, regardless of how low he thinks he may be.

Another truly great thing about God's grace is that he will help you without anyone else being involved, especially if you are sincere and go to him in prayer. You really don't need my mom or anyone else to pray for you. When Jesus Christ died for us on the cross, he fixed it all. He paid the supreme price with his blood.

We can each go directly through him to the Heavenly Father, without anyone else's intervention. The key to remember is that the prayers of the righteous will achieve much. This is a very important point. But, even though you can pray for yourself and have all of your prayers answered, it's always nice to have as many good prayers in the air with yours' as possible. That's one reason that I am always calling home to mom and aunt Dollie, and anyone else I can think of, asking to please include me in their prayers.

The important thing to remember is that the awesome power of prayer that God has given us is a wonderful gift that enables us to instantly connect with him. And guess what! He is never too busy to stop and listen to us. He eagerly wants us to use the awesome power of prayer as often as we want to.

I know for a fact that my mom's prayers work quickly. If it weren't for her prayers and God's bountiful mercy, I would not be here. I would have been killed at Jackson State or died as a small child of my mysterious illness.

I always like to jokingly say that my mom is a card carrying member of the Amen club. She will not let an opportunity pass to testify and let you know just how good God has been to her and her family. While it may seem like I am having fun at my mom's expense, that's truly not the case at all. I, for one, am extremely proud of her for who she is and what she has done for our family. Oh and by the way, I am sure a lot of other people feel the same way about her.

As I was finishing up this book, my mom was honored at her church, Farish Street Baptist church in Jackson Mississippi, as the Woman Of The Year in 2001. She, single handily raised three boys and one girl in the worst of ghetto situations.

I really have to give it to my mom, she is quite a lady. My mom's unshakable belief in the power of prayer, and God protected us time and time again from Satan and the many challenges he threw at our family.

With God on our side, we should never FEAR EVIL, because he is in control of all things.

CHAPTER FORTY SEVEN

SPEAK TO ME LORD, SPEAK TO ME!

My mother once told me a story of how she was able to finally get through to me, after we had a long period of problems. It was right before I moved out of our family home after I entered Jackson State College. I had been out all night on one of my many partying sprees. This period was right after I had gotten shot at Jackson State during my wild partying days before I re-found Christ. On that particular night, my mom said she laid in bed awake; she was unable to go to sleep worrying about me. She knew I had changed drastically after the Jackson State murders and was carrying a gun. She had also heard stories of some of the wild parties that I had been involved in out on Lynch Street from some of my old high school classmates, who I had stopped hanging with.

My mom's efforts to talk to me about my new wild lifestyle had failed over and over again. She said I either would refuse to talk to her about it, would get up and walk out of the room. Or, I would just plain outtalk her, or would cite the fact that I was now grown and/or give a hundred other crazy
explanations as to why she shouldn't worry about me. My mom, while she was a tough disciplinarian when we were small kids, was the type of person who believed in reasoning with us as we

grew toward the end of our teenage years. She would provide you with the information to make a good decision and after being armed with this information, she'd let you learn from your mistake.

This parenting style allowed you to take her advice or leave it. My mother never rammed her decisions down our throats when she thought we were old enough and intelligent enough to make the right choice. This sounded good, and had worked pretty well up to now for my older brothers, but I guess in my case, being the hardheaded person that I was at that time in my life, this technique just wasn't working for my mom when it came to me.

One particular night, my mom decided it was time to take our serious communication problem to the Lord. It was about 2:00 in the morning. Mom said that she slowly eased herself off the side of her bed and got on her knees. She prayed and asked the Lord to show her what to say or do to get through to me. If nothing else, after praying about the situation, she found herself able to go right to sleep. This was a relief in itself, since she had been having many sleepless nights worrying about me while I was running the streets all night!

At about 4:30 AM, she said the Lord awakened her and put this weird thought into her head. The thought came to her in the form of a voice. The voice in her head was rather loud, but was clear as a bell. It said, "Lola, get up and fix Vernon some home made biscuits, he'll be coming in, in just a few minutes." While my mom was certainly an excellent cook and fixing biscuits from scratch was not unheard of for her since my grandmother used to get up and fix them for her and our family all the time, it would be unusual for her (my mom) to make them in the early morning hours. She would normally make homemade biscuits and hoe cakes for us in the evening, and not in the morning. But in any case, she thought out loud, "Who am I to argue with, or doubt the Lord?" She got right on up and did what the Lord asked her to do. After she thought about it, she could see the wisdom in the Lord's plan, because I loved her biscuits with a passion. Now why she hadn't thought of it herself before, she didn't know! The Lord had once again come to her rescue and told her what to do as he had on many occasions before.

My mom said, there she was, sweating over a hot stove, still half asleep, but with a big smile on her face. She was covered with flour and busy making the biscuits that the Lord had told her to get up and make. Sure enough, a few minutes later, here I come in the front door of our house. It was obvious, she said, that I had had a hard night by the way I was dragging in. As I slowly walked past the kitchen door, she sang out, "Oh Vernon, I'm fixing some homemade biscuits for you." Before she could completely get the words out of her mouth good, I tersely responded back, "Homemade biscuits," Mom, you never make biscuits in the morning. She said, I then hollered back down the hallway as I walked away from the kitchen area entryway, "I'm really beat mom! I'm going right to bed!!" Upon hearing this, she said tears started to form a little bit in her eyes.

She thought to herself, that maybe she had just dreamed that the Lord had spoken to her. Or, even worse, maybe she was in fact losing her mind, as I had insinuated by the tone of my voice. But lo and behold, in the next few seconds, she said I surprised her by quickly barging into the kitchen and planting a big kiss on her cheek. I told her I was going to go wash up and I would be back in a few minutes. She knew with this positive response that something was indeed happening because we hadn't been getting along lately, and a big kiss from me during this time was a welcomed surprise.

My Mom said, I quickly returned back to the kitchen and sat my behind down hard in the chair next to the kitchen counter like I had a load of bricks in my pocket. I sat down and without saying a word started eating her biscuits with syrup. During the time I was eating, she said I never said a word. I just kept eating and staring at her with a big smile on my face.

Mom said that she felt that this had to be her opening. She started to explain to me how worried and nervous she would get when I stayed out all night. She also went on to explain how she could not sleep when I was out like that. She said the whole time she was talking, I never said a word. This in itself was a miracle, she said, because usually at the very mention of her talking about my wild lifestyle, I would cut her off and/or begin to mentally try to outmaneuver her, or just plain outtalk her. In any case, our past discussions on this subject would always hit a brick wall.

Our normal verbal exchanges during this crazy period in my life usually consisted of both of us talking to each other at the same time, with neither one of us really listening to the other. But on this special occasion, according to her, everything was different! She said, I listened to her the whole time, while continuing to eat of course. And once I finished eating, I just sat with my hands clasped together in my lap and let her finish talking.

When she finished, she said I leaned over the edge of the kitchen counter and kissed her again on the cheek and said, "Mom, I apologize for hurting you and making you worry. I promise I'll do better." With that, she said I got up and went to bed without saying another word! According to my mom, I did do better and didn't worry her like that again. That was the turning point in our soured relationship. The Lord had given her the answer and the help she prayed for and needed to get through to me.

And even today as a grown man, I find myself frequently driving down the lonely highway on a grueling seven to eight hour drive, desperately trying to get back home to Mississippi so that I can get my mom's famous breakfast and counseling sessions. Until she told me this story, right before I started writing this book, I had never been able to figure out why I have consistently been compelled to get home to the same situation and same spot at the old kitchen counter top to listen and soak up my mom's wisdom.

I've never told my mom this, but I've always have had a burning need from the day of our little talk that morning to get back to that same very spot, get up early and listen to her talk. It's rare even to this day that I will sit at our family table and eat. I usually give my seat up to someone else and sit at the kitchen counter. I guess when the Lord puts some glue in your seat and answers a desperate mother's prayer, it stays with you for a long time.

I know what I'm about to say is going to sound absolutely off the chart, but I really believe that if the leaders of the world would take a few minutes out of their schedule to come to Jackson, Mississippi, let my mom say a prayer for them before they get there, eat one of her famous breakfasts and just listen to her wisdom at the spot at the kitchen counter, that they would walk away with the answers to the world's problems.

Over the years my mom has really helped a lot of people, including my family, friends and neighbors with their problems at that very spot in her kitchen. She is something else. But, I have to warn you. You may not hear what you want to hear, but she will tell you straight and tell you what's right according to how Jesus would do it, if he was in your shoes. And perhaps, that is the answer to any problem. Just put Jesus in your shoes, and after you pray for God's guidance, do whatever you think he would do. There is no way you can go wrong with Jesus calling the shots.

CHAPTER FORTY EIGHT

THE LITTLE MIRACLE

My father died when my brothers, sister and I were very young. This in itself could have easily spelled doom for our family. Even though my mother worked long hours in her hot sewing room, she made time to ensure we all got the love and tender care we desperately needed. I recall on a car trip back to Jackson from Houston how my mom shared with me a story of how she had come upon my grandfather in our house looking really sad and depressed in the early fifties. This was highly unusual for Jeff Stevens. He was a proud man who had come through many a bad time in Mississippi.

My grandfather had just lost his job and was deeply troubled as to how he was going to feed his family, which at that time included my grandmother, my mom and my two other brothers and myself. To add to this dilemma, my grandfather was also really sick at the time, according to my mom, and this was the reason he had lost his job. My grandfather was just too sick to go to work.

In those days, employers weren't very understanding or bound by many of the employment laws we have today. They could and would fire you at the drop of a hat for any reason, including just not being at work one day even though you were seriously ill. As a result of this tough policy, my grandfather's employer let him go. My grandfather felt he had let his family down. Just to show you how much pride my grandfather had, he had decided not to share what was going on with anyone. He chose to suffer in silence, hoping that he could find a solution to his problem.

After seeing him looking down and out of character, my mom said she kept insisting and insisting that he confide in her. She was finally able to get my grandfather to tell her what was wrong. Although he was deeply humiliated by his inability to come through for his family, he finally, and painfully I might add, shared what was going on with my mother. She quickly told him not to worry anymore about a thing. She went on to say, "Daddy, you have taken care of us all our lives. It's time for you to rest. I'll find a way to take care of the family in this hour of need." She said she tried to sound as upbeat as possible, because she didn't want granddaddy to have a clue that she didn't have an idea as to how she was going to feed our family. She felt she was successful in making my grandfather feel better because the worry in his face seemed to ease a bit.

She was happy that she could lighten his burden somewhat. Perhaps, my grandfather felt better because his big secret was now out in the open. Who knows!! He walked away looking better and that was all that mattered to her. My Mom was relieved that she was able to ease his pain.

My mother said that as my grandfather disappeared down the hallway, the weight of the world seemed to settle down on her shoulders. All of a sudden, she felt tired and very old. She thought to herself, "Lola, get up and go to the kitchen and see how bad the situation is." After arriving there, she opened the refrigerator and found that there was nothing more than a piece of fatback in it and some water. My mother, who was a good seamstress and had made a pretty good living up until this point in that line of work, was also just recuperating herself from a serious illness that involved a lengthy stay in the hospital.

After taking another long, hard look in the refrigerator, my mom said she went back to her sewing machine and put her head down. Realizing that she didn't have any sewing work to be done that would bring in any money for the next week or so, she began to cry. The tears flowed down her face like rain. She didn't have a clue as to what we were going to do to survive. At that moment, she began to pray and ask the Lord to save our family. She sat at her sewing machine with her head down praying for hours, she said. As she finished, she slowly raised her head and found herself compelled to get up to look out of her sewing room window. She said she couldn't see whatever it was she was supposed to see from her window, so she got up and went to the door. In her mind, she said, something kept saying, " Lola don't you see it?" She said to herself, "see what? Something said, "take a closer look and see the little miracle coming to your door."

She walked out the front door and onto her porch and kept straining her eyes to see whatever it was she was supposed to see. Then all of a sudden, she could see this figure walking briskly towards our house from the direction of Farish Street. The sun was shining directly behind it, still making it very difficult to make out what it was.

At that point, all she could tell was that it was a person, walking like he/she was in an extreme hurry. She didn't know who it was, but as the person got closer and closer, she could tell it was a very old woman dressed rather oddly for a very hot summer's day! My mother said, "The old lady was just too dressed up!!!" She appeared to have her best Sunday-go-to meeting clothes and shoes on, and, she was really gutting it out with every step she made, huffing and puffing coming toward our house. Mom still did not recognize the person walking towards her.

As the figure got near our porch, she realized that it was a lady who looked familiar. She also realized that the lady had paper money extended in her hand. My mom said their eyes were focused on each other in amazement. Thinking that just maybe her mind was playing tricks on her and the lady was going to walk on by our house, my mom said she almost collapsed when the ladies foot turned toward our steps. My mom said the mysterious lady never broke her stride.

She kept making her way up our porch steps, and walked right up to my mom and said. "Aren't you Lola Weakley? My mom, who was almost frightened to death at this point, slowly said, " yes." The lady said, "Well then, this is for you!!!" My Mom said she just stood there looking dumbfounded, trying to figure out who this person was and what was going on. Up until this point, with the exception of asking if she was Lola Mae Weakley, the lady hadn't said another word. Then my mom realized it was a lady she had known many, many years earlier, whom she hadn't seen in years. Quite frankly, she thought the lady, who was a rather old lady when she knew her even then, was dead.

The lady, after hesitating for a few more nerve-racking seconds said, "something kept whispering to me to get up, go to 131 W. Oakley Street and give Lola Mae Weakley this money. I guess I must owe it to you or your family for something ya'll did for me once." My mom tried to hand the lady the money back. She told her, "ma'am, ah, I don't think you owe me anything." The lady said, "No ma'am, I'm right. When my angels come to me and tell me to do something, and they don't come to me very often, they are never wrong.

Oh, it's your money alright! Now why it's yours, that's between you and the Lord. The lady was dripping wet with her sweat from her walk. She went on to say she stayed way across the other side of town. According to the lady, she had no earthly idea where 131 W. Oakley Street was, but God had done a good job as he always had of guiding her feet there. Although she did not know where she was going when she headed out, God had brought her right to our front door.

The lady had walked the entire way fully dressed like she was going to church. My mom, as the lady was walking off the porch asked her, "why are you so dressed up?" The lady said, that she didn't know what it was she was going to face when she got where God was sending her, so she wanted to make certain she made a good impression when she got there.

It was obvious that the old lady was hot and sweaty. She was wringing wet from head to toe. My mom, still completely flabbergasted by what was happening, started to ask the lady to come in so she could rest herself, but before she could get a word out of her mouth, the lady walked off the porch and marched away as mysteriously as she had come. My mom said she couldn't say a word. She went back to her sewing machine, put her head down and thanked the Lord for saving her family.

The lady had handed her two one dollar bills. Don't laugh! In those days, we're talking about 1953, two dollars was a lot of money. A smart person who knew what to get, could feed a family for a month with that kind of money in those days! We are talking 5 cents for a bag of pinto beans, ten cents for a ten pound sack of potatoes and sugar, and the list goes on. My mother told me she took off walking for the grocery store and got enough food to see us through.

To this day my mom said she has not seen that lady ever again. Although my mom was already a firm believer in the Lord making a way when there seemed like there was not one, this incident just solidified her faith that much more!! God is good all the time. And all the time, God is good. He is indeed an on time God, yes he is!

CHAPTER FORTY NINE

THE SHIRT OFF YOUR BACK

"Coming through each and every time without fail or an excuse for a true friend or loved one, when the chips are down."

When I recall my life, I have to think of it in phases. By this I mean that I have had several true to the bone friends that came into my life and seemed to exist for a brief period. Seemingly, so that my life could go on to the next level or take another predestined educational twist on life's mysterious journey. It's as if God was saying to me, "Vernon, I need to tear you away from this crutch, (the person who was with me providing me much needed strength) so that you can be made stronger when you meet him/her again in your life.

In this world I have four true friends. One of these four friends of mine is Ruby Patrick. She is a long time friend of over thirty years. She is incredibly beautiful and has a heart of gold. We met at Jackson State College in 1968 as freshmen. We both just took a liking to each other and from there decided we would be lifelong friends. Strange but true. Generally when people see us together they think we are, or were lovers at one time. This couldn't be farther from the truth. It never happened and will never happen because we are true friends who consider each other brother and sister. To this day, I consider Ruby and her dear sweet mother to be like family to me.

Another one of my famous friends is Rosalind Magee Peychaud, or Roz, as everyone loves to call her. She is the super cool, caring and protective play big sister that every guy should have in his life as well. She has also given me invaluable insight about life, among many other things over the years, that has saved my skin many a day. I can go to Roz with any female problem and she is able to help me analyze it from a woman's prospective and put me on the right track. A lot of people in this world, especially men, cannot understand this type of special relationship. But I tell you this, you had better RUN AND GO find you one, because it's a great one to have. Roz will also not hesitate to blast me when I am in the wrong, and more importantly, tell me precisely what I need to do to come out on top in the game of love and life. Having this incredibly valuable insight on women is like being a mind reader, or an invisible fly on the wall in the hands of a wise man! Need I say more!

Roz also has this remarkable positive insight on life that is always right on point. To show you just how tight we are, she insisted that I be the one to give her away in her wedding in Negril Jamaica. We have had a special relationship over the years that endures to this very day.

It not unusual for Roz to call me, even till this day, at 1:00 am in the morning just to have a word with me, if something was bothering her or if she just felt the need to give me a much needed counseling session. Her husband Joe, who I consider my brother-in-law and who I am very tight with, will often comment that us two, (Roz and I) have got to be the craziest guys on the planet. My big sister Roz is something else. Everywhere she goes people take a liking to her and roll out the red carpet for her because of her extraordinary class, positive attitude, charm and unique people skills. Roz has got it going on!!

People often ask me what is it that would cause a man or woman for that matter, to willingly give his or her life for another. I say it's a mysterious bond that forms out of the love that they have for each other, whether stated or unstated. This bond can be forged as a result of similar life experiences, family ties, or it can be born out of pain and suffering that can derive from crisis in any area. My eternal bond with all of my friends sprang, I believe, from my fraternity connections. Ruby and I got super tight as friends when we both pledged Omega and Delta Sigma Theta at the same time at Jackson State.

Roz and I met in 1969 because she was also a Delta, a member of our sister sorority, who was married at the time to Bill Overton. Bill was one of my Omega big brothers. This means that he was already a Q when I was trying to get in the fraternity. I looked up to Bill, admired him and for years tried to be like him. There was no greater example of a true Omega man than he. I got to know Roz initially through him, because she would feel sorry for us little pledgees and constantly look out for us.

Bill, who is a great guy now and a born again Christian, but in that day in time he was a holy terror as far as us Lamps/pledgees were concerned. He was a first class body builder at that time who could knock you flat out with just one glancing punch. He was a good-looking, light skinned guy who had muscles on top of muscles. I recall one time in the hole, that's where the Qs (the men of Omega Psi Phi) held their meetings, when Bill slapped me so hard that wax flew out of my ear from the opposite side of my head, went clear across the room and hit another one of my line brothers smack in the face.

The force of just the wax flying out of my ear nearly knocked my line brother down. Of course, you know Bill knocked me out with the punch. All of the other lamps/pledgees on line with me thought that he had killed me. They were sure it was my blood and/or my brains that he had sent flying across the room. You know, the funny thing about it all was, Bill really liked me. He thought he was going easy on me.

When Roz heard what had happened, she told Bill and everyone else in the frat that she would look out for me from that day forward. Guess what, she has lived up to her promise. She has been my protective big sister for over thirty years. I visit her and her new husband Joe quite often in New Orleans, even to this very day. The friendship we have is truly a thing of beauty.

When in New Orleans, it's an unwritten rule that I must stay at my big sister, Roz's house. I recall once when some of my old high school classmates threw a party for New Years at their place in New Orleans. I called myself going to sneak in town, stay at Studaway's, the class president's house with his family, go to the party, which was at Matlock's, (one of my old girl friend's house,) and the next day go and spend the rest of the week-end at Roz's crib. After feeling guilty and giving in and calling Roz to let her know I was in town, I was faced with a crazy predicament. The next thing I know Roz is banging on Studaway's door. She calls me outside to say, "Hey little brother, my feelings are deeply hurt because you broke our family rule." I guess you know that I had to pack up my stuff and move to her house.

I consider myself truly blessed to have my big sister Roz in my life. She was running for State Representative of District 91 in New Orleans. I'm not able at this writing to say if Roz won or not, because it was a few days before the final run off in May 2002. Whether she win or lose is up to a much higher power than me. All I can say is, she will have my prayers and support and I also know that if she don't win, it will be a shame and that district would have lost a powerful and courageous champion that could have helped to uplift their neighborhood from the seat of power in that state. I venture to say that ole Roz (WIN OR LOSE) will continue to do what she has done for many years, which is go to bat for and help many, many poor families improve their lot throughout that city. I'll also add that the Lord works in mysterious ways. I'm betting that Roz will win straight away and she will be blessed, regardless of the outcome.

Then there is Joe (Bocula) Neely. Man this guy has saved my butt from absolute certain death a time or two. He has been my friend through thick and thin regardless of the consequences. I don't care how tough the going got, I knew without a shadow of a doubt that my running buddy Bocula had my back.

People don't know how blessed they are, if they have a great friend to rely on and be there for them during the tough times as I have with my boy Bocula. I have been blessed with many great friends in my life, but Bocula is the one who sticks out in my mind when I am down and feeling low. I always seem to find myself missing his hearty laughter and the hilarious madness we always seemed to get ourselves in and out of in our wild days.

Regardless of the degree of trouble I had managed to get us into, Bocula would always be right there by my side, ready to give his life with guns blazing, if necessary, in order to keep me and him from harm. And for the record, I have and would do the same for him, without the slightest hesitation.

Now, I first met Joe Big Dick Bocula Neely as a pledgee on the Omega Psi Phi line that went over the fall after I went over at Jackson State in 1970. He was tall, dark and as crazy as they come. Although I was his big brother and I gave him absolute hell just like the rest of the pledgees, there was something about old Joe I liked. He had a job during the time when he was on line as well as taking a full slate of courses. You would think that these two incredible challenges alone would be enough to overpower a person, but in addition to this, Joe was adamant about making the frat. There was no stopping him. I think his unbelievable desire to be an Omega man is what drew me to him. Plus, he could also take a beating.

In the 60s, 70s and previous, a person trying to get into a fraternity knew beyond a shadow of a doubt that they were going to be brutalized. That was just the nature of the beast back then. In those days, fraternities were the real deal. The big brothers in my day and time would beat the living daylights out of you the entire time you were on line. But, once you successfully went over, by this I mean crossed over the Burning Sands of Omega, it was as if none of it had ever happened.

I personally recall when I was pledging, we as pledgees would be huddled in a corner desperately trying to hold on to each other to keep the big brothers from tearing one of us away from the pack so they could beat him. As odd as this may sound, that was exactly what the big brothers wanted to see. Their goal was to cause us to form an unbreakable bond between each other and a desire to sacrifice yourself if need be to keep a fellow line brother from suffering.

You get to learn a lot about yourself and your line brothers during a pledge period in the 70s. The line between courage, cowardice, fear, bravery, the desire to not quit, and the need to show and demonstrate brotherhood would often smear into each other. It didn't matter how big or how tough a Lamp/pledgee was, or thought he was, at some point in time, his line brothers saw him cry and be broken down. There were no secrets when you were on line in the old days. Pledgees knew each other's pain, fear and at some point had tasted each other's warm teardrops.

Although they did not know it at the time, the willingness to sacrifice ones' self for a brother and feel each other's pain was what we big brothers were hoping to see. In our minds, these sessions created and amplified brotherhood and brought out a basic desire for even the weakest pledgee, to become stronger by willingly putting his body, already racked with pain, on the line for another line brother. I am happy to say that Bocula and his line brothers passed the test with flying colors.

Although, we really dug into old Joe because he was the biggest guy on their line, wasn't the greatest stepper, and was constantly coming into meetings late because of his job, old Bocula hung in there anyway. His love for the frat as well as my line brother, Lee Bernard and many of the other guys on his line like Sylvester (Sam Huff) Thompson, James Prater and Charles Boozell Barnes, have stood the test of time.

I personally believe that the way they were made caused this undying dedication to the frat to occur. Although, the modern day frat does not condone hazing in any form or fashion, I personally would like to see it establish a much longer intake period that has many nonviolent challenges in addition to their regular historical requirements, for the pledgees that could take the form of community service work like painting the homes of the elderly and needy, being the fraternity's out front people for worthy community charity events, providing group mentoring for wayward kids etc. A waiver would be necessary of course, from each potential pledgee, before they got on line. The gain that the individual would get after going over, would be with him for many years and ultimately would be well worth the ordeal. If female recruits in the military can legally endure physical and mental challenges, then we should be as well. That's where perseverance comes in. Plus, Omega is not for everyone. Those unwilling to sign a waiver, should be asked to seek out another fraternity to join. For the record, this is my own personal view, not the view of my fraternity.

I truly believe that the bond that would form over time via the challenges that they face together, would cause them to get to know each other better as brothers and in doing so create that long lasting bond that will span the test of time. In my mind, it was the many challenges that we had to overcome or fail at as line brothers that caused us to get tight, get to know every detail about each other's personality and life and/or weed out the people who lacked the will to show perseverance through tough times.

At the time of this book writing, my Omega line brother Lee Bernard is the District Representative for the 2nd District that covers New Jersey and New York. This is a very high and prestigious achievement for an Omega man. I am truly proud of Lee.

Another brother from my old Jackson State chapter (Upsilon Epsilon Chapter of Jackson State University) who also sprang from the Thirteen Sex Machines Omega line by the name of Kenny Hamilton was once the Basilus (head man) of one of the largest chapters in America, the Atlanta chapter We are all equally as proud of him as well Johnnie Muckie Harris, and Larry Burks who are also currently very high ranking national office holders in Omega Psi Phi Fraternity. We all still get together regularly and live out the true intent and creed of our fraternity.

Old Bocula is now a born again Christian as I am myself and is a devoted deacon in a church in Marietta Georgia. Man, God is good. If he will forgive us for our sins, because we had truly fallen low, there is hope for everyone. All that is needed is that one be sincere and ask God to come into your heart and ask for forgiveness of your sins. He can change your life for the better. Bocula and I are living witnesses.

And last but not least, there is Lee Arthur Bernard who I briefly mentioned earlier. Lee is a very old and dear friend who I have shared many a laugh and tear. While I knew Lee in High school, we did not truly get tight as friends until we found ourselves catching pure D hell together on an Omega Pledge line. I kid you not, I have shared every real secret I have ever had in my life with Lee.

Lee Bernard and I go way back. When I say way back, I mean way back. We have been friends for over thirty years. We graduated from high school together and are old college fraternity brothers who religiously get together for Jackson State's Homecoming and other down-home events.

Lee has seen me through two marriages and the resulting emotional pain and devastating financial aftermath that is inevitable in a messy and hurtful divorce. Suffice it to say, he knows me better than anyone. Although I've done some crazy things to strain our relationship over the years, he has always been there for me when I needed him, in spite of it all. That's what true friendship and brotherhood is all about. YOU HAVE GOT TO BE WILLING TO PUT IT ON THE LINE AND COME THROUGH EACH AND EVERY TIME FOR A FRIEND, WITHOUT FAIL OR AN EXCUSE WHEN THE CHIPS ARE DOWN.

I have truly been lucky to have friends like Lee and Bocula over the years. What also goes along with these life experiences are their knowledge of my wild past life, wild women, and hard core night life, and of course, my knowledge of theirs'. We all were two nasty Q dogs that went over together in the old days, when men were men! That should be enough said!

These four eternal friends, Ruby Roz, Joe and Lee have stood the test of time, in spite of the many forks in the road that we have encountered. I wish that everyone out there reading this book would be blessed enough in their lives to experience true friendship as I have. Friendship is indeed essential to the soul.

CHAPTER FIFTY

THE MUSIC BUSINESS

In the seventies, I became a very successful record producer with records and works known nationally. I had records out on myself as well as several other artists on my own independent record label. I also placed two of my groups with major, internationally known recording companies. This was no easy task. Breaking into the music business from Mississippi was unheard of at the time. If you wanted to make it big in the young folks R&B world, you almost always had to go to a mega center like Los Angeles or New York to get a break.

The only real exception to this rule in those days, was Motown, which was in Detroit and Stax Records which was in Memphis Tennessee. Stax and Motown were for all practical purposes, a closed society. By this I meant that they generally signed contracts with their local talent first before looking at other areas. Another fact that prevented Mississippi from being taken seriously as far as the music industry was concerned was the fact it was still considered a joke across the nation by most standards in the area of economics and race relations.

No one up until this point in time would take anything coming out of Mississippi seriously. Therefore, if you were in Mississippi and sent or took your completed product to any of the major radio stations across the nation for air play. You generally got laughed out of the building before anyone even listened to your product/music. That was just how much disrespect was shown to our state. If you made it big nationally, and you were from Mississippi, you made it because you gutted it out, had to leave it all behind and go out of state, you endured many an insult about being from Mississippi, got ripped off big time in some form or fashion where your contract was concerned and basically crawled on your hands and knees to get even a bad deal with one of the majors. My entry into the music business broke the mold on that historical pattern.

My record company was called Omega Records Inc. To give you an idea of the extent of my music career and label, one of my artists, Michele from London, England, was a joint venture with the great Mohammed Ali. I have also had songs used in major movies and by many well-known famous artists whose music topped the charts across America and internationally.

Mohammed Ali worked in conjunction with my record company to produce an album on Michele. He used his considerable clout to get Michele on a David Frost television special from a Riverboat to introduce him to the world in New Orleans. As a result of this venture, I got to personally meet and hang out with the Heavy Weight Champion of the world and his staff in his glory days. I had an independent record label, several Publishing companies and several other acts that I placed on other major record labels as well during this period in my life.

The first self contained group I signed to my label was called Magni-funk. We were able to get a hit on them called "Do A Little Love." They were a fun group of young teenagers composed of teenage guys and girls. I will never forget the look of excitement on their very young, clean-cut faces when they came running into my recording studio screaming that they had just heard their song on the radio. Boy what youthful energy and enthusiasm!

Magni-funk members were Dale Morris, Reginald High, Wayne Clark, Danny Jelly Roll Mosley, Kim Love, and Varetta Shankles, who while she was in the group, won the national Ms. Black

America Contest. They were a great group of kids with a lot of raw musical potential. Their song, "Do a Little Love" was a major regional hit that established the credentials for my little independent record company. "Do a little Love" and Magni-funk made the big boys in New York sit up and listen to what was happening in Mississippi.

Another one of my acts/groups was called Freedom. While you may not recognize their name offhand, if you were to hear their song on the radio "Get Up and Dance," you probably would say, "Oh Yeah, I know that song." Or what I commonly hear is, "Man, that was the jam back in the day." "Get Up and Dance" was produced by myself and Jesse Thompson Jr. and is owned and published by one of my publishing companies. To give an idea of its lasting popularity, I still receive royalties from it today, even though it came out over twenty-five years ago. It is and has been a very popular cult song for young people regardless of the generation they grew up in for over twenty years. Even till this very day, "Get Up And Dance" by Freedom or Grand Master Flash and the Furious Five, who was one of the many groups who used it over the years, is still often played on the radio and in nightclubs across the world today.

"Get up And Dance" has been used by many major Rappers over the years and has been used in soundtracks in major movies like" New Jack City" and "Above the Rim," which starred the late super star icon, Tupac and the still live and kicking mega star Wesley Snipes. My Publishing Company may have also been one of the first to successfully take legal action back in the seventies against Rap groups who made money by illegally putting their voices on top of our songs and putting them back out on the market.

Occasionally, now as an older man, if I am with some youngsters when "Get Up and Dance" comes on over the radio, I tell them that's one of my songs they are listening to. I usually hear, "Yeah right," in disbelief! Most of them know the song but don't know the song's origin. But that's okay! I just kind of grin and bob my head along with them to the music and try to pick my voice out of the party track in its background. I don't know why, but even the young people of today still love that song. God is good and he definitely works in mysterious ways. When he gives you a blessing, you'd better believe, it last for a long time. I am a living witness to that fact! "Get Up And Dance" is still played routinely in nightclubs all across America and many places internationally. I guess it's hard for young people to equate an old guy like myself with something that teenagers are into! Any how, that's life! No big deal.

Another one of my groups that did well when I was in the music business was a group called "Sho Nuff." This group is dear to my heart because it was the very first group I signed to a major record company. In those days, I either placed groups on my own independent label and released their songs or I shopped their product to a major record company. Placing an act with a major was good business sense, especially with the interest we were getting from the majors. It resulted in the majors taking all of the financial risks, doing the national marketing and legwork. It meant an instant national audience as well, and amplified our chances of success overall.

Lyn Sky Chambers, Lawrence Hot Dog Lewis, Bruce Teddy Bear Means, Freddie Young, Al Bell and James Lewis were the names of the members of Sho Nuff. They were cool, young, street wise, guys straight out of the ghettos of Jackson, with a lot of musical talent. Seconds after they finished their audition the first day I met them, I announced to all in the room, "This group has got "It!" The best way to describe this intangible that I call 'It" is a combination of burning desire, the looks, out of the box thinking, incredible creativity, uniqueness, talent, tireless youthful energy, the ability to learn quickly and a undeniable relentless hunger to do whatever it takes to succeed in the music industry.

Sho Nuff was a mixture of hard core funk and rock with a heavy emphasis on funk. Sky was the leader of their group. He was tall, articulate and very intelligent. While everyone else was kind of wild and out there, Sky was the guy who always kept them grounded in reason. He was the guy I could always go to when the group and I were having a failure to communicate.

After a lot of hard work and sacrifice, Stax agreed to sign

Sho Nuff to a lucrative contract with their renowned company. This deal enabled me to go out and buy a brand new Corvette to sport around the city in. I am not ashamed to say that this was a great time in my life. I was on top of the world!

Although I had done the right thing up until this point and continued to work at the post office while my own record company was getting up on its feet and going on to finally do well, I made a decision to quit my job there and dedicate myself full time to music as a result of the Stax contract. All my friends at the post office gave me a major send-off! I guess they were glad to see someone walk away from that place with his head up and dignity intact! The fact that I had built my music business on the money I had made and saved from the post office also was a source of delight for my buddies there. They called it poetic justice. I called it using the system to get me where I wanted to go!

As a result of the frat and my old reputation as the king of the night life in Mississippi, I enjoyed celebrity status to the max in my hometown of Jackson! My new deal with Stax Records just took my reputation and ego with it, even higher. The day I gave my resignation and two weeks notice to the post office was an incredible high for me. It represented a triumph for me that in my mind at the time validated the fact that my wild, live life at the edge, lifestyle had indeed paid off.

All of the success above in the mainstream of the music business, came about as a result of a tragedy. In the late sixties and early seventies, I had a lot of success playing saxophone in local bands. I also played my saxophone well enough to get a full scholarship to Jackson State. But, getting into the mainstream of the music business would require more than limited success on the chittling circuit. Breaking into the majors would be a different ball of wax entirely.

For years I played saxophone behind some big time local entertainers. But to be honest with ya, the sax man or the rhythm section is always labeled as secondary and is kind of behind the scene. The guy/girl or singing group actually out front on the main microphone is the real star attraction. Up until this point I was content with my behind the scene role, but around 1976, I decided to go for the glory. I decided to be a singer. Of course, any good music person worth his salt, regardless of what instrument he plays can carry a tune reasonably well. But to actually get out front and sing professionally, well that's taking it to another level entirely. When I told the guys in the band that I wanted to sing, or even tried to give advice to the singer, they would all say, "Naw, naw, Vernon, saxophone is your thing. Stick with what you're good at Vernon!"

At that time I worked at the post office. It was a good paying job that kept me pretty well financed. So without anyone's knowledge at first, I secretly began to work on my singing, and recorded two songs at a small local recording studio. These songs were released on 45 RPM on my spanking brand new independent record label called Omega Records. The two songs I recorded, get this now, were called "Tania, The Queen of the SLA" (A side) and "Is It Love or Lust" (B side). Now when you finish picking yourself off of the floor laughing, I will continue the story.

I don't have to tell ya that the A side didn't get very much play on the radio stations. But the B side oddly enough did get a little. Some of the smaller stations in Mississippi picked it up and played it occasionally. So now the cat was out of the bag. I had guys I had known for years teasing me about the deep voice that I used in singing "Is It Love or Lust."

The recording studio that I paid to cut the record for me was not very good. In essence they just kind of took my money and let me go for it. Even though my little 45 was not very good, I for one was pleased with it because it meant a new starting point for me. I was now known as a singer, a not so good singer, but hey a singer nonetheless. I carried my little 45 with me wherever I went and tried to get people to listen to it and critique it for me. Boy, did I get some negative feedback! Thank God that he gave me the strength to handle it all, because I was now the biggest joke in the city in my old music circles, as far as my little record was concerned.

The one thing these guys didn't catch out of this whole thing while they were bursting their guts laughing, was that I now at least

had a record out. They didn't! While they were great on stage in the many little nightclubs they played at, they had never ever even thought about putting a record out themselves. Most would say that they just didn't have time to stop and put this type of long and exhaustive project together. Plus, it also would mean that they would have to take a break from their little money
making gigs they were so used to. In any case, they were not smart enough to realize that I was now one up on them in that I had a record out on the radio and I now kind of had an idea what recording was all about.

The recording process that I experienced, even though it was on a minor level, really piqued my curiosity. I made a decision to get away from my old bands and the nightly nickel and dime gigs that I had been involved in for years, and concentrate on learning more about the recording industry. As a result, I began to take some of the money I was throwing away partying and the money I made at the post office and funnel it into my recording career.

Another gigantic positive decision I made was to do a lot of reading about the recording industry. While it was not spelled out clearly right there in print, I was able to gather that establishing a music Publishing Company was oh so critical to the overall success of a serious recording person. Because, the publisher is the entity or person that actually owns the song. That's where the control, real power and the money making potential is. Many major artists back in the old days were not wise enough to get in on this extremely important area. As a result, while they may have had big names known nationally as a result of their records, they made mere pennies off the records that were actually sold. Additionally, they had no say-so in the control of the record and the many valuable songs they often wrote, because they simply did not own them once they legally signed them over to the publisher. These were very powerful factors that worked against many of the greats of that era and caused them to be dead broke today.

To provide just a little more insight into this critical issue, all publishing companies are registered through the major international music monitoring organizations such as BMI and ASCAP. These powerful companies have the very important responsibility of closely monitoring your song, collecting from the person who used it, and making certain you get paid a percentage each time that song is used in any manner, or even played on the radio. Armed with this valuable information, I immediately established my Publishing Company. It took twenty-five dollars in those days to do it!! It doesn't cost that much more than that to do it, even today! This, along with making a decision to learn more about the music publishing business and switching from playing in night clubs to the recording industry, proved to be a very wise career changing decision for me.

Just prior to making the decision to ease back on my partying, I was a high roller. Baby, you'd better believe, Vernon Steve Weakley partied with the best of them. My partying took me to some rather classy, at that time, expensive apartments called Camelot. I had a lot of White friends who I partied with as well as my old crew.

During this time I also became better acquainted with the now deceased famous hall of fame, super star NFL running back, Walter Payton, Robert (Dr. Doom) Brazile, Ricky Young, Joe the Bowling Ball Lowery and many other famous football payers. I knew Walter and Robert from my old Jackson State days while in college. I was able to form pretty close friendships with them while they were living at Camelot. Walter had unsuccessfully tried to pledge my fraternity in college, so I knew him pretty well. I got to know him even more so in the relaxed Camelot setting. He and all the other JSU football greats would bring their buddies from the NFL back with them each summer during the off season. They worked out daily with the JSU football teams to stay in shape.

One night, I was sitting out at a pool party with a White buddy of mine by the name of David Nance. He introduced me to a good friend of his that used to be in the music business. His name was Mike Daniels. He had been a very successful recording engineer with Stax records. For those of you who are not familiar with the recording industry, the recording studio engineer is probably the most important person in the recording business, next to the artist himself, because he handles the mixing board and virtually all of the recording equipment. Simply stated, he turns all the knobs and knows the electronic ins and outs.

There are many so-called superstars out there that owe their all to the recording engineer. That's why a lot of times when you hear a hit song on the radio and it sounds great, but then you go to the artist's concert and the guy sounds terrible. That's what I am talking about. The engineer made it happen. Believe me, there is a lot of this going on in the music industry, even to this day. The engineer can make or break you. He can bend notes to put them in tune, splice together segments of songs to make them work, change the speed of the song to make people appear to be singing in tune etc. There is a whole world of behind the scenes magic a good Engineer can work to make the performer out front singing come off like hot stuff, that is, if the engineer wants to. Mike Daniel was that kind of engineer. He was incredibly gifted, patient, personable and knew all there was to know about engineering. And to cap it all off, he was a workaholic. If you had Mike Daniels in your corner, believe me, half of the battle was already won!

CHAPTER FIFTY ONE

THE PROFESSIONAL

Mike Daniels had worked with the greats liked Isaac Hayes and many of the big name stars with Stax. I told him that I also had a record out. At first he didn't really seem interested. After asking him three or four times, and I guess sounding desperate that night, he finally agreed to listen to my little record. Man, you should have seen me taking off to go and get my 45, once he said yes. Seeing me take off running to go and get my record, he would tell me years later, was the biggest flattery he cherished the most in his life. If it wasn't for the fact that it was a swimming party and I had appropriately came in my swimming trunks (I lived in the apartment in front of the pool) I probably would have already had my little record with me. Remember, I told you earlier, that I carried it practically everywhere I went. I guess I could have stuffed it in my trunks huh, But naw, it wouldn't have looked right! Of course I kid. Now back to the story.

Mike, while he was complimentary of my musical skills, was very critical on the engineering work on my record. He thought I was robbed plain and simple. Although, I tried to continue our discussion about music so that I could pick his brain, Mike kind of blew me off and acted like I was bothering him. So after a while, I gave it a rest and went on to enjoy the party like everyone else. Mike had brought his small daughter to the party that night. She couldn't have been no more than two years old at the time. Up until that time she had been sleeping in one of the back rooms in David's apartment.

Mike, as well as everyone else was drinking pretty heavily. Unbeknown to us all, his little daughter had awakened, put her little floaters on her arms, and somehow walked out past us and dived in the pool. No one was in the pool. The floaters she had, apparently came off her arms. At that point, neither I nor anyone else at the party had any idea what was going on. The painful ironic reality of it all was that while we all were dancing and having a great time, Mike's little beautiful daughter was drowning in the pool. I had not met her and so I had no idea that a child was even at the party. I don't know what it was that made me get up to walk over to the pool, but I was glad I did.

At first, I couldn't believe what I was seeing in the well lit pool. It looked like a small doll peacefully lying on the bottom. I thought to myself, "this can't be right because there haven't been any kids in that pool." Plus, I had been swimming in that very spot earlier and had not seen a doll before. Then all of a sudden, I saw bubbles start to flow from whatever it was mouth. Its eyes were wide open. Then, it seemed to slowly wave one of its little arms at me. My worst fears hit me like a ton of bricks. I realized it was a small child!

I immediately screamed "There's a child drowning in the pool." I immediately dove in. Apparently, no one believed me at first. In fact some of the people started to laugh. I guess they thought I was either joking with them or drunk. In any case, there I was, not too good a swimmer myself, struggling in the pool trying to save the child. After a few seconds of seeing me thrashing frantically in the pool trying to save the little girl, who was in the center of the deepest part of the pool, David Nance stop laughing, got up from his seat, walked over near the edge and said, very loudly "Swalos (which was my nickname) don't joke like that. Something must be going on!!"

Once he reached the edge and saw that I was coming up out of the water with a child in my hands, he began to scream, " Someone call an ambulance?" As soon as Mike saw his daughter's little angelic face in my arms, he went crazy, screaming and hollering.

He was completely out of his mind with fear. He was shaking so badly that he couldn't even hold his daughter in his arms. I took her back from him and laid her on her side on the ground. Water came out of her like you wouldn't believe. Someone ran to get a doctor who lived in the complex. He was there in seconds. He gave her CPR and saved her. Thank God, I had gotten to her in time. Man what a scary sight! Mike was completely devastated over what happened as well as everyone that was at the party. Mike was also very hard on himself. Even after everything calmed down somewhat, Mike was still trembling unbelievably with fear; he was a nervous wreck.

A few days later, Mike tracked me down and personally thanked me. In my mind it was just what anyone would have done. But to Mike, it represented a lot more. He pulled me to the side, put his hands on my shoulder and said, "Man, I did not treat you right at the party because you are Black. And that's not right! I know it sounds bad, but it is true! I just want you to know, I'm truly sorry! I know a way that maybe I can repay you, if you will please let me. The next time you go back into the studio, I will do your engineering work for free. Believe me, it will be a world of difference in your music and my name recognition may even help you get through some doors and get it played." I knew the value of a great engineer. So, you'd better believe I quickly said yes to Mike's offer.

Mike also went on to tell me that day that he had recently given up his recording career with Stax. He had moved to Jackson from Memphis to give up the music industry entirely. He said that he had lost his wife and kids via divorce because of his obsession with music and all the time it required. He continued by saying that he really had no intention of getting back involved with music ever again. His daughter, who had almost drowned, was on visitation with him for the week-end. Mike viewed what had happened as a sign from God.

Mike, as he promised he would, engineered the session for my next song, which was called "Let Me Be Your Secret Lover." Along with the invaluable help of a super radio DJ by the name of Big John Williams, my song was a smash hit. Big John worked at

WJMI across the street from my recording studio on Lynch street. He was, without a doubt at that time, the most popular DJ in the city.

"Let Me Be Your Secret Lover," was a very slow, old fashioned, romantic, true tug at your heartstrings, boy and girl love song. It required a lot of skill, passion and emotion to pull it off in the final mix. While Mike was a great engineer who knew how to position the microphones and instruments and knew all sorts of other electronic techniques and tricks to get the best possible sound on tape, he admitted he did not have the soul to do the final mix down for "Secret Lover." For that reason, I brought in Big John Williams to help me.

Big John knew all there was to know about Black music. He knew what each superstar artist had used to make his/her song a hit and how to go about duplicating it. I can just see him now standing over the recording studio's mixing board. He would have his eyes closed and be slowly dancing and moving his hands in big circles while he snapped his fingers to the beat, when he participated in mixing the songs. While Big John had to be one of the coolest guys on earth, he was a big giant Teddy Bear looking guy. I'm not saying he was ugly, I'm just saying he was a big guy. While we all teased Big John about his funny looking style (dancing while he mixed his song), it worked, plain and simple!! Although he had never done it before, the mixes he worked on were head and shoulders above anything else that came out of the studio. Big John's mixes had a magic about them that would draw you into the music and captivate you. There was no denying it.

I would be mixing the levels and adjusting the various controls and Big John, well let's just say, would be dancing all over the studio mixing board. He would be adjusting knobs that he had no idea of what they did. His unorthodox antics drove Mike crazy. Eventually, Mike gave us a listing of the general settings to remain within for a song and would leave when the final mix downs occurred. He would be jokingly half screaming, "I can't take it anymore!! I, I, I, just can't take it anymore! I spent years in college learning about electronics and you guys come in, close your eyes, do the funky chicken around the mixing board and pull off a hit.

Damn!!" Of course he was joking! Mike had a great sense of humor!! Once Mike left the building though, the real show began. Talking about the Funky chicken, shoot, we also threw in the kitchen sink and grand moms chicken feet as well. Big John and I would go to work operating on the soul of the music like two mad brain surgeons.

Big John generally focused on the voices and the instruments. He would be slowly phasing them in or out, or up and down volume wise. Sometimes he would slowly change the direction in which a voice was coming from. This was called panning in those days. Generally, you decided what direction instruments and voices etc., would be coming from at the beginning of a mix/song, and from there you left them alone. That was a standard mixing practice at that time in the recording industry. Mike preached it religiously. But Big John and I were about creating something new. We would slowly change the flow and direction of the voices, back and forth, while the mix was actually occurring. Sounds crazy, but the final product was nothing short of phenomenal. Whenever we brought people in to listen to our mixes, they were totally captivated and would be trying to figure out what it was that made them like the song so.

Big John, would be saying Stuff like, " Man, you have got to break away from the norm BABY." "Find and then lock in on that sexy groove and make mad, passionate love to it and from there, just let your inner feelings and emotions run free! That's the secret White Boy," he would boldly say as he looked over at Mike!! Who would be shaking his head no in total amazement and anguish. Then ole Big John would cap off one of his funny comments to Mike by saying something like, "Mike, I'm going to make a soul brother out of you if it kills me. And it may very well kill me, because you are a hopeless, lost cause." Of course, being the funny guy that Mike was, he would quickly throw back one of his funny, good-natured barbs at Big John as well. It was all good natured fun!! Whether it was standard industry practice or not, it was obvious to us all that Big John Williams was on to something!

Big John brought in another super DJ by the name of Danny

Gilmore after "Secret Lover." He also brought a lot to the table on many of our future projects as well.

"Let me be Your Secret Lover," got unbelievable air play in Mississippi and various other states across the South. It sold a lot of copies and established me as well as my company in the music main stream. Having a hit called for me to get out on the road and support it in order to take it to the highest level possible. That's a tried and true formula in the music business that never fails. Once you get decent air play, the artist must get out and push his song up the chart even farther with his or her presence on the chittling circuit.

I have to admit that being on the road was a lot of fun for a while. But, you know what, somewhere out on the road in a little town called Port Arthur, Texas, I lost my desire to be a singer. I will never forget that day. It was on a cold Thanksgiving holiday. I, along with the recording group Freedom and Junior Walker and the All Stars, which was a well established nationally known group at that time, was sitting in this restaurant. Junior Walker was the headliner for the show that night.

Normally, I spent Thanksgiving with my family. I was married at the time and my daughter Shinika was about three years old. Our Thanksgivings, as it had been the long standing tradition in my family, were spent with my mom, aunts, brother, sisters, in-laws and a cast of many other people who normally visited our house on this special day. Thanksgiving was, and still is, a big deal with my family. We all gather at Aunt Dollie's house and just have a stomp down good time! We look forward to it each year. So, as you might imagine, not being there with my family for the first time had me feeling really down.

I recall looking out the window just staring out into nowhere, while everyone else ate. The famous saxophonist and singer Junior Walker, who is now deceased, sneaked up on my blind sign and tapped me on the shoulder. He said, "Vernon what's wrong?" Before I could get a word out he continued, "I don't think I have ever seen a rising star with a big hit out looking so sad before." Boy was I feeling down! I kind of held my head down. Junior Walker slowly commented, "Oh, now I see what's wrong. It happened to me my first few times out on the road during the holidays as well."

Junior Walker continued by saying, "Being in the music business, while it looks great on the surface to the world, is not an easy life son. It's hell on your family and on people physically! Being out here on the road during the holidays can really break your spirit. The funny thing is, is that while we are putting on a show for the audiences with big broad smiles on our faces during the holidays, the people looking up at us just don't know that sometimes our hearts are breaking. If you are going to stay in this business, you will want to get used to what you are feeling right now and being away from your loved ones, because this is what show business is all about." This is it and it doesn't get any better than this I'm afraid.

I didn't say a word while he spoke. I just sat leaning into the window with my hand under my chin. After he finished I showed him a picture of my wife Cookie and my beautiful little daughter Shinika. We laughed and had dinner together and made the best of a very bad restaurant cooked meal!

Immediately after dinner I got up and called my family. As it is customary in my family when someone is missing from a celebration, the phone is passed around and everyone gets to say a few comforting words to the person to let him or her know they were indeed missed. In a small way, this approach eases the pain somewhat. It makes the person feel like he or she, although absent, are still a part of the family celebration. That talk with Junior Walker made up my mind for me. Junior Walker was truly a great man, not only from a music standpoint, but as a human being as well.

CHAPTER FIFTY TWO

THE RISING STAR

Generally, when an artist has a hit record out, going on the road is imperative. The appearances amplifies record sales and provides a lot of immediate income for the artist from his live performances. This on the road income is the big payday for most artists because royalties from records sales are made only twice a year and they are for a very small percentage of the total take of the record. My record "Let Me Be Your Secret Lover," eventually burned out because I did not get out and pump it up on the road like I should. I made a conscious decision to give up my dream as a singer to be the record producer behind the scenes, rather than be the guy out front!! I simply could not stand being way from my little girl and family during the holidays. The cost of being an on the road, all the time recording star was too high a price to pay for me!!

The studio where Mike recorded my song was so impressed with him that they gave him a job being their head engineer. The company that owned the studio at that time was headed by the Frascogna brothers. Most of them were very successful music lawyers. Their company was called North American Recording

Corporation. Rather than compete with the majors and put records out themselves, their corporate strategy was to groom and manage acts that they discovered and developed to sign with the major records companies. Up until this point, they had not placed R&B artists with a major label or had any major hits come out of their studio. They had all of the top notch equipment, but it just wasn't working for them until they brought Mike Daniels on board.

Shortly after hiring Mike as an engineer, they promoted him to studio manager and gave him a position with the corporation as the head of their music division. Of course, you know that he insisted that I join him at North American Recording Corporation.

The only stipulation I offered was that I be able to still run my own little independent company, Omega Records, as well. They quickly agreed and literally gave me the run of their fine studio on Lynch to boot as a bonus for coming to them. Although North American Recording Corporation had been pretty White oriented, until Mike brought me in as Black Music Director. I had only been in this position a month or so and "Bam" it happened. Lightning struck! Sho Nuff, my first group was a smash hit! I recorded them along with Mike and we were able to quickly sign them with Stax records for a very large, long-term deal.

This was a great period on the recording scene in Jackson. It was as if Black and White record companies had now come together as one to take on the entire international music scene. Everyone was making money and everyone was very happy. We were all one big happy family. I was called by magazines and newspapers all over America and asked to do interviews. People wanted to know what was the incredible music magic that was exploding in Mississippi. We began to make a major mark on the national as well as international music scene.

The Frascogna boys were ecstatic. They had been trying for success for years without getting an act on a major label. And here we were, coming in and hitting home runs the first time at bat. Unbelievable!! Our success legitimized their company and gave it the credentials necessary to move into the mainstream of the national music industry. Mike's talents, name and the big name people he knew also helped North American Recording Company to take wings and fly.

One very instrumental figure who also helped Mike and me get our first record deal was a guy by the name of Peter Fontenberry. He was a very successful manager in the music business in the sixties. As I understand it, he had managed Paul Revere and the Raiders, his father owned some of the first stock in one of the major Hotel chains and he was very close with Elvis Presley. Peter was out of Memphis and had known Mike back in his hay days at Stax. Peter and David Porter, the then new president of Stax, were friends and were on a first name basis.

Peter was a super cool, hey just because I am filthy rich don't mean I can't get down with you po folk, middle-aged White guy. He was the height of class. He looked filthy rich, his mannerisms screamed, I am of royal blood, but he never looked down on or judged anyone. He always had great advice to offer, if a person wanted it!! He had this charm about him that everyone liked. He not only fit in anywhere, but within a few minutes of arriving, Peter would be the center of attention. People, both Black and White, would flock to him all the time. I always teased Peter and told him he had a giant magnet in his pocket, because of the crowd he always seemed to draw to him.

All of these variables combined with raw talent, hard work and excellent producing skills translated into a big time record contract with Stax.

Shortly after Sho Nuff was signed to their deal, another college group called Freedom came on the scene in my studio. Unlike Sho Nuff, who were pretty earthy guys, the youngsters in Freedom were a clean-cut, well mannered bunch. Where we would constantly be trying to pull the members of Sho Nuff out of nightclubs and/or get on them for smoking a joint or two at the wrong time, Freedom was just the opposite. They were truly church going boys and were always doing the right thing.

Another big difference between Freedom and Sho Nuff was that Sho Nuff's talents were more natural. By this, I mean that with the exception of their band leader, they were self taught musicians.

They played music basically by ear. Freedom was very different in that like me, they had taken music lessons all their lives and in many instances were on music scholarships at Jackson State, or were in the Jackson State College band. So, they knew their stuff backward and forwards. They were managed by one of my frats. His name was Jesse Thompson, Jr. He was also a superstar in music in his day as well. He had been one of the singers in the famous group called the Composers.

Jesse (Doc) Thompson formed a group called the Composers that performed in and around Jackson State College. James 'Wild Man' Staples, BB, Willie Ray 'Swamp Dog' Norwood (Brandy, the famous singer's father) and Doc Thompson were the lead singers of the group. I played saxophone and Howard (Dolemite) Levite played drums. Along with a kick ass rhythm section, (AC, Johnny Cool and Trinidad) we routinely turned nightclubs out.

BB and I had a pretty short run with the group. We came to grips with the fact that we really didn't have the time needed to give to it. Given the choice between a wild, anything goes party with a half dozen beautiful girls or a hot, steamy, five hours of rehearsal with a bunch of hard legs, you had better believe old BB, Dolemite and I chose the party every time. Ole Doc, Staples and Norwood though, went on to make quite a name for themselves with the Composers.

Doc's group, Freedom, had the music theory down as well as the natural feel. He was a great coach and mentor for them as well. The members of Freedom, Ray, Tyrone, Adolph , Robert Black, Mason, Thigpen, and Addison, really gave new meaning to the words self-contained. They could do it all, which included practically producing themselves. Although these guys on paper seemed to have it all, I secretly wondered though when I first met them if they really had what it would take to make it in the business. This doubt did not spring from their abilities. It was that Freedom, if anything was just too clean-cut looking. For whatever reason, people, (the buying public) , when it comes to music, seem to want to gravitate to or support the more earthy, radical looking types, rather than the mama's boy looking guys. Now go figure!

Although it took a little longer than Sho Nuff, Freedom was able to get a major record deal as well. I do remember a couple of embarrassing moments in trying to place them though. Once we received a call from Motown Records or let's just say someone representing himself to be with Motown. He told us that Motown was interested in signing Freedom to a major recording contract. He asked that we set up a showcase, which meant in those days getting a nightclub and let them come down and check the act out while Freedom performed. Of course, after checking out the call we put together an elaborate showing for Freedom. Everything was perfect.

Freedom rocked the house like you would not believe. Man they were absolutely incredible. The crowd was dancing in the aisles, overflowing the dance floor and danced in their seats the entire concert. Another call to Motown confirmed that the person was on his way, but the plane was running late due to a storm.

At the beginning of the concert, we had announced that Motown would be in the house checking out Freedom. That announcement sent the crowd through the roof. Their support for Freedom was nothing short of amazing. Guess what though! The guy never showed!!

I recall calling back to my studio and asking Peter Fontenberry, the big name music personality who had helped us get our deal, who just happened to be in town, to come down along with some of the other executives over at North American Recording Corporation. I called in my markers and asked that they come over and sit at the guest of honor table, so as to shield the group from the blunt of the embarrassment. Of course, being the great guy that he was, Peter went and put on his best suit and tie and came down to help the guys out! He looked like a million bucks. Some of the Frascogna boys did the same thing. They were all good people. Their appearance helped to cover up what had happened. The so-called record executive not showing up that night really hurt! But the guys in Freedom kept their chins up and tried to not let it bother them. They worked that much harder. And while Sho Nuff had records that hit the charts and practically lived in Japan because their music was so popular over there. It was freedom whose music has stood the test of time. "Get Up and Dance" has made a lot of money over the years and is still very popular even today.

Mike and I won Producers of the Year that year and jetsetted back and forth to Memphis where Stax was located, and across America supporting our acts. People jokingly called us "Salt and Pepper." I guess I don't have to tell you who was Salt and who was Pepper. Mike and I had gotten pretty tight with each other. Stax was so pleased with the situation that they sent many of their regular acts down to us in Jackson Mississippi, if you can believe it, to record for them. It was much cheaper than flying them to New York or LA.

As Stax producers, we often had to go to Memphis to do recording sessions there for them on the spur of the moment. I recall this funny time once, when we were on a very tight schedule to get an album out. The president of Stax Records who at that time was David "Can't See You When I Want To" Porter, called and said.
"Hey Salt and Pepper, I need you in Memphis at six am tomorrow to do the mix down on some of the songs on Sho Nuff's new album. David, as you may have already gathered by the song title I put in between his name, was also a pretty good singer himself in his day, before he took over the reins of the resurgent Stax Records.

The mastering company that Stax used in those days was located in New York. They had a small window of opportunity to get our product out. If it was to be done, we had to be there. It was our contractual obligation. As fate would have it though, a full blown winter's blizzard started shortly after we received David Porter's phone call. Normally, we would just pick up the phone, call the airline and say, "This is Vernon Weakley and Mike Daniels with Stax Records," and our free tickets would be waiting for us at the airport when we got there because of Stax's open account with them. But because of the blizzard, all the planes were grounded. I had just bought a brand new PEARL WHITE Corvette Stingray. Mike called and said, "Hey Swalos, we're going to have to put that new car of yours on the road to get to Memphis. My car is in the shop and hey its already eleven p.m. now.

It's going to be tight, given this storm situation to get there by the session, even in your car." It was also too late to rent a car as well. Everything was closed in Jackson. I was still a little fussy over using my new car. Oh, you know how it is when you buy a new car. I recall saying, "Mike, man I am not taking my new car out into that blizzard!" Mike laughed and said, "I know how you feel my brother. I will take any suggestion you got, but based on what I can see, that's just the way it is." He followed up by saying, "Don't even sweat it Swalos. I promise you I will have Stax buy you two more just like it if you mess it up." I quickly snapped back with, "Yeah right! And how are they going to replace us when we kill our fool selves out on the highway." Mike laughed and said, "You worry too much my brother."

There we were, the only crazy people out in the blizzard, zooming down the highway. I was raising hell the whole way. Mike just sat there calmly laughing at me. He was making comments like, "Damn, my grand mammy drives faster than you. Stop babying this so-called high powered performance car. I thought these Corvettes could haul ass." While he kidded me, I could tell he was just as scared as I was. The highway was slippery as ice. We were both scared to death. Snow and ice covered the road. We could barely see how to drive. My extreme caution probably saved our lives.

I remember once, a highway patrolman who we passed parked at a restaurant, getting behind us and pulling us over and saying, without getting out of his car, on his car speaker system , "Where in the hell are you two fools going in this weather." The patrolmen then got out of his car and came over to us. As he leaned over to see a Black guy and a White guy in a spanking brand new Corvette, he sarcastically said, "I've checked the wire and there has been no bank robbery committed, no presidential assassination that has happened, no White women been raped or no nuclear war going on. SO WHY IN THE HELL ARE YOU TWO ASS HOLES SPEEDING UP AND DOWN MY HIGHWAY?"

Of course, the highway patrolman was being funny. In that day in time, it was nothing for the highway patrol to pull people out of their cars and beat them unmercifully. Plus, in my mind, they probably had pulled my tag information and knew exactly who I was as a result of the shootings at Jackson State. I was almost ready to use the bathroom in my pants. That's just how scared I was!! I figured this guy would see this as an early Christmas present, take us deep in the woods and blow our brains out. Mike jokingly said as the patrolmen walked up to the car, "Swalos, these guys hate hippies like me and Black people. Besides that flaw, hey, they are good people." Then he breaks into one of those little grins of his! Then Mike said "Just be cool man and let me handle this shit." Mike was much older than me. I'd say he was in his middle thirties at the time. I was about twenty-six.

Mike quickly told the patrolman who we were and where we were going. The patrolman said, " hum, big time record producers huh! You fools are going to die tonight, if you keep trying to make it down the highway to Memphis. I suggest you do what I am about to do and sit the Blizzard out at the restaurant. Mike said, "thanks for the tip officer, but I think we'll make it." Mike wasn't scared at all, Mike could charm the skin off of an anorexic snake. As the patrolmen began to walk away, he slowly stopped, and then came back to the window, he then looked in at Mike with a stern face and said, "You! You get out of the car now, and come with me." I quickly thought to myself, "Oh shit, this is it!!"

Mike got out the car as the officer instructed and walked back to his patrol car. They talked quietly for a few seconds. Although I stretched my ears to the limit, I could not hear what they were saying. The next thing I know he and the highway patrolman were both moving side to side dancing and humming a tune. I'm thinking, "what the hell is going on back there?" Mike then walked back up, reached into my back seat, hands the officer one of the records I had and said, while laughing, Now there goes a happy man! Ah the little pleasures of life. It's really great to have loyal fans!" The patrolman then walked off and drove away. Before I could get a word out to ask, 'What?" Mike says, " You see there Swalos, (Swalos is my nickname) all White people aren't bad. Plus, it didn't hurt when I told him that you were Isaac Hayes' cousin and we were going to Stax to remix your new hit single." I quickly responded. "hit single?" Mike said, "Yeah! I hope he likes Tania Queen of the SLA." And with that we both almost tore up my car laughing. Tania was the first song I ever recorded. It had to be the worse song ever recorded in music history.

As we continued to drive down the icy road to Memphis that night, Mike told me what being in the music industry was all about.

He said, "Hey brother Swalos, remember the night we first met and you were struggling and all excited about the possibility of making it in the music business?" Not knowing where Mike was going with all of this, I slowly gave out a long "yeah." He then said, "Well guess what, we have fast forwarded one year my brother. And look at yourself. You're at the verge of making it very big in the music industry. You've got successful records out there on yourself as well as with others with your own company. And if that's not enough, you've got two major contracts on two acts who right now, as we speak, have records climbing the chart nationally. You've got plenty of money in the bank as a result!"

Mike continued by saying, "Now here we are driving down the highway in a brand new Corvette. Your brand new Corvette, to boot! If it wasn't for the storm we would have been riding first class on a major airline. SO THIS IS IT!! MY BROTHER, YOU GOT YOUR WISH!! Sure this could be happening in LA or New York. But the fact that it's happening in Mississippi, where there has never been this type of recording success before, makes it just that much more incredible. Hit record producers jump start their careers in LA and New York all that time. But in Mississippi, man come on! You have got to know that God is behind all of this! Hey, we've got the Lord on our side my brother! It doesn't get any better than this! You asked for it! And the Lord has blessed you with it!" In a laughing high pitched voice, Mike then said, "So stop your complaining."

About this time the city lights of Memphis were starting to peek through the darkness!! Mike continued, "Now as far as our having to make this dangerous trip. There was never a doubt in my mind that we wouldn't make it!! I quickly jumped in and said, "yeah right, you looked pretty scared to me when that highway patrolman pulled us over!" Mike jumped back into the conversation before I could get another word out. He held his right hand up as if to testify in court and said, "No, No, No, my brother I am serious! I will admit now that I was scared at first when the highway patrol pulled us over. But it all went away when I looked over and saw you sitting over there saying a prayer.

After all you went through over at Jackson State, I could see why you'd be scared. But you know something, I knew that when you started to pray, we would be okay!!! Do you think the Lord was going to bless you like he has (giving you all the success that he has blessed you with in the music industry and letting you survive out there at Jackson State) for it to all end out here on this lonely highway. I don't think so! The Lord is too good to work like that!" With that comment, I agreed with Mike and continued to put the pedal to the metal to get us through the last few miles to Memphis. We made it! And, we made the session on time.

CHAPTER FIFTY THREE

THE K. K. K.

If you arrived on earth from another planet and asked the first person you encountered, "what comes to mind when you hear the word Mississippi?" They would automatically think of the Ku Klux Klan, extreme poverty and ignorance. They probably would go on to say its citizens, both Black and White, suffer from a strange disease called racism. Although this disease is not uncommon to the rest of America, it takes on a uniquely different twist, smell and texture when it oozes from Mississippi's earth.

To illustrate, as small children in Mississippi in the fifties and sixties it was not unusual for Black and White kids to play innocently together like little angels. Brothers and sisters if you will, who couldn't be closer even if they sprang from the same mother's womb. The amazing thing is that Mississippi's children during this era, both Black and White in the fifties, sixties and prior, played lovingly together with the full knowledge and consent of their parents. This was especially true in many of Mississippi's small country towns. It was as if people had chosen to be impervious to an evil so strong and powerful that it could totally consume its so-called church going, God-fearing White citizens. Even to the point that they could stand by, watch, condone, and even participate in public lynchings and murders against the very kids, or parents of the kids they lovingly played with as children.

Rumor has it, that it was not uncommon in many of the Klan strongholds for Mississippi Klansmen to come home from a lynching, sit down with their family, bow their heads to say grace and then in graphic detail laughingly recount to their wives and small kids that they had just castrated and lynched the father or relative of their own child's playmate. This is so sad, but even sadder is the fact that this type of thing occurred in many small towns, not only in Mississippi, but in the deep South in the fifties, sixties and prior.

The end result of this madness in Mississippi's case, in the fifties and sixties, was a state mired in ignorance and poverty, lost in time, with bloody hands and no desire to better itself or its struggling population. This beautiful state along with its loving and outwardly friendly and hospitable majority, as a result of a pitiful few, was adrift in a sea of darkness and severely crippled by its racist White leadership in their quest to gain wealth and retain its self-proclaimed superiority. In many ways, Mississippi's obsession with racism and White power kept Whites down, lower than the very Blacks they intended to suppress.

To truly keep a man down and ensure his permanent plight, you must stay down with him! So ironic are these words that ring so loud and true; they reverberate and echo so clearly throughout Mississippi's blood-stained history. It is no wonder that Mississippi, along with several other southern states, during the fifties and sixties were the butt end of every state joke, and was nationally known for its sickening racism, poverty and ignorance.

Consider for a minute or two the new types of prejudices the Ku Klux Klan and other hard-core racist organizations would have to create when the aliens get here from another planet, just to keep their place in the food chain. I can just hear them now saying, " Golly Bubba, we ain't figured out how to get a handle on the Niggers yet, so how are we going to lynch these funny looking critters. They ain't even got no necks." Of course, I jest with my facetious comments but I truly have to wonder what it is the Klan think they are going to find in heaven. Of course, I am stretching it here by a mile or two because we all know that none of them will ever make it there. But just take this giant leap with me and pretend, that maybe one did make it to the front door and was able to peek in as they were slamming the Pearly Gates in his face and see what was in there.

Do they think that White people will be the only ones there? It's absolutely mind boggling to me that a lot of their rhetoric has a basis in Christianity. A lot of their ceremonies also contain references to the Bible. You've got to wonder why can't these guys figure it out!!! Don't they know that they're working for the Satan and not the Heavenly Father. How dare they think that the Heavenly Father could condone and agree with their evil behavior.

At one point in my life I used to feel sorry for the Klan. I recall once telling some of my friends, "Well they're just ignorant, misguided people who don't have sense enough to know better." I'd also find myself saying they "they are just poor, ignorant fools and lost souls who are being used for someone's else's profit and evil purposes, Ignore them, avoid them and eventually they will die out and fade away!"

As a teenager and young adult working up close and personal with some guys who were rumored to be Klan members at the post office, I found their real problem was that they simply didn't know anything about Black people in general, other than the foolishness they have been fed by their handlers. Most of them I would come to find out had never really given themselves a chance to get to know anything about other races.

At the post office where I worked years ago in Mississippi, I would always find myself getting into face to face arguments with these guys. Even though, I knew they were not worth of the effort, or time, I would be right up in their face, blasting them intellectually and making them look stupid. The bad thing though, is by getting down on their level, it also made me look to be as bigger fool as they were. Rather than employ the old tactic, 'Let them rage on, so that all will know them as mad.' I unfortunately gave them a public forum and perhaps some degree of creditability by wasting my breath even talking with them. In any case, these two different methods would now come to the fore in my life. All of this came about as a result of a rather odd decision I made while working at the post office.

For some crazy reason or another, I decided in about 1978 to volunteer, along with another Black guy by the name of Stringfellow, to be the first Black people on a tour that heretofore had been occupied exclusively by Whites. It was rumored to be a strong hold for hard-core racists and Klan members at the post office.

Although, many of my friends warned me and pleaded with me not to go to this tour because of the possible danger it presented, I went anyway. In my mind, we were the problem. Fear was our worst enemy. It worked in the racist's favor on this tour because they had already won the battle of the minds. They didn't have to openly object or protest Blacks coming to the tour to work with them, because they knew we were afraid to come.

Sad but true, all they had to do was posture a little bit, throw out a few evil stares, talk a little off the record racist trash and we cowered in fear. I had been with the post office roughly seven years at that time. Up until this point I had never given any thought to trying to get on this tour. I guess I was kind of happy where I was at the main downtown post office. A lot of my college friends were on the tour I was on as well. When the announcement came out for the job, I almost let it go past. It wasn't until I heard two older and more senior White workers laughing about how Blacks in years past had been afraid to even put in for this tour of duty at the old annex that I even gave it a thought.

Of course, no reasonable, peace loving person goes looking for trouble. This factor in itself, I believe, caused Blacks in the past to never try to get on this tour. But I was young and crazy in those days, and besides, this so-called White only sacred tour was nowhere from where I stayed. It was off of 80 highway a block or so over from Lynch street. So it was convenient for me in that I now wouldn't have to fight the downtown Jackson traffic to get to work each day, or pay for parking. Plus, working from 5:00AM to 2:00 PM made it easier for me to continue to go to college because of my new work time and the fact that the location was very close to Jackson State.

It would take a million years to describe the crazy looks that ole Stringfellow and I got the first day that we reported for work. Man, what a laugh!! Ole Stringfellow and I would be slapping hands and saying "You'd better get used to it baby, because we are here to stay. And, guess what, let us say it for ya, there goes the neighborhood!" We really got a kick out of this funny verbal hand grenade.

Stringfellow was from Meridian Mississippi. That was practically the birthplace of the Klan in our state. So he knew about the Klan firsthand. He could tell some stories about the courage that Black people had to display and demonstrate in those little country towns surrounding Meridian that would make you shiver with fear. If nothing else, Black people can truly hold their heads up and say they have paid their dues here in America. Whatever doesn't kill ya, makes you stronger. That is a true statement! One of these days the Klan will realize this and come to grips with the fact that they are fighting a losing battle and they are only making matters worse by making us stronger. Resistance is truly useless in this situation. Our mental and physical toughness was tempered like steel in our long, hard, death deifying, epic journeys across the sea in slavery times. ONLY THE STRONG SURVIVED! and now, America will have to deal fairly with the consequences it brought on its self.

Although, I had seen Stringfellow around before, prior to getting on that tour with him, I really didn't know him very well. But boy did we get tight when we were thrown in that snake pit out at the old annex. At first we were totally ostracized. I don't even think the supervisors wanted anyone to see them talking with us. They would walk past us and quickly bark out an order without even looking in our direction. That's just how bad it was. At the very beginning any little slip up we made, although the supervisors had not really taken time out to show us what they wanted to be done, we received a written negative note correcting us connected to our time cards.

One day, while standing behind my supervisor when he was checking my personnel folder for some insurance information, I spotted copies of the many negative notes they had been giving me in my folder. Man did I hit the ceiling. I demanded to know why hadn't I been told that the little half scribbled, broken English notes on paper were going into my personnel file. Sure enough the supervisor explained that that was how they normally did it on that tour. It didn't take Stringfellow and I long to put a stop to this mess. We were both sharp enough to know where they were heading with their little negative write-ups. We quickly raised hell about this nasty tactic, took it to the union and it was stopped.

We had a very strong union at that day in time at the post office. They did not take any mess like that off of management. Although ole Stringfellow and I usually only had each other to talk to when we first came on the tour, eventually their curiosity and bravado got the best of them. Dialogue, although laced with ulterior motives, did slowly occur. From there, they were like little lambs walking into the lions den begging to be devoured. Curiosity definitely killed the cat.

Before this uneasy dialogue began, we engaged in an odd war of wills. No one spoke to each other, unless it was absolutely necessary. They stared us down and we did the same! If looks could kill, we could have easily filled the Ross Barnett Reservoir with the dead bodies.

Ole String and I would be sitting there with our arms folded looking at these guys, as if to say, "Superior race huh! You racist, Mississippi Rednecks have got to be the worse pieces of good-for-nothing trash on this earth. That look, rocked them to their core. They just couldn't take it! Within ninety days ole String (that was my nickname for Stringfellow) and I had the best (the meanest, ugliest and the most ruthless Rednecks) they had to offer in a complete dither. They simply didn't know what to think? Although there had to be at least five of these hard-core guys mixed in with another ten who just hated our guts for GP, we were not afraid of them and we let them know it.

I kept an open invitation to meet them in the parking lot, any day they wanted. We could outwork them. We definitely were better educated than they. Stringfellow and I were college guys. Most of these guys were considered highly educated if they had even finished the sixth grade.

When we first arrived all we heard behind our backs was, "They are lazy, stink and are going to hurt our production." I recall once, shortly after arriving on this tour encountering something in the bathroom that would forever stick in my mind. Someone had newly wrote on the bathroom wall, "NIGGERS AND FLIES, NIGGERS AND FLIES. DAMN, HOW I HATE NIGGERS AND FLIES! BUT YOU KNOW WHAT? THE MORE I SEE NIGGERS, THE MORE I LIKE FLIES! That little slap in the face was just a small sample of what I would face on this heretofore sacred tour. This negative attitude towards me, caused me as a young foolish, immature young man, to act in kind. Although as an adult, I now know that reacting in kind to this type of ignorance is wrong, I was drawn in nevertheless.

This open, outward attack on Stringfellow and me caused us to form an even stronger alliance. We saw this as necessary in order for our dignity to survive. We agreed that rather than go to blows with these guys, we would fight them with our minds. And when possible, rather than get mad and do something stupid, we would draw on each other's strength and resolve, and yes, laugh at their foolishness.

While this plan of taking the high rode sounded great, it was especially difficult for me, because of being shot and seeing my fellow students killed at Jackson State. Plus, just prior to coming on this tour, I had, had a major run-in with a so-called, go for bad, racist highway patrolman while picking up mail in front of the Governor's Mansion. I was blessed to be alive after these incidents. Both of these near misses were very traumatic for me and left a bitter taste in my mouth when it came to racists. SIMPLY STATED, MY FUSE WAS ALREADY SHORT! IT WASN'T GOING TO TAKE A WHOLE LOT FOR ME TO BLOW UP AND OPEN A SCOLDING HOT CAN OF WHIP ASS ON SOMEBODY, IF THEY GOT IN MY FACE AND/OR LOOKED HALF-WAY LIKE THEY WERE GOING TO PUT THEIR HANDS ON ME.

But, I have to give it to ole Stringfellow though, he was a big calming influence on me. He was about ten years older than me and could quickly reason things out and arrive at a great conclusion, without breaking a sweat. Now, one thing I personally teased him about was being on the country side a little bit. Of course, he was from a little small town right outside of Meridian Mississippi, so I guess it wasn't his fault. Ole Stringfellow never got angry. But he could beat you down intellectually and reduce you mentally to the lowest denominator, when you rubbed him the wrong way. When he finished breaking something down to you, you'd want to run off and slap your mama for birthing you. I think he invented the old Star Wars 'Jet Eye Mind Trick!' He would twist these guys words and thoughts and totally confuse them. They would walk away from him in a dazed and confused state. Man it was hilarious. Ole String and I would just shake our heads and laugh at these guys.

The supervisors on this tour were racist themselves. Even still, they knew the value of getting the job done. They would constantly be playing us against the middle with these guys. They'd say stuff like, "You guys had better git going if you're going to keep up with old Stringfellow and Weakley. While you guys are criticizing them and telling everyone how lazy they are, they are working rings around ya'll!! Shut up, stop your jaw janking, criticizing and git going."

During breaks and our down times, the inevitable had to happen. We would have some knock down, drag 'Em out,' head on discussions with these guys about race. All in all, it kept coming back to plain ole, give me another chaw of chewing tobacco ignorance. Their vocabulary, we found was very limited, but we chose to continue the discussion anyway. Over and over again, we would be diplomatically challenging them on their knowledge of Black people and the world in general. String and I would have these guys stuttering and gasping for air to defend their dis-jointed and incoherent positions. Eventually, one by one, more Blacks came on the tour. This made it a little better.

We would constantly be in their faces, (the guys rumored to be Klansmen) in one of these up close and personal sessions. They would have one or two of their so-called spokesmen talking for them and the rest of them would be standing around behind them grinning and kicking their feet into the dirt, wanting to get an Amen in, but being afraid to because they knew that they were going to get blasted and be made to look like utter fools in front of everyone. People (Black and White) would be cracking on them like you wouldn't believe. Several of those guys were borderline retarded and they would cause even their own guys to burst out laughing at them when they tried to sneak in a comment or two. We would all turn around and look at them as if to say, "Fool please shut up!"

Without having to repeat some of the unbelievably silly and grotesquely vulgar and ignorant comments I got at the beginning of these discussions, suffice it to say that there were days when I almost went to blows with some of these guys. The fact that none of us wanted to lose our great paying job at the post office made our verbal sparing sessions interesting to say the least. Call it the war of the wills and forked tongues because we couldn't do more.

It was common knowledge that the first one to throw a punch on the post office premises was history, fired, gone without discussion, plan and simple. I suspect they tried to get our goat just to get us fired and out the door and we in turn did the same thing to them.

We could all talk trash, but not touch each other physically. The post office absolutely did not tolerate fighting. One punch, or shove and the person who threw it was fired on the spot. I was Twenty-four in those days. I was in great physical shape and I knew I could hold my own in an out and out fistfight, or whatever, with these guys. And if worse came to worse, I knew I could count on the Qs, (Big Dick Bocula, Sam Sylvester Thompson <Don't make me stomp a mud hole in your ass> Huff, BB, Prater, Boozack, Dolemite and the rest of the Boys) to gladly give me more than enough backup if I needed it.

    I am ashamed to admit it now, but there were plenty nights that I stayed up late coming up with some good, take that, and Hooa in your face, verbal jabs/insults to throw back at these guys when these discussions arose. I'm sure, it's pretty safe to say that they probably did the same thing as well.

CHAPTER FIFTY FOUR

AND THEN, THE LIGHT SUDDENLY CAME ON!
(GOD IS TRULY GREAT)

I guess after a while, we kind of all ran out of nasty barbs to throw and funny things to say, because we eventually were able to talk to each other without anger and vulgar insults. Oh, don't get me wrong, just because we took the tone of these little conflicts down a peg or two, didn't mean we still didn't get into our little verbal battles. The same questions seemed to always surface in these little, "Is that the best you can come up with sessions."

"All Black people are lazy," they would say. We would reply equally in kind with a stinging retort like. "Lazy! How can you even say that! String and I have been carrying ya'lls' lazy, pathetic butts all day!!! Is that all you got? Come on Man! Get out of my face with that corny mess!" Of course they would respond and we would dig in the spurs with some stupid throw back comments as well. After a while, I think we all kind of looked forward to these funny little sessions. I have to admit these funny sessions were a welcomed aside, as we all worked side by side, elbow to elbow, sweating away on the hot conveyor belts in our little dusty areas at the back of the post office annex. I would throw out stuff like "Hell, I used to like White people before I started working with you lazy Rednecks here at the post office.

Ya'll are the laziest people I have ever seen in my life. Shoot, I have to wonder if White people really did discover America or go to the moon. You sure you guys didn't have Black people steering the ships for you and doing all your work while you hid down below deck, just waiting for the ship to finally hit land, so that you could jump out, push the poor Black guys out the way and scream, "Look at us everybody, WE DISCOVERD AMERICA!!!"

We'd laugh at our jokes and they would retaliate with a funny barb or two and get their laughs in as well. They would say stuff like, "Let you and Stringfellow steer the ship and drive us somewhere. No way man! Ya'll would be too demanding. We couldn't afford to buy chauffeur outfits for you two, with all the fancy frills and shiny shing digs ya'll would have the union make us give you. And besides that, we couldn't take the embarrassment. The outfits and the boat would just be too fancy and frilly. They would probably look like a pimp outfit and car. Every navy around would be laughing at us because of yawl's sissy outfits." Of course we would body slam them back with another funny comeback. There was no way we would let them get a funny comment up on us. And so, as you may have already guessed it, our little tour of duty was always full of laughter. That laughter probably was God's way of bringing us to our senses. If you can fathom that thought. It is true, God does work in mysterious ways.

All in all, our conversations with each other slowly turned into good-natured ribbing, rather than the truly malicious attacks we had engaged in at the beginning of our relationship. And then, based on where our relationship had started from, something truly miraculous happened. Truth began to come to the fore! Once we finally got all the nonsense out of the way, the truth began to seep out and we would get down to the real nitty-gritty and nut cutting.

"So do you guys even know why you hate Black people so much, I would say? Tell me, what did I personally do to you?"

They would respond, "Ahh nothing man!" Then they would throw a funny barb, to keep their true selves from shining through and try to keep their old tough guy guard up. "The last time I looked Weakley, this was America and I had the freedom to hate who I want to hate! I guess you want to take that away from me now too huh? Of course at this point in our significantly improved relationship, they were kidding. When we finally got to the root of it all, we all had to laugh at how stupid we had been sounding. I include myself and String in this comment as well. WE WERE JUST AS BAD AS THEY WERE.

Eventually, we learned how to talk with each other and say what was really on our minds, albeit, still on the stupid side. Our conversations went something like, "Well Weakley, I don't really hate you. You're all right because you're different! It's the other bad Black people we're talking about." I would say, "Come on Man! I'm not special at all. And what other Black people are you talking about anyway? You don't personally know any other Black people other than me, now do you? You know and I know that the White guys on this shift have never really been around Black people until String and I got here!!"

The true problem was, that they really didn't know anything about Black people, other than the garbage they had been told. I would often ask, "Have you ever given yourself a chance to really get to know someone from another race, so that you can truly decide for yourself, if they are no-good?" Of course, the old joke defense would be thrown up again. They would throw in something like, "Hey, that sounds like you're trying to get an invitation to my dinner table. No way man, my wife would poison us both, trying to kill you." Everybody listening to these funny comments on the sidelines (Black and White) would be picking themselves off of the floor laughing. Finally though, these guys showed they had a heart and would break down and tell it like it was. The conversation would go something like, "Well Weakley, I really don't know what I think right now," But I know I like you and old String. I can't say, if I would like all of the other Black people out there. I just know I like you two guys and you're cool with me," they would say.

In the end, Ole String and I were able to convert a few of these guys by having frank and honest, face to face, man to man, without all of the foolish posturing, conversations with them. They found out in our discussions that Black people were plain old people just like they were!! Sure we have our problems, but basically all of God's people and creations are the same!!!

We finally were able to agree that there were good White people and there were bad White people. Just like there are good Black people and bad Black people. Probably, the biggest hurdle was getting them to realize that all Black people were not criminals who were trying to rob them and/or rape their women like the television seemed to always be reporting. This seemed to be a very big issue with these guys. Let them tell it, we were all thugs and sex addicts. Wow what utter nonsense!

One point that really seemed to crack their skin/armor and get beneath it all was the point we made that the only reason the news media focused on Blacks, is that we are in the minority, and not in power. The people in power always need someone to point the finger at to be the bad guy, to keep the focus off them, while they are stealing everyone else blind. Plus, it makes great copy to shine the light on the poor minority so that the people just above them and higher are constantly reminded just how good they have it. And, if they know what's good for them, they will stay on the side of the guys shining the flashlight to keep from slipping into the hell that the minorities are catching.

Hey, no one in their right mind, especially those that are in the moneymaking business, as is the news media, is going to criticize those in power and/or, for the lack of better words, those who hold the purse strings who are able to regulate their industry. 'Point at the least among you and the one who is least likely to have the clout to take you on.' That's what corrupt big business is all about. Besides, it's always good to be able to make the people in the majority feel like they are holier than thou and especially better than the guy on the bottom. We would tell these guys, "Call it your reward for being king." And it's damn good to be king, isn't it? The bad Black people, sadly enough, would probably do the same thing if they had it like that. But they don't, and therein lies the dilemma for us as a people. The bad thing for us all is that we are all in the same boat and just don't know it!!!

Statistics will prove that White people, if only by sheer numbers alone, commit far more crimes than Blacks. But, even still, it seems that Blacks are the ones who fill the television screen each day and are the majority rotting away in prisons.

The situation got so good between us eventually at the post office, that occasionally they would ask us to bring them food back when we went out to lunch to some of the soul food places. Imagine that! Ole String and I would gladly invite them to come along and they would jokingly go back into their song and dance. "Man, I ain't gonna let your people catch me in the hood and kill me. I can see it now, me in a big ole black pot with a bunch of pig feet and chittlings floating around my head. Of course they would get another good laugh in. But that was okay because they, (these so-called hard-core racist) were the ones begging us for soul food. Now ain't that a kick in the head!!!

They would go on to say, "You and String are cool with us, but I don't know if yawl's people would go for us running around in the hood with yawl." String and I would get a big laugh out of this. They would be shuffling their feet wanting to go. Or if we brought back food to eat for ourselves, they would sit in close proximity hinting around and trying to get up the nerve to ask us for some of our soul food. You know this couldn't hold out for long. They would be breaking down and getting their grub on like the rest of us. Of course, this in itself sparked another round of jokes we would throw at them about how they would be tearing into that soul food. While they were in full flight eating, we'd say stuff like, "Damn, yawl had better slow down eating before you accidentally bite off some of your fingers."

CHAPTER FIFTY FIVE

THE TRUTH CAN REALLY HURT SOMETIMES

Even though we were finally able get the lights to go on in all of our heads. We agreed that it was very easy to think that this problem is exclusive to the other guy when being told this on a daily basis by the news media. Or, it was easy to hate others for no legitimate cause because they were being fed this garbage by someone like the Klan leaders, who were trying to exploit the situation so that they can perpetuate their own evil purpose.

Another source of laughter for us was when these guys once argued us down that Black people committed more rapes in America than White people. To hear them tell it, it was rare, according to their Klan literature, for White people to commit rape. Can you just see String and me (in looking for our next wise crack to hit these guys across the head with) pouring through the racist literature they brought in for us to take a look at. We would slowly go through each item line by line and rip it to shreds intellectually. Sometimes, they would keep their hands on one end of the pamphlet as we read it, as if they were afraid we would take it away and show it to others. String and I would sound something like, "Hey, what idiot wrote this mess?" We would stop, and look them square in the face, while keeping a straight face, pause for a second and say,

"Do you really think Black people have tails as it says here? Come on!! Even you blithering retards can't be that stupid. And you call the idiot who wrote this mess your leader?" You should have seen the wild eyed, hurt to the bone, embarrassed looks on their faces after that exchange.

I recall once bringing in some national statistics to prove our point that White people committed far more rapes in America than Black people. They had a hard time believing the data that was staring them right in the face. I recall one old guy saying, "Well those figures were put together by Black people and Jews to hurt the White man." I'd respond to this foolishness by saying something like, "Well Billy Bob, the last time I looked there were no Black people in control of the government. I wish we were in control of the government. We would throw ya'll down and make you eat the government cheese we've had to eat when we were on welfare." Of course I kid!! Everybody knows that government cheese was good. (Smile) DO THEY EVEN MAKE IT ANYMORE? Man, I wish I could get my hands on some!!!

What was even more funny was the fact that the breakdown in rapes by Whites for the state of Mississippi was almost through the roof. They simply couldn't believe that at first. No, No No, No, No, tell me it isn't so Weakley, is what they would sadly say? "Not in Mississippi, tell me it isn't so?" After picking myself off of the floor laughing at these guys, I loved telling them that, "While you guys are out at night policing and watching the Black man, and looking for one of us to lynch, some White guy is sneaking in your back window having his way with the little woman." Boy, you're talking about the mother of all cheap shots.

After we provided that rather eye-opening and sobering revelation, several of them called in sick for a few days just to get over the shock! Everyone on our shift had a big laugh at their expense about their having to take off sick when they returned. They even had to laugh at themselves.

Another point ole String made with them that sealed it, was on the subject of welfare. Some of these guys actually bet us money that there were twice as many Black people on welfare than White people in America. Once I happily rolled out the statistics, and they were able to verify them, these guys fell all over themselves laughing at how stupid they had been. A couple of them jokingly commented that a lot of their Klan buddies had been missing out on getting welfare all these years so that they could keep the White man's figures down. One of them went so far as to say that the government should make up their lost back payments in one big lump sum.

One point they did make and I found myself also agreeing with, was that able bodied people who could work who had no legitimate reason to be on welfare, should not be on it.

Quite frankly, I could not have afforded to not have my good paying job at the post office, prior to going to the music business at that point in my life. I'm pretty certain that these guys were probably in the same boat as me. I'm glad that I didn't do something stupid, like throw a punch at one of these guys and lose my job when I first arrived on the tour.

After being forced to work shoulder to shoulder and sweat to sweat with each other for the first time in our lives, and seeing that our old prejudices were false, we all eventually learned how to get along with each other. By the time I left the post office many of these guys had completely changed their racist philosophy. One of them who was very old, boldly claimed that he had put me in his will, along with his family. Of course, I never showed up to collect when he passed away. I took it as a compliment though, based on how far he had come, and never thought twice about it. Many of these guys were upset about the time and energy they had needlessly thrown away by being led down the wrong path.

Once we were able to take a hard, objective look at the facts, we were all able to realize that our racist views simply did not make sense. What a change! The Lord worked it out in the end.

CHAPTER FIFTY SIX

SHOOT FIRST AND ASK QUESTIONS LATER!

Each person I truly believe has his or her breaking point. It is at this point, that you will either go off the deep end completely and lose all control and go well beyond your pre-set standards of logic and reason, or you somehow will gather all the strength you can muster, yield to what you know in your heart to be right and find the strength to pull yourself away from the brink. I wish I could say that I chose the latter in the life circumstance I am about to share with you, but I didn't.

People often ask me what it was that finally caused me to walk finally away from my beloved home state of Mississippi. Shortly after the Jackson State murders, I was probably one of the wildest of the wild during the period that I spoke about in this book. I was the undisputed leader of the pack! I had a successful music career going and as a result, was on top of the world.

I left Jackson Mississippi in March of 1981. While I will occasionally visit my mom, daughter and other family members there, I knew the moment my foot crossed the state line that I would never go back to Mississippi again and call it my home. I was like a runaway slave, fleeing that state with all the speed I could muster. Now of course, Mississippi has indeed changed over the years. In fact, the change is rather remarkable, given the brutal racism that was so much a part of it, prior to the 70s.

Mississippi has now, believe it or not, clearly emerged as one of the better places to live and raise your family in America. Black people who now reside all over America, who fled Mississippi in the 50s, 60s, and 70s are happily returning back to make their homes there in droves. But for that day and time of the Jackson State murders and prior, Mississippi as well as its sister states like Alabama, Georgia and Louisiana were hell on earth for Black Americans.

As a young Black man committed to trying to stay and right the system in Mississippi, it was almost bearable until one day, I just couldn't take it any more. The incident which finally made living there unbearable, had to do with a head to head run-in that I had with the Ku Klux Klan. Now I'm not talking about the rudy poot, fair-weather, maybe I am and maybe I'm not, so-called rumored to be Klansmen I just spoke about at the post office. No, No, No, No, NO!!! I am talking the real deal guys.

Although Mississippi to most outsiders represents what is truly bad about the Klan, in the years previous to the seventies, in my home city of Jackson, the Klan, had to my knowledge, never made a public appearance in the capital city. If they did, they did it in total secrecy. It was not until roughly 1980 that I personally ever witnessed the Klan marching in its streets.

I will never forget the hatred that sprang from that march. The event that sparked this open display by the Klan resulted from a Black lady being shot and killed by the Jackson police department. The resulting marches by Blacks in the city to protest this tragedy, prompted the Ku Klux Klan to also march. As I recall, the lady who was killed had been drinking and after a short altercation with her husband, where the police were called, she came out of her home with a gun. As it was reported in the news, the lady when asked to put down the gun by two White officers, was shot and killed by them. To be as fair as possible to the Jackson police, I believe the issue was not that the circumstance did not call for their presence, it was how quickly they elected to use lethal force, rather than use more patience and restraint to try and bring about a peaceful end to this situation.

As a result of this tragedy, the Black community announced that they were going to sponsor a major march on City Hall to demand better methods of dealing with all citizens of Jackson by its police force. As my grandmother often said, "When the lights go out, then will come the roaches." Shortly after the Black community made their announcement asking Blacks to show up in record numbers for this march, The Ku Klux Klan reared its ugly head and surprised everyone and also made an announcement that they too would be donning their robes and full regalia to march in Jackson as well.

This announcement was like a nuclear bomb going off when it hit the airwaves. People both Black and White in Jackson were in total shock. The Klan had never marched in Jackson before, as a result, I understand of an agreement that had been made with the 'White Powers that be' many years past. Sure they were free to march and have a heavy presence in the small country towns of Mississippi far away from Jackson, but to march in the streets of the capital city would negatively broad brush the entire state as one that supported their goals and more importantly their methods in accomplishing their infamous objectives.

So the dilemma for the 'Powers That Be' at that time, was not whether to support the Klan; it was how not to openly show total support for them to the world. The Klan marching in Jackson would be a small victory for them. But it also ran the risk of bringing down the seats of power, not only in Mississippi but all across America who financed them. There is just something about the Klan that makes people feel dirty. The Klan also stank of trailer park trash mentality and crudeness that most well-to-do, behind the scenes racists just did not want their names and faces associated with. The odd thing is that the Klan was alright with this, (the high rollers not wanting to openly claim them) and understood this methodology perfectly! I guess as long as they were getting their secret contributions, the KKK didn't care if, (the elite of Mississippi) got down in the dirt with them for the world to see and play in their little racist sand box.

For many years, White politicians without even mumbling a word for the Klan, could with a wink and a smile or probably more importantly, with their complete lack of effort to move against them, show their approval of the Klan without tipping their hand to the public. Their lack of action to move against them and/or stop their violent acts towards Black people, said all that needed to be said. This was particularly true in the small one-horse country towns. When a Black person was dragged out of his home and lynched and/or was beaten unmercifully by the Klan, everyone in the city, including the sheriff or police chief knew more than likely who it was that had done it. Why, they probably sat right next to them in church that Sunday.

But you know something, whose to say that the Evil 'Powers That Be" were not once again letting their big bad dogs out. Perhaps they wanted to again use a trump card as they did with the murders at Jackson State and use the Klan to intimidate the Black community into submission. In stead of using the Mississippi Highway Patrol this time as their pawns, they raised the stakes considerably, pulled out all of the stops and decided perhaps to throw the dreaded KKK into the equation.

The KKK was a seemingly unbeatable ace up their sleeves that would be hard to trump, if this in fact was their plan. Whether I liked it or not, the KKK struck sheer terror in the hearts of Black people. This fear went back many years and would be hard to shake off. Throwing this variable into the mix may have been done to scare Black people from showing up at the march in large numbers as they had promised they would. In any case, only time would tell. I didn't know about anybody else, but I damn sure was going to be there, Klan or no Klan. The truth as to why the KKK inserted themselves into this already potentially explosive mix, was out there some where. All in all, it didn't really matter if anyone had sent them. The bottom line of it all was that the dreaded Ku Klux Klan was definitely going to march in our fair city, whether we liked it or not!!!

CHAPTER FIFTY SEVEN

TOE TO TOE WITH THE K.K.K.

The good old boys in the Ku Klux Klan in that day in time in Mississippi accepted the ambiguous position of not openly getting public support from the top Mississippi politicians. In fact, I think they saw it as downright good politics. Neither a yea nor stone cold dead silence hurt them. Both oddly enough translated into support. The fact that the Klan had now broken this unspoken rule of not marching in the streets of Jackson and were getting ready to march, may have also signaled that a major split had occurred between them and the 'Powers That Be.' In any case, as far as Blacks in the city of Jackson were concerned, the up coming march by the Klan was a major slap in the face.

So there you have it. You have Blacks on one hand now going well beyond the original issue of the shooting of the lady to something even greater. Which in this case, was the fact that the dreaded and hated Klan would be occupying the streets of Jackson. And then, you had the Whites in Jackson, especially the city administration, concerned about the city's image as well as the danger that the Klan would cause in the streets of Jackson, by their mere presence. Mixing these two explosive opposing groups clearly spelled disaster for the city.

Now add to this, the fact that the city of JACKSON would also have to shoulder the enormous financial expense of providing the police manpower to protect and separate these two powder kegs.

The fact that the Klan was marching caused me to say, enough is enough. I wasn't alone either. The entire Black community was in an uproar. The law-abiding White community also appeared to be equally upset that the Klan, who on the surface appeared to be outsiders from other states coming in as a result of our march, would be stomping the pavement as bold as you please in their hooded sheets, in the capital city of Jackson.

Many of Jackson's prominent White citizens openly spoke up and tried to revoke the license to march that the Klan was issued. In the end, they as well as the Black community, received licenses to peacefully march. The final decree that was published in the media was that America is not only for Blacks who want to protest, but it was also for any other Americans, be they Klan or otherwise, who would abide by the law and peacefully march in the city of Jackson. So whether the Black community or White community liked it or not, this little dog and pony show would indeed go on. This insult, added to the tragedy that had already occurred at Jackson State, caused me to snap.

At that time I was heavily armed as a result of the paranoia that consumed me after being shot at Jackson State. I willingly chose to fight fire with fire if need be. I was also blessed to be surrounded by my frat brothers. While the Qs, (The Omegas of Jackson State) were a college fraternity, we were also well respected throughout the city as some guys who could hold our own in a good fight. I knew that my frat brothers would not let anyone steal my life from me while they were around!

There was a period after the murders occurred at Jackson State and prior to the Supreme Court ruling that represented a strange period of metamorphosis for me. I kept having the same recurring dream of me, standing over one of the dying students trying to protect him. But, in the end, I would fail to save him from a big burly Highway Patrolman who would push me to the side, as if I wasn't there, and shoot the poor student over and over again, unmercifully with a shotgun.

Over and over, night after night in my re-occurring dream, I always seemed to fail to save the student. I could not understand why I was so powerless. It was as if I had no strength in my arms at all. Sometimes during the day I would try to figure out new angles and wrestling holds to use against the patrolman, but of course, I could never remember them in my dreams when the time came. The results would always be the same. The poor student would be unmercifully shot to death. I would awaken from these dreams feeling so worthless, sad and full of mistrust in the system. It was as if everything I had been taught about the world and people up until the murders at Jackson State had suddenly had a head on collision with the cold, hard facts of life.

As a child you think that grown-ups will always be there to protect you! Your naiveté also leads you to think that you are going to live forever, and you foolishly think that everything should, and will, come easily for you during the course of your lifetime. And, why shouldn't it? " GOOD THINGS ALWAYS COME TO GOOD PEOPLE!!" That's what one of my favorite old high school teachers used to say. All you have to do is be a good person, believe in God and work hard. Your family and the system will take care of you and keep the evil people and the unfair things in life away from you. What happened at Jackson State knocked the hell out of that theory for me! I had to come to grips with the cold hard fact that life isn't fair and bad things do happen to good people whether we like it or not. " It's just a part of God's master plan. "

The murders that I witnessed and the gunshot wound I received at Jackson State brought me to the realization that life is indeed short and precious. I decided that I would live life to the fullest because it could be snuffed out at any moment without notice or fair warning. "Tomorrow is truly not promised to any man." To this end, at that point in time in my life, I made a decision to quickly give my life if necessary, to show the Klan and the evil racist 'White Powers That Be' that I was not going to put up with their bullshit anymore!

CHAPTER FIFTY EIGHT

THE VERY LAST STRAW!

As a result of what had happened at Jackson State, my friends and frat brothers that I ran with had armed ourselves to the teeth. We made a decision that we were not going to take anymore mess off of anybody. This included the evil racist Powers That Be, the Klan, the Highway Patrol, the Jackson police force as well as the local Drug Dealers, Dope Heads, Thieves, Go For Bad Asses and two cents Pimps who infected Jackson. As a result of the money I made in the music industry and the post office I was well financed. I personally bought and carried a brand new .45 automatic in the small of my back when I was in the streets. I also had a .357 magnum pistol near by and a pump shotgun that I carried in the truck of my car during this period in my life. The kill or be killed mentality that the Jackson State murders drove me to, made me feel I was justified to take whatever measures necessary to survive. It had now been made crystal clear to me that the state of Mississippi, and especially the evil 'Powers That Be,' who were running it, cared little for Black life.

Just prior to the march in Jackson by the Klan, I met with my tough as nails buddy, Big Dick Bocula, and several of my frat brothers at a place called Peaches' Café on Farish Street next to the Alamo Theater. It was not too far from downtown and was relatively close to the parade sight. WE WERE ARMED TO THE TEETH.

Our intent was truly not to start any trouble with the Ku Klux Klan, but I tell you this, if any started, we were not planning on coming out on the short end of the stick. After throwing down a few beers, we basically made a blood pact that this was our dying day, if the stuff went down wrong!! There was no way we were going to let the Klan get the best of us and live.

I recall walking out of Peaches' Café that day with my frat brothers and after walking merely a hundred yards, feeling like I had the weight of the whole world around my waist. My guns were just that heavy. I had a 45 automatic with several extra clips and a .357 magnum tucked around my waist with extra bullets in each pocket.

Walking to City Hall that day, we looked like the guys in the famous old western "Shoot Out At The OK Corral." We had our game faces on and we were ready to take care of business.

I remember silently saying my prayers as we pounded the pavement in a hard walk. They were my final prayers as far as I was concerned. As I walked the last few hundred feet to City Hall, I asked the Lord to forgive me for what I was about to do and receive my soul into heaven, if he could be merciful enough to do so. That's just how serious we were that day!! All hell was going to be unleashed on the KKK with just the slightest provocation. Mississippi and the South may have been where the Klan got its claim to fame, but as far as we were concerned, it would also be where the Klan met its end, or at a minimum got its biggest defeat to date.

As we walked to City Hall, we could see a large crowd forming. It was made up mostly of Blacks with some White supporters sprinkled throughout it. The crowd was very angry. No doubt, many of the Black marchers were loaded for bear as we were that day as well. There was no way that Black people in Jackson were going to be trampled by the Klan. We had, had enough of their murderous rein!!! The crowd, all of a sudden, seemed to swell uncontrollably, float above the street and move all together in the same direction as if it was a raging herd of wild buffalo.

We were very loud and vocal. People were screaming to the top of their lungs. The crowd was made up of young and old. It was composed of many prominent Black citizens in our community as well as the poor. We stood shoulder to shoulder. We repeatedly screamed. " Bring On The Got Damn Klan! Bring on the Klan! Bring On The Got Damn Klan!" We were at a fevered pitch!! It would not have taken much to cause this powder keg to explode. It took mere seconds for us to reach City Hall. There had still been no sign of the Klan at this point.

I recall thinking to myself that perhaps they had chickened out after seeing the size and resolve of the opposing crowd. Then we heard voices in the air about a block or two over, a different type of tone and flavor. Their voices were definitely different than ours. They had a different ring and texture to theirs. It seemed more high-pitched with a deep southern drawl and twang to it. It was indeed the Ku Klux Klan. Most were fully robed in their white sheets and hoods and several even dared to march without their hoods over their heads. How dare they be so bold as to show their ugly faces! They held several big confederate flags up high and waived them defiantly.

My eyes and neck strained to get a better glimpse of them. There could have only been thirty or forty of them at best. Compared to our hundreds, they seemed tiny and insignificant! My blood began to boil. I silently repeated a portion of the 23rd Psalm. "Yea, though I walk through the valley of the shadow of death, I will FEAR NO EVIL, for thou art with me!!! I will FEAR NO EVIL!!!!" I could feel myself getting angrier and angrier. My hand moved to the palm of my back to grip my .45. I looked around at my frat brothers faces and the were just as enraged as I. I kept my hand under my coat but yet now connected as if as one, to the butt of my gun. My palm and finger tips danced around its cold steel edges.

A portion of the crowd that I was in, all of a sudden broke

away from the body and surged toward the Klan. The Klan appeared surprised by this, our sheer numbers and the seething rage that was moving quickly towards them. It was obvious by the look on their face that they had gotten themselves into more than they had bargained for. At this point, we were close enough to see the whites of their eyes. Their eyeballs were bulging from their sockets as if to better peer through the eye holes in their hoods to see the terrifying sight they were facing. While initially, when we first saw them, they were proudly moving towards City Hall, they now seemed scared and frozen in their tracks as if hoping we would turn away from them and move back to City Hall. It was obvious to all that they had now abandoned their well publicized intent to take City Hall by storm.

You could see the fear in each of their eyes. As we moved ever closer, the air grew thick, stale and hard to breathe. Although it was spring time, an odd sort of steam, haze and stinky mist hung over our heads. I don't know if it came from our feet kicking up dust or our nostrils breathing hot with anticipation of the confrontation that surely was about to erupt. Many lives were on the verge of being lost.

My mind, all of a sudden, then did the craziest thing. It raced me away from that scene a thousand miles an hour in a mere instant. First it took me to the night of the murders at Jackson State. I could see myself lying on the ground witnessing the students being shot in the back and being severely cut by flying glass as they frantically tried, oh so desperately, to get inside the narrow glass west-wing doorway. Then a brilliant flash occurred and I was transformed again and could now see the pain and anguish on my own face as I lay in the dirt withering in pain that night from my gunshot wound. I appeared seconds from death, injured much more seriously than I remembered that night. Then all of sudden, I was transformed back in time there in the city streets of Jackson facing the Klan. All I could think of was taking the full measure of my rage and anger out on them for what they and the "Evil Powers That Be" had done to me and my fellow students at Jackson State. I now suspect it was Satan playing a trick on me! Tempting me to willingly kill!

We had now moved within thirty to forty yards of the Klan, picking up speed even more as we surged forward. I recall looking around at the faces in the crowd. We were indeed, a bloodthirsty mob. The anger and hatred for the Klan shined brightly through our eyes. Then all of a sudden the group made a final surge towards the Klan to close the small distance between us and them. The Klan members' faces were sheet white with fear. Sweat poured from their faces and out of their eye holes for those who had sheets on, like water from a fire hydrant. They appeared to brace THEMSELVES AND then all of a sudden, SEEM TO COLLAPSE INWARD UPON EACH OTHER. The flags that they had been holding high proudly when they first came on the scene dropped down and completely disappeared into their midst as if they were about to try and break and run.

And then, as if by magic, a thin line of blue appeared. It was the Jackson police force. They came from out of no where. They quickly and bravely, I might add, moved between the two groups separating them completely.

Thank God, I guess, that the Jackson police force did its job very well that day. They quickly took control and begin to create more space between the two factions. Pushing and shoving with all their might to get every inch of space they could between us! Although we were also struggling trying to break through their ranks to get to the Klan, they somehow were able to keep the two groups away from each other. The Klan, being a much smaller group to dislodge, were quickly pushed to a distant side street. Seeing this, we stopped, and turned back to continue our surge back to the steps of City Hall. City Hall, as I had just come to notice, appeared deserted. But that didn't matter. FOR IT WAS A GREAT SYMBOL. IT WAS NOW OUR PRIZE ALONE! It represented the righteous and the ultimate victor. Whoever possessed it fully and exclusively, had won!!!!!

The news media was everywhere. The Klan had now totally dispersed/disappeared as if into thin air. We went on to loudly protest, pump our fists and scream our demands. Several speakers spoke through bullhorns. They made it clear that we, the tax paying citizens of Jackson, would not put up with the Klan or the Jackson Police Department's, shoot first and ask questions later method of dealing with Jackson citizens. After about an hour or so the crowd, who had been at a constant fevered pitch, eventually burned itself out.

Bocula and the boys and I, dispersed with the rest of the crowd. The next morning, a friend called my home and asked had I seen the newspaper. I quickly opened it! There I was, the centerpiece of the photo. I appeared angry and completely out of control. I had my hand thrust into the air with my mouth gaping wide open as if caught in full sentence, screaming to the crowd.

Other calls began to come into my home. They all seemed to be praising what I had done. But you know, for whatever crazy reason, I did not feel proud. Just the opposite was true; I was ashamed that I could let my anger get so far out of control. Although it was definitely a picture of me in the photo, to me, it just didn't look like me. I recall later on that day looking at the picture again and again and again with my mom and family. Although, I didn't share this with them, I truly could not recognize myself.

They too appeared proud that Black men had faced down the Klan and practically ran them out of town. Although it should have been a sweet moment of victory for me, something indeed was wrong. It bothered me deeply that a city, a system, the Ku Klux Klan, An Ungodly Evil Called Racism, could drive me to such an out of control state. There I was, a taxpaying, college educated, well-known, successful God fearing citizen openly packing guns in downtown Jackson in the middle of an enraged mob. It turned my stomach!

I wondered to myself, why should any American citizen have to be pushed to the edge as I was to make their justified grievances known. There has to be a better way. I could not stay in a state that would demand that its taxpaying citizens take to the street and put their lives on the line so that their voices could be heard and justice would prevail. Good government should be about the business of truly serving and protecting the people that so graciously elected it. The issue that sparked this event should have been a no brainer.

Someone, a high ranking, God fearing elected official, should have stepped forward and said, "YES YOU ARE RIGHT! Our citizens should not be mowed down in the streets in a shoot first and ask questions later manner, as the lady had obviously been." That wild eyed look of primal rage on my face in that picture was a driving force that caused me to take it to the Lord for guidance. It was God's guidance that said, "Vernon it's time to leave Mississippi," and so I did!

I left Mississippi over twenty years ago. I left with a bitter taste in my mouth and a deep lingering sadness in my soul. Although it broke my heart to leave my home state, I had to leave because there were just too many good people (Black and White) who were being brutally victimized by the racist smoke screen created by the 'Evil Powers That Be.' At the time that I left, they had a death grip on the state of Mississippi. My wild lifestyle in the nightclubs, gun battles out in the streets of Jackson, frequent run ins with the evil racist 'Powers That Be' and the final last straw for me that involved the Klan, was it for me. I had, had enough!!!!

I am sure a lot of people would say that I was merely taking a stand that day at City Hall and doing what must be done to correct injustice in this country. I do agree that some circumstances, such as this, do call for extreme measures. However, it was how I behaved, namely my out of control state and the accumulation of all the crazy things I had done up until that point that screamed that something was indeed wrong with me and missing in my life.

In choosing to fight fire with fire, I had evoked Satan. Satan, as a result, oddly enough was also winning the battle over me and my eternal soul, by drawing me deeper, and blindly I might add, into the battle against him with my hatred and anger for the Klan and the evil 'Powers That Be.' Plain and simple, he had brought me down to his level. No Christian should ever go there!!

I had to stop and realize that this was not the answer for me or anyone else. The answer for me was and is Jesus Christ. It was time to let the seething hatred and bottled up anger I harbored over what had happened at Jackson State go. This was the true root cause of my unknowing dance with the Devil. It was time for me to come out of my denial and just let it Go!!!

"FEAR NO EVIL" is the title of this book. I am sure that some would say that based on the ungodly evil that is and was the KKK, that it would have been alright to unleash a righteous fury on them and completely slaughter and wipe them off the face of the earth. And they, (the KKK) many might say, would only be getting what they deserve. BUT IT WOULD HAVE BEEN WRONG! This is Satan's way!!! This is what Satan would want a God fearing person to do! And in doing so, lose his soul in the process.

The very fact that they, (the Klan) that day, were only and are, even to this day, are nationally only a few in number clearly support the fact that righteousness has won already. The Lord God has already gotten the victory over them. All his people has to do is have faith, pray and watch the walls of Jericho crumble before them AS GOD PROMISE THEY WILL!

Plus, this is America. Everyone, and I mean everyone, (including the KKK) should have the right to peacefully protest in this country. When we, by force or intimidation, take that right away from anyone or group. We do this country a great and grave disservice. This is ironic, but I am so glad that it was the Jackson police that stepped between us that day and kept us from slaughtering the Klan.

Ignore the Klan as far as their rallies go, demand that our law enforcement agencies, as well as ourselves, closely monitor them to ensure that they do not break the law and they, (the KKK) will eventually, completely disappear. The few that remain today, are only a tool for Satan. We should not give them more publicity and yes sympathy, than they deserve, as we would have that day with that confrontation, if it would have occurred.

I am a born again Christian and I truly believe that
~ GOD IS IN CONTROL OF ALL THINGS. ~
Sometimes he allow bad things to happen or let evil, for a short time rule the day, to test us to see if we truly have faith in HIM, as many of us openly say we do.

One of the great things about God's grace is that he loves us oh so much. He will not forsake us! He may not come when you want him to, but believe me, he is always right on time! We must wait on him!!

Additionally, **God is willing to forgive even the worst among us**, if they are willing to truly repent their sins, depart from their evil ways and from there honestly try to live a Christian life! I know that I have chosen the right course. And now, my life is in total balance and in order.

As an adult, I now know without any uncertainty that there is a God. I also know that Jesus Christ died on the cross for my sins and he loves me and everyone else very much in spite of the crazy things we may do. I also know that I must continue to strive to live a Christian life, (strive to be more Christ like, rather than like Satan as many of us unknowingly do) not necessarily because of the terrible consequences of being damned to hell or the countless wonderful blessings that the Heavenly Father will shower me with, but because it is simply the right thing to do. And, more importantly, it is what God (The Heavenly Father, Son and Holy Ghost) wants us to do.

ALL GOD ASK IS THAT WE **FEAR NO EVIL** AND PUT OUR FAITH STEADFASTLY IN HIM. THROUGH HIM, ALL THINGS ARE POSSIBLE!!!

ALL PRAISE BE TO GOD!!!

~ EPILOG ~

(SO WHERE DO WE GO FROM HERE?)

I THINK EVERYONE READING this book would openly agree that racism is wrong and has no place in our society and the world. But still, it remains a thriving cancer eating away at us no matter how hard we try to wipe it out. There is a reason for this. That reason, is that racism has many other uses that go far beyond what meets the eye. We must all open our eyes wider and go a step farther to get behind the evil of racism. We must arm ourselves by finding out what causes it, what motivates it and what sustains and fuels it. Then and only then will we be able to defeat it!

Racism in itself, is truly a terrible thing. But its negative effects are greatly amplified when its used to confuse and keep the masses at each others' throat. Generally, the hidden purpose, when its used in this manner, is to be a diversion used by unscrupulous people in order to obtain monetary goals and/or to gain absolute power over others.

This book is entitled " Fear No Evil!!! It was meant to not only be a testament to the resilient spirit of Black people, but also a living testament to all Americans. In spite of the terrible consequences we face in trying to do what's right, we must suffer them. That is the cost we must bear for God and the freedom that we love so dearly. Beyond these righteous purposes, we are truly insignificant in the grand scheme of things.

ALTHOUGH THE STORY LINE in "Fear No Evil!! focuses on my family and my personal experiences, it also I truly believe embodies the full spectrum of the human experience. Whether you are on the receiving end or the giving end, is the only separating variable in how you receive the lesson it reveals. Black people initially did not ask to come to this country. We were forcibly brought here and made to work to help build it into the great country it is today.

I am absolutely certain that within twenty years all surviving Black Americans from slavery time will someday, rightfully receive reparations for the many years that we were in slavery, and for the resulting years of indignity and suffering we were forced to endure as a result of being forcibly brought to this country.

One comment I generally hear from White America, when this subject is broached, is that African Americans are in far better shape, as a result of being brought to America. They generally, in trying to make this argument, point to the terrible conditions that the continent of Africa is currently in. The point that I always like to retort with, is yes! You indeed have a point. But, no one knows, just how great Africa may have become, if we (millions and millions of its finest daughters and sons) would not have been stolen away and brought to this country. The very greatness that is now America's, could have easily been Africa's, as it was at the dawn of man. For it has been proven that the first man, came out of Africa. It is also a fact that the earliest known great civilizations sprung from Africa.

Along with America's success are a lot of tears and pain that all people, not just Black people, have encountered along the way. It took us all working together to make this country great, that is true. However, from our blood sweat and tears, we built the foundation and from that strong foundation has sprung the roots of this mighty nation.

A SOLUTION I OFFER TO REDUCE RAMPANT RACISM in America, is taking a pro-active approach to it. For too long we have waited until something terrible occurred like the dragging death of an innocent Black man in Jasper Texas, or the sodimizing of a young Black prisoner by two police officers with a broom stick in New York, or racial profiling, be it in New Jersey or anywhere across the nation, before we give an out cry. Oh yes, we can raise a lot of hell after these incidents occur. Jesse Jackson, Al Sharpton, Tom Joyner, Johnny Cochran, Tavis Smiley etc. thank God for them, because they are truly courageous and will champion a just cause and aggressively take the fight to the evil doers. That's one thing we have been blessed with! Strong Black leaders over the years who will step forward and do the right thing. Although I gladly take my hat off to these brothers for their great work, I submit that it is now time that we also GO ON THE OFFENSIVE in this great fight against racism in this country.

I believe that immediately after a new mayor, police chief, political representative in any office, President or an Attorney General is sworn in, regardless of their politics and most especially in those areas where there have been trouble, we should meet with them in numbers, (march to the court house or to the white house etc. if necessary) and tell them that we will not tolerate any injustices on Black people or any America for that matter, from them or their administration. We must let them know, in no uncertain terms, that we will be watching them closely and will hold them, along with any others perpetrators accountable. To ensure that these people understand that we mean what we say, we should meet with them regularly while they are in office to gauge their performance. Good performance should be publicly acknowledged and bad performance should be quickly met with the utmost in non-violent public protest and/or legal action to bring about their immediate political demise.

I recommend that a national general legal fund be started immediately and put on stand by to fight these battles when they rear their ugly heads. In the past while we were busy crying, trying to scrape up money and wondering what to do, the perpetrators had either made their get away or had gotten their alibi and ducks in a row. THIS WILL NOT DO!! We must formulate a proactive strategy that would make a local, state or federal official/evil doer think twice before trying this mess.

This fund should not only be about growing money, it should also fund a continuous think tank, to find and devise effective strategies, analyze tried and true methods and finding new ways to defeat racism in the court room. I would like to think that this legal defense fund could be initiated by our wealthy Black citizens and constantly replenished by donations from all Americans.

My experience and observation is that problems occur, because those in power, higher up in city and state government, in many cases, set the tone for abuse, thereby causing the public and/or those who work under them, such as policemen or radical organizations within their jurisdictions such as the KKK, by their leadership (negative or positive) to act the way they do. If the KKK knew that they were indeed being closely monitored and knew without any doubt that their illegal actions or remote involvement in a future plot to deny any American his civil rights would result in each responsible member of their organization being dragged out into the streets, and from there on to a dark and dank jail cell, then you would have far less incidents of this unacceptable behavior. The same holds true with our non-law abiding policemen. If they knew that any abuse will not be tolerated by their leaders, then we will have far less instances of it.

I am also certain that if organizations like the KKK knew for a certainty that their organization and each member in it would be held financially liable to the point of losing their homes, cars personal assets etc, then you would see real change from these organizations. Immediate, stiff, merciless, punitive measures are the key. This is where the rubber truly meets the road. Most cowards are not willing to see their very own skin peeled away to further their cause. They prefer to operate in secret are in the shadows of the tolerance of others.

Sadly enough, the latter is usually the case because these evil doers know they have an invisible, unspoken line of protection by those in power. It is those behind the scenes, that we must warn, or better yet point at and shine the light on, even before they sow their evil seeds. Their lack of action, or an all to familiar nod and a wink, generally leads to serious abuses by the rank and file, or the not too intelligent.

Good leaders instead should send the right message down the line by their actions, that if even a hint of an injustice occur, the guilty will not be supported and furthermore, they will be quickly prosecuted to the fullest extent of the law. IT IS AT THIS POINT, that justice and the American way will truly be given wings to soar to even greater heights. It is time for this country to set a new standard of justice. It is at this zero tolerance point that we will have far less incidents of hangings, racial profiling, physical and mental abuses of our citizens in this great country of ours.

Quite often we get so caught up in the disgust in the ones who carry out an evil act that we often let those behind the scenes, pulling the strings or allowing this mess to go on, sneak away in the confusion. We must now reach back and drag those responsible into the light of day as well. It is time for a new day as far as justice is concerned, in America.

MY BOOK HAS SEVERAL OTHER very important, powerful themes running through it. One is how the incident at Jackson State caused me to lose my faith in people and God and how I was able to regain it. God is boundlessly merciful. He allowed me to come back to him after sincerely repenting my sins. I had fallen as low as I could right after the Jackson State murders. I filled my life with destructive behavior. If God allowed me to come home. Then there is hope for every sinner. For those of you out there who do not know God, I urge you to give him a try!

Another theme in this book is having the courage to do what's right, although the odds are stacked against you. Moreover, in more specific terms, having the courage to challenge and correct injustice at all levels of our society. Persistence is the key in challenging and gaining the victory over rampant racism and injustice in this country. Persistence, Persistence, Persistence! I can't emphasis it enough! Whether you are rich, poor or consider yourself just the average Joe Blow on the street, I'm hear to tell you today that it's every citizens responsibility and duty to God and our country to do something about it. We must not turn a blind eye to injustice. Especially racial injustice because It Diminishes Us All!!

I RECALL A GOOD FRIEND OF MINE ONCE CONFIDING in me that he wanted to go into politics, but was afraid to do so because he felt that he would have to be ruthless and corrupt to be successful. He also felt that a person at a minimum, would have to at least hang out with those who were that way and/or pretend to act that way, if he was going to be successful in the profession.

Some may say he has a good point. But the key point I was able to make with him was, just because others are not acting right, doesn't mean you have to be that way or become that way. Bad behavior by others is not a disease or a stain like ink that rubs off on you just because you come in contact with it.

You must show courage and do what's right, regardless of what others may do. That is why God has given man the magnificent gift of "Free Will." Our charge by God is to use it and do what's right, regardless of what others may do or think. The only way that corruption in politics will be wiped out is that good people cause it to be wiped out. You have got to have courage and jump in there and change things. Your voice may very well be the one needed (the catalyst if you will) that sparks true everlasting change. Sometimes the courage in others may just need a little push (or jump start) to get them going.

IT IS ALSO IMPORTANT for people not to make the mistake of thinking that it's just the people on the receiving end of the abuse etc. that feel that bad situations should be changed. There are good people at all levels of our society. Remember Black people just didn't magically free themselves and change the laws that gave us our freedom. It took good people realizing that what they had done or what was being done to others was wrong, and realizing that it needed to be corrected, in order for real change to be made.

IT APPEARS THAT THE TRAGIC EVENTS of September 11th, may have a ironic silver lining hidden deep within its underbelly. In the midst of our tears, all Americans, regardless of race, social status, religion or color, have felt a powerful and undeniable need to draw closer to each other, unify and build our country up. This is truly a good thing that I for one hope will be contagious for future generations, and to our neighbors in other countries across the globe. It is truly amazing how death seems to sober people and bring them together.

The fact that the seemingly HERETOFORE invincible country of America was laid low by such a ruthless and unfair low blow, appear to have revealed to the world that we too are human and can hurt, and yes openly weep. I know for me personally, it was the first time I had ever seen an American president openly cry on television. This slip in character, spoke volumes. Not only was the 911 attack humbling for the United States, it was an even bitter blow because racism and religion (how ironic) seemed to be at the very core of the evil that made us stop, think and put life back into a sobering perspective.

PRIOR TO 911, primarily Black people only had to concern themselves with racial profiling. After 911 we found ourselves, a people who should completely despise racism because of feeling its sting and injustice for oh so many years, also participating in the profiling of Arab Americans. While I do believe that because of the unique circumstance of the event, that it is prudent in security circumstances to be ever mindful of the fact that it was Middle easterners who did this terrible thing to us, we should be careful not to let our hatred rule the day and make us act without good reason, cause or logic in these trying circumstances. Not all Arab Americans and middle east countries support the evil cause that led to the 911 tragedy. We must remember this!!!

I think it is very important to look to the root cause of why the 911 tragedy occurred. I truly believe that it is 'Greed, Power and Racism' that we will find at its rotten core. Although, Osama bin Laden claims his cause and ultimate purpose is a religious one, I truly suspect his goal is to over throw Saudi Arabia and gain its GREAT wealth, resources (oil) and seize the vast power that would come with it, as being the undisputed head of the Muslim world. We have seen this brand of madness before with evil people like Hitler! With God's help, bin Laden will fail too!

Also consider this, America sadly enough have played a role in helping bin Laden's quest.

A few years ago when Russia opposed Afghanistan, we supported bin Laden and the evil he did even then. Now it is us who oppose him and condemn his evil ways. Is it like Malcolm X said? Are the chickens (the evil we once sowed) finally coming back home to roost and haunt us? I think they are!! America must learn to do better and never bend its principles to achieve an end. The end does not justify the means.

I BELIEVE IN GOD and I truly believe that God gave each one of us The Ability To No Right From Wrong. Whether we choose to use what God gave us and to listen to our hearts and conscience to discern it, and from there, reject it or not, is a different matter entirely. But I believe that for sane people, the ability to know right from wrong is there. It is up to each individual to choose what's right and from there show courage to do it! That's why God gave us the wonderful gift of 'Free Will.' He wants us to make the right decision on our own.

I truly believe that that is why God has set us here on earth in Satan's domain. He wants us to shame Satan, by doing what's right in spite of Satan's many temptations, tricks, pleasures and rewards etc. Of course man is not perfect and is no match for Satan. We will often fall short. God knows this! But the key thing is, I do believe strongly in my heart, is that God wants us to FEAR NO EVIL, keep picking ourselves back up and keep trying again and again and again. Because, we realize IN OUR HEARTS AND KNOW THAT it is the right thing to do. God does not want mankind to wallow in evil and be content with it! Or worse yet, be willingly seduced and lost to the dark side completely. If this be the case, then Satan's would have won not only earth but ultimately his heavenly insurrection/war and subsequent exile from heaven.

I TRULY BELIEVE AMERICA IS THE GREATEST country on earth for a reason. I believe America stands where it is today not by accident. I believe that God made it that way so that it can be a shining example to other nations of what a country with many different ethnic backgrounds and religious beliefs can achieve, if we just pull together.

Of course, America is far from perfect. But that my friends means that even though we are the greatest country on earth, we still have a lot of work to do. I have to wonder if the terrorists who killed all of our innocent people on September 11th realized that they would also be killing many Americans of Arab ancestry as well. Their evil, mis-guided vengeance also served to hurt their own beloved Muslim brothers and sisters who are welcomed and practice their religion freely here in America. It makes no sense for Muslims to feel they should wage war against America because of religious differences particularly, when America welcomes their own religion into our country with open arms.

IF THEIR RELIGION TRULY BE THE BEST, then it will thrive and ultimately rise to the top in America. They should not want to use force, out right murder and terrorism as intimidation to achieve this end. The latter clearly runs contrary to God's gift of free will and I am absolutely positive that God (or Allah as they call him) would not condone the 911 murders.

If they (the Terrorist) were truly sincere, then they would realize that they only spite themselves and hurt their religion with their violence rather than help it!!!

AMERICA IS TRULY A MELTING POT. It is now well beyond the pointing out of one race, religion, nationality or gender to shoulder any perceived blame. It is completely ludicrous for another nation to think that they can strike out at any one race etc. here in America without in someway (direct or indirect) hurting their own and in doing so shaming themselves. We (America) truly represent the world. We are the only nation that holds this distinction. If not for this reason alone, America should be looked to as an oasis to be encouraged, rather than one to be feared and destroyed .

ON A RECENT TRIP to my beloved, former home state of Mississippi, I ran into my favorite hero, (Constance Slaughter Harvey) from one of my previous books, "Standing At The Edge Of Madness." If you've read this book you would know that she is the brave, smart and tenacious attorney who stood up for justice and challenged the state of Mississippi in the courtroom for the murders that occurred at Jackson State on May 14, 1970.
There is no doubt that Constance risked her life to take a stand for me, the other JSU students, the surviving family members of the deceased students and all good and decent Mississippians who believe in justice in taking this bold stand. For this, she will forever have my gratitude. Constance, was willing to give her all so that the voice of the downtrodden and oppressed could be heard. In that day in time in Mississippi, her defiance and stand for what was right, could have easily been her death sentence.
Constance is truly a beacon of light for all the world to follow and set their standards by. She is still as beautiful and tenacious as ever and is still fighting the good fight to correct racial injustice wherever it may be throughout the state of Mississippi and the deep South. She was recently inducted into the Toogaloo College Hall of Fame for her outstanding work in the legal arena, and the community in Mississippi. This is just one of the many awards and recognitions she has received during her many years of service to her fellowman. I strongly

recommend Constance Slaughter Harvey, as a role model for our young people today. Young people, I say beat a path to her door to soak in her pearls of wisdom and courage.

ON AUGUST 25, 2001, I went home to my old home state of Mississippi and attended a dedication of Lanier High School's new gymnasium. It was dedicated to an extraordinary teacher named Leroy T. Smith. I personally remember him as a very friendly man who I often went to for advice and an encouraging, uplifting word. Coach Smith, as we in my class lovingly called him when I was at Lanier, has soundly demonstrated the embodiment of what dedication to duty and hard work is.
This event was attended by many people. A lot of the participants came in from out of town, as I did myself, just to honor Mr. Smith. While there, I also got chance to share a few words with my favorite principal, Mr. Buckley and many of my old teachers, like Mr. Rigsby, Ms. Dow, Ms. Pittman, Mr. Williams and many, many more. These were truly great memories.

Although I was tremendously impressed with the scope of his life and the outstanding dedication and program that was put on by one of my famous classmates, Randall Pinkston (the CBS News Correspondent and his beautiful wife Patricia) and the committee, I was also impressed with something else that occurred that night as well. That something was the Governor of the great state of Mississippi attending this event. Imagine that! Not only did he attend, he actively took part in the ceremony. What was even more earth shattering was that, if he had not walked to the stage and from there told us his identity, I certainly would not have known who he was. I'm sure there were many more people in the audience who did not know who he was as well.

Prior to the fifties and sixties, not only would a Mississippi Governor not have given the time of day to a predominately Black school, he probably would have sent some good ole boys to the neighborhood to intimidate and ticket the participants just because they had dared to insult him by sending him an invitation.

Before the program began, I had seen him, (this rather odd, out of place looking White gentlemen) standing out front in the middle of the crowd. He eagerly chatted with some of the people gathered outside when the opportunity presented itself. I'd bet serious money that the people he talked to (especially the ones that were from out of town as I was) were just being nice to him, and did not know who he was either. He certainly did not look like the previous Governors of Mississippi! They generally were all flash, pomp and the epitome of pretentiousness. But this guy (Musgrove) was different.

There were no army of armed bodyguards or sea of state troopers, a ten thousand dollar Rolex watch, fingers adorned with expensive diamonds, or a two-thousand dollar suit and shoe outfit to put everyone to shame as we have seen in the past from other Governors. He, as best as I could see, was just another down-home person in the crowd. And guess what, he seemed to be loving it. He appeared to be having a great time without the fanfare that his predecessors in days of old would have been licking up and wallowing in. He appeared to be very comfortable in the surroundings.

When this gentleman took the microphone, he seemed right at home and genuinely interested in what the program was all about. He told several funny stories that had the crowd laughing in the aisles, about how far the state of Mississippi had come as far as race relations were concerned. He even joked that he often had to show identification and provide other evidence to prove that he was indeed the Governor of Mississippi when he traveled out of state. I assume this was because of his positive views about all races getting along with each other.

In years past, (the sixties and earlier) Mississippi as well as many of its sister southern states had a terrible reputation where racism was concerned. Boy what a change from the old days. Don't tell me that the South, are a state for that matter who in years past was known for its murderous, hard-core racist views, can't change. And, although the old racism from the past may still very well be there in Mississippi, just seething just below the surface and now just putting on a show, (which in my heart I do not believe) real change, I am certain must start at the top, be faithfully put into practice and be wholeheartedly demonstrated in the light of day. Viva the change Mississippi!!!

I'm sure that some of the now long deceased 'Evil Powers That Be' who for so many years eagerly led Mississippi into the evil abyss of self-serving, racial hatred are now turning over in their graves with disgust from the many positive racial changes that are occurring. I say let them turn! Stay the course Mississippi.

DURING A TRIP TO NEW ORLEANS on the week end of the 6th of April 2002, I ran across an old friend of mine by the name of Warren. Warren was an old drinking buddy of mine before I became a born again Christian that I first met in a wild party setting in Jamaica. In his hey day I'm told, long before I even knew him, he was the very best, if not one of the best bartenders in New Orleans. I understand, that he was quite the showman doing incredible stunts with liquor bottles and glasses long before the antic in the famous movie "Cocktail" came along. As I jokingly once told him, I would not be surprised if that movie was not about his famous exploits in one of New Orleans old night clubs. Yes Warren, like myself, has had his share of night life.

I was indeed surprised to find that my good friend was now a born again Christian, settled down and married with his own ministry. Although I was there on this trip in New Orleans to visit my dear old friend Roz, I found myself stealing away to Warren's house next door for some good old fashion bible study with him his wife, family and friend. God is truly great! He also works in mysterious ways.

All these years I had been avoiding Warren because I was now a born again Christian who did not want to back slide by, in my mind, hanging out where maybe I shouldn't be. Here it was, that my old friend was now deep, and I mean deep, in the word of

Christ himself. If anything, I should have been tearing up the road to hang out with my old friend. On my trip to New Orleans, Warren gave me some incredible insight to the bible and God's awesome power that I will cherish for the rest of my life. His words of encouragement will aid me on my journey to Christ's kingdom.

Warren really knows his bible and is truly a walking testimony for God's mercy and grace. He knows exactly where to go in the bible to find strength or an applicable solution for any life circumstance. He was able to help me tremendously and resolve several dilemmas I have been wrestling with in my life. While Warren will be the first to admit to you that he does not have a college degree, he is without a doubt one of the smartest men I have ever met in my life. I strongly recommend a visit with Warren on Milan street for any lost soul who truly wants to repent or any good Christian who want to rejoice in God's wonderment and love with a fellow Christian. Your soul will truly be fed.

While there on my trip, Warren and I, along with an incredible young man by the name of Chris, had a great time praising God. Occasionally, as Warren and I would come to find, we were able to discuss Chris' second passion which was politics. Chris, has incredible insight into not only the plight of New Orleans but the history of religion as well. He has dedicated himself to improving the quality of life in New Orleans for all its citizens. As a young man of 23 at the time of this writing, he has already been to Rome and the Vatican to see and study the history of the world's great religions.

He told captivating stories about the beheading of Paul and personally seeing the fountain where the water bounces three times to signify how Paul's head bounced as he was beheaded. He even told of how another one of Jesus' disciples asked to be crucified upside down to avoid comparison to his beloved Lord and savior, Christ. He also told of viewing the actual remaining skull of Mary Magdelene, learning of how the church of England was formed and he also gave unbelievable insight as to the purpose and actual making of the King James version of the bible.

Chris, has done all these things in order to better understand human nature. It was truly fascinating hearing Warren and Chris, uniquely marry good solid Christian, religious beliefs with politics. Their ideas to improve their city through the righteous church going community was awe inspiring. It was truly fascinating. These two are definitely on to something. Perhaps the time has come for religion to take center stage in politics today. In any case, I predict Chris will be a future mayor of New Orleans, mark my words. I also predict he will be the best mayor that city has ever had. I also am certain that my old friend Warren will help many a lost soul find their way to heaven.

AS AN ADDED FEATURE IN THE EPILOG SECTION of my books, I always like to offer a definitive and quite often controversial solution to the ills of our society. I never want it said that I was always griping about things and never tried to do anything about them.

The solution I offer today may sound a little materialistic to many out there, but before you pass judgment, please hear me out. For years it's been said that money is the root of all evil. Quite frankly, I do believe this, but I also submit that there just may be a way to turn this powerful motivating force into a positive factor. I would like to recommend that some of our prominent super well off Black Americans like Michael Jordan, Oprah Winfrey, Michael Jackson, Bill Cosby, Tiger Woods and any other wealthy people who would participate, follow Tom Joyner's lead to give scholarships to Black kids, but also take it a step further by, individually giving a million dollars to each predominately Black college (HBU) in America whether independent or publicly owned. Sounds like a lot, but each one of the people I named above, could do it with ease and still have at least three hundred million dollars in the bank. Okay you guys, (Bill, Tiger, Michael and Michael and Oprah) you can't take it with you. I know you already have and are doing great things out there, but do this as a unified effort as well. This is the one!!

Hopefully when the smoke clears, each school will have gotten at least ten million dollars to aid in their improvement. This will significantly lift up the smaller independent schools tremendously and also be of major benefit to Black state supported schools. This noble effort, will help save our kids and take them and future generations, to even greater heights.

The announcement of these charitable gifts should be publicly made (which is a departure from the past) so that someone, who may not have the ability to give 300 million dollars, will also step forward and give what they can. This public pronouncement will send a powerful message to our kids. It will also send enormous positive, improvement shock waves into our community for many, many years into the future.

I will serve as a contact point, if necessary, for any celebrities, individuals, etc. who would like to start an administrating Foundation to quickly get this project off the ground.

IN HUMAN HISTORY there have been many civilizations that have come on the scene on mankind's stage, made their mark, if there was one to be made and exited the scene. There were those who lasted a long time whose influence are still with us even today. And there are those who barely made a mark at all and who we would have to scourer the history books just to find mention of their name.

Historians in trying to find the one distinguishing attribute between those of note and those of little note, say it is the ability to take a critical look at itself, and know that it is not perfect and from there take the often painful steps necessary to improve itself, by lifting up the least among it, that makes it great! For this is the true greatness of any society.

I PRAY FOR AMERICA'S SAKE THAT WE POSSESS THE GREATNESS AND WISDOM NECESSARY TO MAKE OUR TIME IN THE SUN, A MEANINGFUL ONE.

ABOUT THE AUTHOR:

VERNON STEVE WEAKLEY was born in Chicago Illinois. When he was very young, his Mother relocated him, his two brothers and little sister to Jackson, Mississippi. And there, in the super charged racial climate of the deep South, he was influenced, (both positively and negatively) and raised to adulthood. In addition to the love, guidance and spiritual foundation provided by his Mother, his grandparents also played a major role in his upbringing. His parents and the many experiences he encountered in Mississippi influenced the way he perceived the world and the people around him. His Mother and grandparents gave him the strength necessary to survive the trials and tribulations that he endured while growing up in his beloved home state.

As a result of a strong desire to change his life and renew his relationship with God, and, what he perceived to be an intolerable racial climate in Mississippi, he decided to move to Texas where he now resides. The stories he chose to share with his readers in this book are only a few of the adventures he experienced while growing up in the deep South. The stories that were chosen for this book were selected based on their relevance to his own personal healing process. The author's eternal hope is that America, and Mississippi in particular, is also ready to heal with him.

FEAR NO EVIL!!!

BY
VERNON STEVE WEAKLEY

c Copyright 2002, Vernon Steve Weakley
This book may not be reproduced in any form without the written consent of the author.

AN IMPRINT OF
ZWORLD-NET PUBLISHING INC.
ISBN 0-9712310-2-8 /// A SPECIAL PAPERBACK EDITION

Z-WORLD-NET PUBLISHING INC.

THE POWER OF THE WRITTEN WORD!

www.ingramcontent.com/pod-product-compliance
Lightning Source LLC
Chambersburg PA
CBHW032032150426
43194CB00006B/245